FROM THE BANANA ZONES TO THE BIG EASY

FROM THE

BANANA ZONES

TO THE BIG EASY

West Indian and Central American Immigration
to New Orleans, 1910–1940

GLENN A. CHAMBERS

Louisiana State University Press   Baton Rouge

Published by Louisiana State University Press
Copyright © 2019 by Louisiana State University Press
All rights reserved
Manufactured in the United States of America
First printing

DESIGNER: Mandy McDonald Scallan
TYPEFACE: Whitman
PRINTER AND BINDER: LSI

Portions of chapter 2 were first published in the author's article "Vigilando al Otro: Raza, crim-
inalidad y violencia sancionada por el Gobierno en la Costa Norte de Honduras, 1910–1940,"
Mesoamérica 54 (2012): 27–53, and are reprinted by permission of *Mesoamérica*.

Library of Congress Cataloging-in-Publication Data

Names: Chambers, Glenn Anthony, author
Title: From the Banana Zones to the Big Easy : West Indian and Central
    American immigration to New Orleans, 1910–1940 / Glenn A. Chambers.
Description: Baton Rouge : Louisiana State University Press, 2019. | Includes
    bibliographical references and index.
Identifiers: LCCN 2019008844| ISBN 978-0-8071-7049-6 (cloth : alk. paper) | ISBN
    978-0-8071-7180-6 (pdf) | ISBN 978-0-8071-7179-0 (epub)
Subjects: LCSH: Immigrants—Louisiana—New Orleans—History—20th century. |
    New Orleans (La.)—Emigration and immigration—History—20th century. |
    Caribbean Area—Emigration and immigration—History—20th century. | New
    Orleans (La.)—Race relations—History—20th century. | New Orleans
    (La.)—Social conditions—20th century.
Classification: LCC F379.N59 A23 2019 | DDC 305.8009763/35—dc23

The paper in this book meets the guidelines for permanence and durability of the Committee
on Production Guidelines for Book Longevity of the Council on Library Resources. ♾

To Langston Malcolm Toure,
you truly are the best of me

Contents

Preface and Acknowledgments

When walking through the streets of New Orleans, it is impossible to avoid the ghosts of the past. In a city where the physical and supernatural worlds are often intertwined, the past remains ever present in the cultural and political landscape. The ghosts of the past, or rather memories, abound. While the Vieux Carré (French Quarter), with all its charm, attracts tourists from all over the world and has become a defining symbol of the city's French and Spanish colonial heritage, it is the neighborhoods of New Orleans that reveal the city's true story. Down the narrow streets and back alleyways, the tales of countless individuals from all walks of life who lived and worked in the city are obscured, but one has to only scratch the surface to uncover a wealth of history. The Caribbean and Central American immigrants who called some of these spaces home during the first half of the twentieth century followed in the long tradition of immigrants to the city, most of whom left a lasting and visible imprint. Areas such as the Irish Channel, the German Coast, the Faubourg Marigny, and the Faubourg Tremé reflect the city's European, African, and Creole heritage. The legacy of Africans from the Congo and the Senegambia region who were enslaved in the city for the first 150 years of its existence is particularly strong and permeates the cultural heritage. In many ways, this heritage serves as the cultural foundation from which all others descend, whether directly embracing it or reacting against its influence. Italians, Jews, and numerous others have added to the vibrant culture of New Orleans.

Unlike the previously mentioned groups, West Indian and Central American immigrants from the first half of the twentieth century left few cultural markers to memorialize their presence in the city. There are no neighborhoods, schools, shops, or other vestiges documenting their presence. Dilapidated buildings, street corners, old wharves, train tracks, and run-down warehouses are what remain of the areas they frequented, relics from an era in which New Orleans was a major transshipment point for the banana industry from Latin America and the Caribbean to the United States. In recent years, urban renewal and gentrification have erased what time did not. Many of the areas in Central City that served as rooming houses, restaurants, and corner hangouts for so many West Indians have become tourist hotels or condominiums. A certain amount of change is normal. It reflects the transformation over time that occurs in large cities such as New Orleans, whose boom-and-bust economies create periods of perpetual transition. One might ask, why dedicate an entire book to the Central American and West Indian community if so little remains? Answers to this question first emerged in 2007 while I was teaching a Caribbean history survey.

Several of the class discussions focused on the migration of West Indian workers from the Anglophone Caribbean to Central America in the early twentieth century to work on the various railroad projects, the Panama Canal, and ultimately in the banana industry that came to dominate the region. I was nearing completion of a book on West Indian immigration to Honduras in which the banana industry factored prominently. Therefore, significant attention was given to that historiography throughout the course. During one particular discussion, a student in the class who self-identified as "white" revealed that her grandmother was Honduran (but not Spanish-speaking) and had immigrated to New Orleans as a young adult. The student had never traveled to Honduras and knew very little of the nation's history or that of her English-speaking ancestors except that they were originally from the North Coast and the Bay Islands. The student recalled that although her grandmother had spoken of Honduras on a few occasions in passing, she had not passed on any traditions from her native land. Many of this student's aunts, prompted by the growing field of genealogical research at the time, had made attempts to reconnect with their Honduran roots in later years, with limited success. Because the grandmother had married a white American from New Orleans and culturally raised her children as white, American, southern, and New Orleanian, the ties to Honduras had quickly withered and were relegated to family lore. In this instance, as with many individuals throughout this book, the desire to fit in with the local culture (whether black or white) had superseded the need for cultural preservation. However, it is important to emphasize that the fact that immigrants outwardly embrace the social, political, and cultural status quo of their host societies does not mean that they have forgotten who they were before coming to the United States. The past has a way of resurfacing in the most unlikely spaces.

I could not have written this book without the love, patience, and support of my wife, Terah, and our son, Langston. I first began this project in the summer of 2008. Having been married for roughly a year at that point, I thought it was a "good idea" to celebrate our anniversary in New Orleans. I thought I would work in the archives for a few hours a day and have the afternoons and evenings to explore the city with my wife and introduce her to the culture and history of the place I have known and loved since I was a child. Well, my emergency appendectomy and a few days in the Tulane University hospital abruptly put an end to those plans (and that trip). There have been countless trips to New Orleans, Washington, DC, Honduras, and other places since then. Through it all, Terah, an eternal optimist, has been by my side. When I thought of giving up because researching the lives of a constantly moving population seemed impossible, she reassured me of the importance of telling their stories. Terah, thank you for believing in me. I love you "even though . . ."

I also wish to thank my mother, Toxi, and sisters, Samaria and Caire, for their unconditional love and support through the years, as well as my entire extended family in Texas and Louisiana. While I know they did not always understand the nuances of academic research and publishing, or the life of a professor, as long as I was happy and living the life I wanted they were on board. On many of the research trips, there was also peace of mind knowing that my mother-in-law was available to help Terah with Langston. Thank you, Rhonda, for always having our backs.

I conceived of this project while an assistant professor in the history department at Texas A&M University. Albert Broussard, a senior colleague in the history department who had chaired the search that hired me fresh out of graduate school, advised me to "stick with what you know." I wisely took his advice. As a scholar of the Caribbean and Central America well versed in the history of Louisiana, I could combine all my interests in this book.

I also wish to thank Verna Keith, then director of the Race and Ethnic Studies Institute (RESI) at A&M, for providing the initial funding for me to explore the possibilities of this project. The Africana Studies program, under the direction of Kimberly Brown and later Violet Showers-Johnson, provided me the intellectual space to interrogate the history and culture of the African diaspora. My colleagues in the A&M history department Rebecca Schloss, Jason Parker, Harold Livesay, Cynthia Bouton, Violet Showers-Johnson, Andrew Kirkendall, and Walter Kamphoefner shared advice and expertise as I worked through early conceptions of this project. Special thanks are in order to Carlos Blanton, Felipe Hinojosa, and their respective partners, Kristine and Maribel. In addition to being colleagues, Carlos and Felipe became two of my closest friends and created a space for me to be "human" in an academy that has become less so. Felipe and I went on archival trips together, and he challenged me to really explore the complexities of Latinx identity, an area of scholarship that was new to me. I am forever grateful.

Halfway through researching this book, I moved from Texas A&M to the history department at Michigan State University. It was at Michigan State that this project really progressed. Special thanks to LaShawn Harris and Pero Dagbovie for their genuine friendship and encouragement. Special thanks also to Nwando Achebe, Jessica Johnson, Ed Murphy, David Wheat, Peter Beattie, Walter Hawthorne, and the late David Bailey for offering suggestions and challenging me to focus on the connections between "everyday" people and to be true to their stories. I also want to acknowledge Jeanna Norris, Elyse Hansen, and Debra Greer for answering administrative questions, processing reimbursements, and making my professional life easier. The history department at Michigan State is a great place to work in no small part because of their tireless efforts.

In addition to the history department, the African American and African Studies program (AAAS) at Michigan State has been an important space for me. I became director of the program in 2016 and have since had the pleasure of working with some exceptional and brilliant faculty and graduate students. Special thanks to Blair Proctor, Janelle Edwards, and Michael Wilson for their help as research assistants, whether formally or informally, on this project. The bibliographies they compiled, the archival-database searches they conducted, and the firsthand knowledge of New Orleans or the Caribbean immigrant experience they provided helped me navigate the intellectual terrain around issues of culture, identity, and citizenship.

Though living in Michigan has been a wonderful experience, I am a southerner at my core. This is especially true from November through April (and sometimes May), when the brutal cold never lets up. Family, friends, and community are very important to me. Terah and I have worked hard to make Michigan "home." A big part of that effort has included surrounding ourselves with great people. The "Crew" (as we call them) have become our family. Thank you, Yomaira Figueroa, Tacuma Peters, Tamara Butler, Delia Fernandez, Django Paris, Rae Paris, Terry Flennaugh, Chezare Warren, Dylan Miner, Estrella Torrez, Maribel Santiago, Jeff Wray, Tama Hamilton-Wray, Lucía Cardenas, Xhercis Mendez, Leslie Gonzales, Ruben Flores, John Yun, and Patricia Marin for being a part of our lives. While some of you have since left Michigan State, we appreciate all of you and all that you do for the Chambers family.

In any research project, there are times when it is easy to get stuck in a rut. It can be simple writer's block, the inability to make sense of a source, or just the frustration of managing the profession. When this happens, I know that I can call Quito Swan and Louis Woods, who will undoubtedly have the answers or at the very least ask the right questions to help me figure out how to move forward. This has been the case since we were struggling graduate students at Howard University and continues to be so. I can never go wrong with you as friends. Thank you.

A few years ago, while at a social gathering at the Association for the Study of African American Life and History (ASALH) conference, I ran into Sowande Mustakeem and was explaining my project to her. She offered encouraging feedback and challenged me to focus more on the dynamics of the merchant ships, particularly how blacks navigated that space and its implications. Her questions led me to the National Maritime Union and the participation of black seamen in organized labor. The wealth of archival materials related to this subject and the many paths it took me down ultimately enhanced the project. I would not have structured chapters 3 and 4 in the same way had it not been for that chance encounter. Thank you, Sowande.

In the age of digital humanities and online sources, the work of archivists and librarians can be underappreciated. While digital sources in many ways enhance traditional research, it is simply not possible to study the late-nineteenth- and early-twentieth-century Caribbean, Central America, and New Orleans without spending significant time in a physical archive. I am indebted to the librarians and staff at the Texas A&M University Libraries, the Michigan State University Libraries, Tulane University's Latin America Library, the University of New Orleans, the New Orleans Public Library, the University of Texas's Nettie Lee Benson Collection, Howard University's Moorland-Spingarn Collection, the Rutgers University Libraries, the Wayne State University Libraries, the Schomburg Center for Research in Black Culture at the New York Public Library, the Clayton Library Center for Genealogical Research at the Houston Public Library, the British National Archives, the Archivo Nacional de Honduras, the US National Archives, and the Library of Congress.

Lastly, I wish to thank Rand Dotson and the Louisiana State University Press for believing in the project, and the anonymous reviewers whose critical reading greatly improved the final manuscript.

FROM THE BANANA ZONES TO THE BIG EASY

Introduction

The story of West Indian and Central American immigration to New Orleans does not begin in the French Quarter, Jackson Square, the Garden District, or any of the other tourist and cultural landmarks that have come to define the city. Nor does it commence with border crossings, immigration officials, or diplomatic fallout. Instead, some of the first accounts of this population in the city emerge haphazardly in the African American press and in literary works focused on other matters. In his 1929 novel *Banjo: A Story without a Plot*, Claude McKay, the renowned Jamaican writer of the Harlem Renaissance, navigates the intersecting lives of residents of the Vieux Port section of Marseilles, France. He highlights their jaunts as they negotiate a diverse and fragile existence, frequenting the bars, brothels, and other establishments in the underbelly of the famed French port city. As with many Atlantic port cities, the racial and ethnic composition was diverse, reflecting a host of races, languages, and nationalities, as well as a sizable population of immigrants, migrants, and transients. Many of the novel's characters arrive as sailors on merchant vessels and decide to remain in the city, either hoping for a new beginning in France or waiting to move on to the next adventure. One such character, Buchanan Avis, known to his friends as "Malty," is a West Indian sailor, most likely Jamaican based on McKay's own background and the style of patois he employs to voice the character throughout the novel. Malty begins his working life as a sailor on fishing boats in the Caribbean. Once he reaches adulthood, he boards a cargo boat for New Orleans and from there becomes a seaman on international vessels, never returning to the Caribbean.[1]

Literary critics have focused on the fact that the novel takes place largely in 1920s France, following the First World War, in which a loss of innocence, rejection of the old order, and disillusionment with the world and its established institutions were common themes.[2] The representations of North and West Africans, Asians, and other groups in the city are interpreted as contributing to the ethnic, racial, and religious diversity that distinguished Marseilles from other parts of France. The literary scholar Michael Chaney notes that the central character in the novel, Banjo, relates to members of the community as he drifts among them by becoming "the energizing locus of a bacchanalian fraternity of vagrants based in a culturally heterogeneous Marseilles."[3] This drifting, moving beyond national, cultural, and racial boundaries while remaining both at the mercy and at the margins of society, evokes a sense of exile that according to Graeme Abernethy is both transnational and perpetual.[4] However, these transient wanderers are not entirely rootless. McKay underscores the fact that Malty begins his professional career as a sailor in New Orleans (and not the Caribbean of his birth), a point often overlooked by both literary scholars and historians.

Though the characters created by McKay are fictional, they are based largely on the real-life experiences of the author and thousands of other West Indians in the late nineteenth and early twentieth centuries who traveled far from their island homelands in search of economic opportunity, political freedom, and adventure. That the city of New Orleans plays an unassuming but integral role in shaping the path of the main protagonist mirrors in many ways the experiences of West Indian and Central American immigrants to New Orleans during the first half of the twentieth century, particularly during the interwar years, from 1918 to 1940. The stories of these immigrants are transnational, rooted in the expansion of US empire, the internationalization of labor, racism, migration, and the sense of longing and loss that these experiences created. However, despite all this, New Orleans was always present. Furthermore, New Orleans as a space of refuge and reinvention for newcomers was a concept that continued to resonate in the political, economic, and cultural fabric of the city from its inception.

Like other American port cities, Thomas Fiehrer writes, New Orleans was the "recipient of nearly all major migratory movements to North America: French, Spanish, British Isles, German, Italian (Sicilian), Yugoslav, Latin American, Canadian, and African (through the Transatlantic Trade)."[5] The fertile soils of the surrounding region and thriving commercial activity throughout the late eighteenth and nineteenth centuries made New Orleans attractive to those seeking to advance their economic prospects.

The Colonial Origins of the New Orleans–Caribbean Connection

Though the realities of early Spanish colonial enterprises differed significantly from those of late-nineteenth- and early-twentieth-century New Orleans, the role of the port city as a link between the commerce, ideas, and cultures of diverse populations has remained consistent throughout history. There is a wealth of scholarship on colonial New Orleans and its ties to the larger Atlantic world dating from the French and Spanish colonial eras through the acquisition of the territory by the United States. Therefore, I do not revisit the bulk of that literature here. However, an understanding of the historical relationship between New Orleans and the Caribbean (particularly colonial Saint Domingue) is fundamental to understanding the ways in which the city historically embraced immigrants from the larger Latin American and Caribbean region over generations. When the French Canadian explorer and future governor of the colony of Louisiana, Jean Baptiste Le Moyne de Bienville, founded New Orleans in 1718, the city had very few means of sustaining itself. Gwendolyn Midlo Hall notes that many of the early settlers of Louisiana were prisoners convicted of random acts of violence, murder, drunkenness, and debauchery, among other crimes. However, most were beggars and vagabonds taken from the streets of Paris.[6] This metropolitan French population added to the preexisting group of French Canadian *coureurs du bois* (fur traders) who lived in Indian villages and took Indian wives. The fur trade never developed in Louisiana, owing to the humid climate and the inferiority of the pelts compared with those of the Upper Midwest and other northern areas of the continent. The presence of the small population of French Canadians, metropolitan French, and the few settlers from the French Caribbean of dubious origins, combined with the high instances of disease, indigenous resistance to colonization, and unsuitable terrain for subsistence farming and other agricultural endeavors, created a situation in which colonists were forced to rely on commercial ties with France, through the thriving French Caribbean colony of Saint Domingue, to supply and sustain them.[7]

Nathalie Dessens suggests that Louisiana, unlike Saint Domingue, stagnated for much of the eighteenth century, with nominal population growth until the arrival of large numbers of refugees from Saint Domingue following the successful overthrow of the French by enslaved Africans and free people of color during the Haitian Revolution.[8] She further notes that whereas an independent and somewhat antiauthoritarian sentiment developed among the economic and political elite in Saint Domingue prior to the French Revolution (and later the Haitian Revolution), Louisiana remained indifferent to the idea of colonial rule.[9] Because the French neglected the colony economically, no self-sustaining economy emerged. This reality, combined with Louisiana's proximity to British and Spanish North American possessions, necessitated a dependence on the French. Hall suggests that this dynamic also fostered an openness to people of other races and cultures. The high number of interracial marriages between Europeans and Indians and, later, relationships with Africans is a testament to this. Survival often depended on establishing connections across racial lines.[10]

What the French were unable to provide economically, the contraband trade, based in the Caribbean, supplemented. Lawrence Powell notes that the smuggling business permeated every level of Louisiana society, from the office of the governor and his elite circle of economic and political leaders to the masses.[11] The smuggling networks also linked the rural communities of southern Louisiana to New Orleans through the numerous bayous and rivers. This web of illegal activity ultimately connected Louisiana to the larger Caribbean (specifically Saint Domingue), with New Orleans operating at the center. Dessens maintains that because of the high degree of mobility between New Orleans and other spaces in the Caribbean and Latin America, people in Louisiana were "acutely aware of the opportunities offered by the greater Caribbean."[12] In no group was this more evident than in the Saint Domingue refugees.

For most of the Saint Domingue immigrants, Louisiana was a secondary destination. At the onset of the Haitian Revolution, fewer than one hundred individuals sought refuge in Louisiana. Paul Lachance posits that the largest movements out of Saint Domingue were to the Eastern Seaboard (New York, Boston, Philadelphia, Baltimore, and Charleston) in 1793, Jamaica in 1798, and Cuba in 1803. It was not until the Louisiana Purchase that New Orleans began to see an uptick in the numbers, with roughly 1,000 people arriving from Jamaica. In 1809 and 1810, roughly 10,000 individuals arrived from the eastern Cuban cities of Santiago and Baracoa.[13] When Napoleon Bonaparte occupied Spain in 1808 and the Spanish royal family was essentially held captive in France, Cubans attacked French refugees from Saint Domingue in retaliation and burned their homes, forcing most to flee the Spanish colony and seek asylum elsewhere.[14]

The refugees from Cuba were a diverse group. Roughly 2,700 were classified as white, another 3,200 were enslaved or reenslaved,[15] and the remaining population comprised free people of color.[16] Free people of color in Louisiana represented varied origins. Some were descended from the early French and Spanish settlers of Louisiana and enslaved Africans. Others were previously mentioned exiles and migrants from Saint Domingue. Despite their legal efforts throughout the nineteenth century, narrowing definitions of freedom that were closely tied to race in an Anglo-American-ruled Louisiana following the Louisiana Purchase meant that their claims to full citizenship in Louisiana were never honored. In spite of this, Rebecca Scott maintains, free people of color and their descendants built educational and philanthropic institutions that encouraged broader Caribbean and Atlantic perspectives. Trade networks also linked free people of color in urban areas to their relatives who elected not to settle in Louisiana but instead remained in Cuba, Jamaica, Trinidad, France, and other areas throughout the Atlantic world.

Relatives in backcountry areas along the rivers and bayous of Louisiana also remained connected to these networks, extending Francophone Caribbean culture and connections beyond the limits of New Orleans.[17] Powell further asserts that people of color exemplified the multicaste racialism of the Caribbean and that Afro-Creole intelligentsia were inspired by the revolutionary ideas of the Francophone Caribbean world.[18]

Virginia Dominguez writes that in addition to maintaining ties with the larger world, Creoles, as the free people of color and their descendants came to be known in Louisiana, adopted sociopolitical connotations of the word *Creole* that placed little emphasis on racial identification but more on culture, language, religion, status, and ethnicity.[19] In fact, during the plantation era, family ties and other bonds often existed between free people of color, whites, and enslaved and free blacks.[20] Dessens suggests that many of the bonds were established in Saint Domingue and persisted well into the nineteenth century, indicating a strong Caribbean diaspora consciousness.[21] Carl Brasseaux depicts a similar situation in the prairie parishes of southwestern Louisiana.[22] However, despite such initial racial inclusiveness, after the acquisition of the territory by the United States, the subsequent expansion of the plantation economy, and increased migration of Anglo-Americans and their enslaved populations from all over the South, those Louisianans from the French and Spanish periods found themselves negotiating between a rigid Anglo-American racial system centered on the black-white racial dichotomy and a more fluid Latin American and Caribbean racial construct that afforded space for identity negotiation. This problem persisted through the Civil War and following Reconstruction, in that laws of hypodescent (the "one-drop rule") left little room for racial ambiguity.

The persistent economic ties between Louisiana and the Caribbean and Latin America during the nineteenth century were reinvigorated in the early twentieth century, when New Orleans reemerged as a central port for trade and commerce between the United States and the region. As merchant vessels transported goods between the United States, Central America, Cuba, Jamaica, France, and other areas, they were in many ways retracing well-established routes. Additionally, the complexities around issues of race and culture in Louisiana resurfaced

when immigrants and migrants from familiar yet "foreign" lands arrived in the city. The twentieth-century manifestation of New Orleans
as an entrepôt to the United States and a gateway to the world raises
several questions. Were these later immigrant or migrant experiences
isolated incidents, or was New Orleans at the epicenter of a much
larger international wave? Was there a sizable community of West Indians and Latin Americans in the city, or was New Orleans simply a
way station? How did this somewhat marginalized group interact with
an African American population dealing with the historical legacy of
slavery and the ramifications of a federally codified racial policy legally rendering them second-class citizens (Jim Crow) that had only
emerged in 1896 from a US Supreme Court case originating in New
Orleans (*Plessy v. Ferguson*)? The attempt to answer these questions
and others serves as the foundation for this book.

New Orleans: An American "Latin" City

In her recent work on Mexicans in the US South, Julie Weise asserts that
in New Orleans the lives of "African Americans, capitalists, Caribbeans,
Central Americans, sailors, labor activists, and other marginalized peoples crossed paths in one of the most historically and culturally diverse
spaces in the United States."[23] However, within this space Caribbean
and Central American peoples lived on the margins. As Weise further
suggests, an examination of those marginal actors "illuminates more
clearly the main characters and plotlines that have long preoccupied
historians."[24] The major plot in this study involves the ways in which
Caribbean and Central American peoples negotiated their distinct identity in the racial laboratory that was New Orleans during the first half of
the twentieth century.

The question of immigration from the Caribbean and Latin America
into the United States as it pertains to the South has a special topicality
and relevance given the contemporary prevalence of border crossings
into the nation from the region. Contentious rhetoric on immigration
from all sides of the political, economic, and cultural divide reveals that
there is insufficient appreciation of the nature of immigration into the

United States over the centuries, particularly from Latin America and the Caribbean. The tendency to treat all immigrants from the region uniformly and the culture in general as a monolith ignores the profound differences among the region's numerous nationalities, races, and cultures. More importantly, such rhetoric fails to articulate the diverse experiences of Latin American and Caribbean immigrants in recent decades and the process by which many have assimilated.

In New Orleans, much of the recent debate on immigration from Latin America has centered on the post–Hurricane Katrina realities of a visibly larger Spanish-speaking Latino presence in the city. In 2006, then mayor C. Ray Nagin maintained during the rebuilding efforts after the storm that New Orleans would "be a chocolate city again,"[25] a comment rooted in the historically adversarial relationship between blacks and whites in the city. However, Nagin's words also highlighted the anxieties within the African American community about the increased Latino presence in the city. The assumption by many in New Orleans was that Latinos represented a new cultural reality, an assumption that totally ignored the long history of Spanish-speaking immigrants to the city from Central America and the Caribbean. This pattern began in the late nineteenth century and continues to the present day, with the majority of immigrants arriving from the Republic of Honduras. Honduras (both the British and Spanish territories) and New Orleans shared historical links that fostered strong economic and cultural ties dating from the early nineteenth century. At various points throughout the French and Spanish colonial periods, government officials were forced to allow Louisianans to trade directly with Latin American and Caribbean ports in an effort to curtail the previously mentioned smuggling activity, which resulted from the colony's inability to produce enough essential goods to supply its citizens. After the transition to American rule in 1803, smugglers continued to circumvent the new tariffs and trade laws and provide Latin American goods at reduced rates to Louisianans. New Orleans served as the main hub for this activity. Over time, people from the Caribbean and Central America in particular began to follow the trade goods and settle in the city. The geographer James Chaney notes that by the twentieth century there was also a steady flow of migrants from Honduras to New Orleans because of its centrality to the banana trade.[26] This latter trade was built largely on the preestablished routes from earlier eras.

This book centers on the immigration of West Indians and Central Americans (particularly those of British West Indian descent from the Caribbean coastal areas) to New Orleans from the turn of the twentieth century to the start of World War II. I look at the methods by which this population of diverse racial and ethnic backgrounds integrated into New Orleans society and negotiated their distinct historical and ethnoracial identity in the Jim Crow South. The transitory nature of immigrants in New Orleans and the shifting political and economic realities that fostered this instability make it difficult to ascertain the number of West Indians and Central Americans who permanently settled in the city. According to official US census data, at no point in the years from 1910 to 1940 did the "foreign-born Negro" population or the Latin American population ever exceed 1 percent of the total black population in New Orleans. The numbers peaked in 1920, when roughly 1,136 West Indians and 1,072 Central and South Americans were present in the city. Of these, 52 percent (1,148) were identified as "Negro." The 1930 census indicated 593 West Indians and 1,268 Central and South Americans, of which 36 percent (670) were listed as "Negro."[27] Table I.1 offers more detailed data for the period. Whereas there was a steady decline in the "foreign-born Negro" population after 1920, the census data for the years 1930 and 1940 provided more statistical categories to determine the complexity of the population. Categories requesting naturalization status, immigration status (first papers/no papers), and whether citizenship from any nation was reported presented an opportunity to explore available US documents related to immigration and naturalization.

If we relied solely on US census data to quantify West Indian and Central American immigration and its implicit influence on New Orleans during the period of study, there would be no story, or at best a limited one. The US government has recorded an official census every ten years since 1790. For the purposes of this study, the 1910, 1920, and 1930 censuses are the most relevant. However, if an immigrant arrived in New Orleans in 1922, applied for US citizenship in 1928, received it,

TABLE 1.1. Foreign-Born Black Population of New Orleans, 1910–1940

POPULATION GROUP	1910	1920	1930	1940
"Foreign-Born Negroes"	377	1,146	666	389
"Native-Born Negroes"	88,885	99,784	128,966	148,645
"Naturalized Negroes"	—	—	204	225
Citizenship Not Reported	—	—	66	44
Obtained First Papers (Immigrants)	—	—	62	34
No Papers (Immigrants)	—	—	334	86
Total	89,262	100,930	129,632	149,034

Sources: US Department of Commerce, Fourteenth Census of the United States: 1920, 729; US Department of Commerce, Sixteenth Census of the United States: 1940, 427.

and relocated to Chicago, California, or Texas in 1929, then the seven years spent in New Orleans would never appear in a US census. If that individual chose to forgo US citizenship entirely and return to his or her home country or was simply "passing through" New Orleans, the impact of that individual on the city or, more importantly, the city's influence on immigrant notions of what it meant to be an American (black or white) is indeterminate. Therefore, we must look beyond the numbers to reach a more accurate assessment of the immigrant presence in New Orleans. Arrest records, ship passenger records, reports of foreign consulates, draft registrations, declarations of intent to apply for citizenship, naturalization applications, residential patterns, and city directories give a much clearer picture of the lives of immigrants. I have chosen to focus extensively on those West Indians and Central Americans who applied for US citizenship in New Orleans and/ or worked as merchant seamen for the major fruit companies. These numbered roughly 375, or one-third of the total population of West Indian and Central American immigrants of the period. Though this small sample did not reflect the entirety of the population from the region, there was an established paper trail from which to reconstruct aspects of their lives.

Throughout this study I employ numerous minibiographies of individuals, an approach borrowed from the recent works of scholars of early New Orleans such as Rashauna Johnson and, to a lesser degree, Rebecca Scott. Minibiographies provide a means to situate the experiences of West Indian and Central American immigrants within the rapidly changing and politically charged environment that was New Orleans. Not unlike the enslaved African populations of the eighteenth and nineteenth centuries that Johnson studies, twentieth-century immigrants witnessed an environment in which seemingly rigid lines of empire, race, color, and (legal) status were routinely crossed.[28] The individuals I emphasize in the minibiographies represent the diversity that existed within the larger immigrant community. Whether or not they were counted in official records, West Indian and Central American immigrants and migrants worked, married, had children, went to school, organized politically, went to jail, and ultimately lived full and complete lives during their time in New Orleans. For some, New Orleans became a permanent home, but for the majority it was simply a moment in time. Not unlike the lives of the characters in Claude McKay's *Banjo,* the lives of the subjects of these minibiographies, lives spent under the radar, expose the nuances of the larger society and its connections to national and international realities.

Among Latino immigrants to New Orleans, Central American immigrants have been invisible from the beginning, in part because most did not fit the stereotypical profile of a Latino in the North American sense. They were of African descent, had English surnames, and in some cases held British passports. They lived their lives in between established US and Latin American racial classifications, citizenship designations, and cultural and linguistic spheres. Nevertheless, US immigration officials saw them as black, or "African" (the US census designation of the period), thus ignoring their complex experiences and subsuming them within the larger African American community. Moreover, their political status as Central American, their cultural identity as British West Indian, and their racial classification as black underscore the difficulty of identity negotiation among transnational migrant populations.

There is precedent for documenting the invisibility of the black immigrant experience within a southern US context. The anthropologist Susan Greenbaum, in her assessment of Afro-Cuban immigrants to Tampa, Florida, in the late nineteenth century, noted that they found themselves invisible because in popular constructions Cuban identity was defined in opposition to blackness.[29] In Jim Crow Florida, Cubans were white and successful, a stark contrast to images of African Americans as poverty stricken and, by extension, morally and culturally bankrupt. For Greenbaum, Afro-Cubans resided at an intersection of race and ethnicity and negotiated multiple identities. They were "black when with Cubans and Cubans when with African Americans."[30] However, in the eyes of the state they were legally black and therefore subjected to the harshness of Jim Crow racial policies. West Indians and Central Americans of African descent in New Orleans negotiated a similar political and racial terrain. However, because their numbers in New Orleans were much smaller than in Tampa, a cohesive community the likes of Ybor City or Key West never emerged in New Orleans, and these unique diasporic identities existed under the radar.

Central Americans of West Indian descent in New Orleans did not generally shy away from a black identity upon arrival in the United States. In fact, available evidence suggests that most in New Orleans embraced their African American brethren. They worked with African Americans on the docks as porters and day laborers, as merchant seamen on United Fruit Company and Standard Fruit Company steamships, and in the trades and professions. West Indians married into African American families, were active in African American cultural institutions, attended historically black colleges and universities (HBCUs), and fought alongside African Americans for an end to racial discrimination through civil rights and Pan-African organizations such as the Universal Negro Improvement Association (UNIA) and in labor unions such as the National Maritime Union (NMU). However, to limit the lives of these migrants solely to an African American experience diminishes the complexity of the African-diaspora immigrant experience in New

Orleans. It also creates a missed opportunity to demonstrate the long history of cross-cultural interaction between blacks in the United States, the Caribbean, and Latin America, particularly within the context of the southern United States.

The sociologist John A. Arthur, in his assessment of contemporary African transnational migrant communities, notes that for many Africans who can establish immigrant identities in migrant host societies, "these identities once formed, are non-linear." Arthur asserts that "these identities become circulatory, lived and experienced in their host societies and at the same time transposed, acted out, shared, modified, and recreated back in Africa."[31] Rashauna Johnson emphasized a similar dynamic in New Orleans under slavery, in which a slave's circulatory movements throughout the city were essential in mapping the social and cultural history of a rapidly shifting city, nation, and world at the crux of empires.[32] I contend that Arthur's assessment, though based in a contemporary continental African immigrant experience, also holds true in analyses of the historical experiences of blacks within the larger context of the global African diaspora, especially West Indian migrants from Central America during the early twentieth century. These migrants transcended the borders of nation-states by economically incorporating into their host societies, while maintaining connections to their cultures back home. Many even passed this culture on to their offspring. Others opted to embrace an African American identity.

West Indian and Central American immigrants to New Orleans resided in a host of countries prior to settling in the city. Their West Indian and Latino culture shifted to New Orleans and was confronted with a rigid racial-classification system. However, New Orleans's strong historical and cultural ties to Latin America and the Caribbean provided these immigrants with a unique opportunity "to add to," as Arthur posits, "and enlarge the ethnic and racial tapestries of their host society by contesting newer forms of black identities against the backdrop of the vestiges of entrenched racial hierarchies and ethnic categorizations and labels common to U.S. society."[33] Though their numbers were small, the impact of this population in the city was significant since a West Indian presence was visible in every aspect of black New Orleans life. Because of the rigidity of the Jim Crow system, West Indian and Afro-Latino identities would publicly be subsumed by race but privately augment an African American community on the cusp of real social change. This concept was not new to New Orleans. As the sociologist George Lipsitz maintains, "New Orleans is always African (Black), but never only African."[34] Historically, the African culture of the city has interacted with European, Native American, and other immigrant cultures in complex and contradictory ways to enhance the vitality of the city. Lipsitz's assessment does more to explain the ways in which the African diaspora is lived in the daily lives of Africans and their descendants than do theoretical frameworks.[35] In this instance, Africa (and, I would argue, later blackness) in New Orleans is constantly evolving and making room for others, particularly black immigrants, to be incorporated into the community without giving up all of who they are.

Theoretical frameworks, particularly in studies of the African diaspora, are helpful in explaining the phenomenon of Africans and their descendants navigating multiple spaces and identities simultaneously. Particularly useful is Monique Bedasse's concept of "trodding Diaspora," with its explanations of movement "within, between, and beyond boundaries of any particular nation-state."[36] Much as with the Rastafarians in Bedasse's work, to study the history of West Indian immigrants to New Orleans is to encounter a multinational reality that incorporates and transcends traditional archives and narratives.

The global dispersion of West Indians, the emergence of a Caribbean cultural identity in their host societies based on a common language (English), religion (Protestantism), and social practices, and the idea of maintaining connections to their respective Caribbean homelands and the larger black world places them firmly within traditional definitions of the African diaspora. The story of this migrant black population also mirrors the experiences of countless other colonized peoples during the late nineteenth and early twentieth centuries, whose movement, according to Tiffany Patterson and Robin D. G. Kelley, was shaped in part by "many of the same needs of capital, the same empires, the same colonial labor policies, and the same ideologies" that forced other groups to leave their homelands in search of economic opportunity.[37]

Colin Palmer linked this initial mass movement of peoples to the Atlantic trade in enslaved Africans and the economic conditions following its immediate demise. For Palmer, this diaspora constitutes a "movement of peoples among and resettlement within various societies in which racial oppression and resistance to it are two of its most salient features."[38] Building on the work of these authors, this study also grapples with how West Indian migrants in New Orleans negotiated their multiple identities, balancing a strong sense of black consciousness with the external economic and political forces that facilitated their mobility.

The fact that West Indians maintained multiple identities warrants further discussion. Stuart Hall argued that identity operates under erasure in the interval between reversal and emergence. For Hall, the relationship between identity and political location is pivotal to understanding the difficulties and instabilities that have impacted identity politics. However, he notes the occurrence of a reconceptualization of identity within displaced or decentered populations.[39] In the case of the West Indians and Central Americans in New Orleans, what does it mean to be "West Indian" when the persons migrating and in some cases even their parents were not born in the West Indies? In the case of Central Americans, how does one grapple with this "West Indian" cultural identity when their political identity (citizenship) is Honduran, Costa Rican, or Panamanian? A distinct West Indian culture does not emerge in New Orleans. Rather, a West Indian set of practices intertwines with existing African American traditions, a process intensified by New Orleans's established tradition of incorporating (and often absorbing) new peoples and cultures.

The West Indian population in New Orleans was truly transnational, multinational, multilingual, diasporic, and constantly evolving. Its members remained conscious of their West Indian roots but were not bound by them. Their experiences were transnational but not politically internationalist, as was the case with the larger West Indian communities in the northeastern United States.[40] Patterson and Kelley argued that "black internationalism does not always come out of Africa, nor is it necessarily engaged with Pan-Africanism or other black movements. Sometimes it lives through or is integrally tied to other kinds of international movements."[41] In this case, postemancipation realities of depressed West Indian economies and US corporations' need of cheap labor to fuel their commercial exploitation of Central American agriculture, combined with Latin American racism and xenophobia, served as the unifier for many West Indians and expedited their movement abroad. Their internationalism was tied partly to maintaining family, economic, and cultural ties across multiple nations in which issues of citizenship proved challenging. Philip Howard contends in his analysis of West Indian migrant workers in Cuba, some of whom eventually settled in New Orleans, that their "internationalism was also tied to anarcho-syndicalism in which black Caribbean workers developed a conscious identity (often formed simultaneously with organized labor) that felt that the internationalist approach could help expose how capitalism and imperialism degraded and alienated workers regardless of racial and ethnic identities."[42] Some framed their situation in class terms. Other West Indians, influenced by the Pan-Africanism of Marcus Garvey and the UNIA, linked their situation directly to race.

Blackness in Latin America and the Internationalization of Labor

The concepts of internationalism and Pan-Africanism as interpreted by West Indian migrants within Latin America gave rise to the larger issues of blackness and citizenship in Latin America. Though identity and culture in New Orleans shifted among West Indians, it cannot be ignored that most "West Indians"[43] who arrived in New Orleans were coming from the Central American republics to which West Indians had immigrated a generation earlier. Though nations such as Costa Rica and Panama (with the exception of the Canal Zone) did not grant citizenship to children of West Indian immigrants born in their territories until decades after the bulk of West Indian migrants arrived in New Orleans, citizenship in the Republic of Honduras was a birthright granted to all born in the nation regardless of the citizenship of their parents. Therefore, those "West Indians" arriving in New Orleans born in Honduras were Honduran citizens and therefore Latin American. However, Mauricio Meléndez Obando writes that in the Central American republics

(Guatemala, Honduras, Costa Rica, Nicaragua, and El Salvador) during much of the late nineteenth and early twentieth centuries, recent immigrants and their descendants were viewed by the state and the local citizenry as "foreign to the history of the isthmian (Central American) nations."[44] As a result, the citizenship of groups like the West Indians and their descendants was deemed inauthentic by the masses because the historical reality of recent immigrants was detached from the pre-Columbian and/or Spanish colonial legacy of the region. Because Latin American nationalizing discourse centered on notions of hybridity, particularly between Europeans and Native Americans, Africans and their descendants were peripheral to or completely excluded from the nationalizing projects of most nations. As a result, to be black and Latino was deemed incompatible with citizenship.

Recent scholarship on Central America has attempted to broaden the historiography of the region by engaging in research that moves away from this traditional Hispanophile narrative based in the colonial era, which centered on contact, conquest, and other facets of European-Amerindian relations. Lowell Gudmundson and Justin Wolfe maintain that within this "traditional" framework, the history of Africans and their descendants in the region has focused either on the colonial past or on the Caribbean enclave of the late nineteenth and early twentieth centuries, which are "worlds apart in time and place."[45] In discussions of the former period, the topic of blacks is too often treated as an appendage to larger discussions on racialization. In discussions of the latter period, largely owing to its focus on immigrant West Indians, blacks are viewed as separate from the nation. New scholarship integrates the black experience in Central America across all eras of the region's rich history, giving voice to previously marginalized populations such as blacks, women, and others. This historical shift is centered overwhelmingly on issues of race, class, and national identity and the ability of these previously excluded groups to negotiate a distinct identity while embedded in a political and cultural environment dedicated to the creation of a nationalistic and artificially constructed culture of modernity that favored patriarchy and European heritage. West Indian immigration in the region coincides not only with the shift in discussion on nationalism and identity but also with the growth of foreign investment in the region and the subsequent dominance of the United States in Latin American political and economic affairs.

In Central American and Spanish Caribbean societies with large concentrations of West Indian immigrant workers, blacks were viewed as undesirables, and government policies and local populations protested their recruitment into the region by the foreign companies who dominated the economy. Honduras, Costa Rica, Cuba, and Panama exaggerated the potential threat of a highly racialized, English-speaking, black population to early-twentieth-century constructed national identities that, while claiming to transcend race, reaffirmed the colonial era status quo, which glorified whiteness.[46]

The perception that West Indian immigration, which was closely tied to US expansion in the region, was a threat to the survival of national identities remains an underlying theme in most research pertaining to blacks in Central America during this historical period. Most intellectuals during the late nineteenth and early twentieth centuries feared that black immigrants would undermine the already fragile national identities of Central American nations. Scholars of communities of West Indian descent throughout Latin America and the Spanish-speaking Caribbean have made significant strides in discerning the political and social ramifications of such fears. Lara Putnam, Michael Conniff, Aviva Chomsky, Ronald Harpelle, Philippe Bourgois, and other scholars in North America, along with Central American scholars such as Quince Duncan, Darío Euraque, and Elizet Payne, have documented the social, political, and cultural impact of the massive immigration of West Indians to the region during the late nineteenth and early twentieth centuries.[47]

Most of this work, according to Lara Putnam, has been viewed through the lens of local and national debates.[48] This ultimately makes West Indian communities in Central America appear disconnected, when in reality these communities, regardless of their location in the region, are products of the same international rise of the agro-export industry, West Indian economic decline, and the massive mobilization and resettlement of labor by North American companies to the Caribbean coast of Central America. Putnam's incorporation of a regionwide analysis to explain the far-reaching impact of antiblack legislation on West Indian economic and cultural realities is one of the few comprehensive approaches to the West Indian experience in the region. However, previous scholarly work has centered largely on Costa Rica and Panama, with Honduras remaining on the periphery. The immigration of these Central Americans to New Orleans offers fertile ground for examining the complexities of migration and cultural-identity retention within British West Indian communities, as well as the impact of this movement on the national-identity debates within their host countries.[49]

Noted Honduran scholars Darío Euraque and Elizet Payne Iglesias have extended the historical debate on blackness in Central America, particularly as it relates to Honduras, by integrating the history of British West Indian immigration and its effect on broader discussions of race, nation, and identity.[50] Euraque's work emphasizes the multifarious interpretations of black identity in Honduras during the early twentieth century and the often ambiguous use of the term *black* as it applied to Hondurans of African descent, whether they were West Indians, Bay Islanders,[51] or Garifuna. While the term *black* was applied monolithically to very diverse Afro-descended populations in Honduras, it was a label synonymous with criminality and a reminder to nationalists of the economic and political dominance of foreigners in the country.

Ben Vinson notes that as Latin Americanists write the history of Afro-descendants in the region, the emphasis on hybridity and mixture can delimit the understanding of the social space that was available to blacks.[52] In the Central American context, because West Indians and their descendants have been viewed as an obstacle to notions of *mestizaje,* or racial mixture, they have been seen as inauthentic "Latinos" and reluctant citizens. Their Caribbean roots and black racial identity precluded their full inclusion into society. The study of the migration of these Central Americans to New Orleans and their negotiation of multiple ethnic and national identities contributes to an emerging field in African diaspora and Caribbean diaspora studies that looks at the implications of the cultural and demographic phenomenon of migration within the diaspora and the ways in which these new inhabitants and their descendants negotiate their multiple experiences and identities in foreign, often hostile nations.[53]

Though Central Americans of all racial and ethnic backgrounds arrived in New Orleans throughout the late nineteenth and early twentieth centuries, the greater part of this study focuses on those of West Indian descent arriving from Honduras. Honduras represents a Central American reality in which identities were in constant flux because of the early development of the multinational banana industry and the subsequent importation of West Indian workers into the country that led to the internationalization of its Caribbean coast. Issues of race, class, citizenship, labor, and national sovereignty were recurring themes throughout the period that galvanized both local and national responses. The mobilization of foreign capital (mainly British and US) into the country and the subsequent introduction of West Indian labor represented one of the first instances in which race and citizenship were linked. The status of the immigrant black population in Honduras was often uncertain. The antiblack political and social climate of Honduras led to the tense relationship between Hondurans and West Indians and their descendants. Putnam notes that beginning in the 1920s, governments across Central America outlawed black immigration on the explicit basis of race and employed legal sanctions and extralegal measures to expel West Indians, some of whom were second- and third-generation residents of the nations they were forced to flee.[54] This population's ostracization in Central America and the political and social antagonism they suffered based on their racial and ethnic identity prepared them for the realities of Jim Crow society in New Orleans. West Indians in New Orleans were racially aware, politically astute, and economically savvy as a result of their previous experiences. How they used this knowledge to navigate the Afro-Caribbean, African American, and Afro–Latin American experiences in New Orleans is pivotal to this analysis.

Chapter 1 focuses on the longstanding historical connections between New Orleans, Latin America, and the Caribbean. Though the economic and political realities that tied Louisiana to Latin America and the Caribbean dominate the scholarly discourse, the commercial activity also set the tone for future cultural and intellectual exchange. New Orleans for many Latin American and Caribbean people became the epicenter of economic and cultural life, whereas for New Orleanians of all racial backgrounds the Latin American region offered the prospect of a world not bound by the rigidity of a growing Anglo-American political and cultural reality. The myths associated with both regions ultimately shaped the flow of immigrants into New Orleans and the expansion of US business into Latin America.

Chapter 2 turns to Central America, specifically the Republic of Honduras, and the political and economic events that led to the deportation of West Indians from the Caribbean coastal areas to New Orleans. Hondurans' anti–West Indian sentiment was closely tied to fruit-company labor policies and local manifestations of xenophobic nationalism. Strategies in Honduras resembled those employed by other Central American nations to remove West Indians from their nations. Regardless of national origin, many of the West Indians who arrived in New Orleans had spent time on the Honduran North Coast (Caribbean coast) prior to their arrival. The removal of West Indians fom the various Central American republics coincided with US expansion into the isthmus and the subsequent connecting of fruit companies to the port of New Orleans. These events provided a major catalyst for West Indian immigration.

Chapter 3 centers on the ways in which West Indians navigated the political and racial terrain of New Orleans and established themselves as a viable presence in the city. It situates the arrival of West Indians in the city within larger movements occurring in the United States during the period. As Jim Crow laws became institutionalized and structural changes within the agricultural-centered economy of the South displaced many (mostly African American) workers, New Orleans became the terminus for large-scale rural-to-urban migrations, as well as the launching point for migrations to the northern and western United States. In addition, New Orleans remained one of the few destinations in the South that received significant numbers of European immigrants. All of these factors, combined with an increased Latin American trade, created a complex environment for West Indians to navigate.

Chapter 4 demonstrates the ways in which West Indians made New Orleans their home. An examination of issues around citizenship, labor organization, and connections to larger African diasporic movements within the United States and abroad shows West Indians in New Orleans to be a very small but important group. While most West Indians ultimately became US citizens and embraced a larger black identity, a few of those who identified as mixed-race or white challenged the black-white racial binary of the United States and either became "white" or developed public and private racial identities rooted in their West Indian past. While New Orleans became home for some, for many West Indians it served as a launching point for their racial, cultural, and political journeys to other parts of the United States.

Chapter 5 looks at those Latin American immigrants (whites and mestizos) who encountered many of the same challenges their West Indian and Afro–Latin American counterparts did. However, because they were Spanish American and therefore "white" according to US racial classifications at the time, they had access to opportunities and resources that their fellow citizens of visible African phenotype were not afforded. Some used this status to challenge the United States and their home governments to confront the political and economic realities that forced Central Americans to leave their countries in the first place. Others embraced US racial notions and assimilated into whiteness.

Throughout this book, I incorporate a style that is part narrative and part commentary and analysis. This approach allows the lives of West Indians and Central Americans to guide and in some cases define the discussion. This style was determined in part by the nature of the sources—immigration files, labor unions, and political-organization records—which tell the stories of individuals. However, the lives of immigrants and migrants are not linear, and the twists and turns and subtle nuances that define their lives are reflected here.

CHAPTER ONE

New Orleans and Latin America

*Disparate Destinies and Shared Imaginaries in the Late
Nineteenth and Early Twentieth Centuries*

From 1918 to 1934, Central American republics with sizable black minorities employed a heavy-handed political strategy to rid themselves of
the population of West Indian descent working in the banana enclaves
along the Caribbean coast. Their methods included, but were not limited to, passing restrictive immigration legislation, intense diplomatic
negotiation (with Great Britain and the United States), and in some
cases state-sanctioned violence targeting West Indians and others of
African descent.[1] These actions served as deterrents to many would-be
migrants to the region from the West Indies, which in previous years
had supplied large numbers of laborers to the agricultural and construction industries in places such as Costa Rica, Panama, and Honduras. By
examining the experiences of these laborers and the centrality of New
Orleans to creating and fostering the political and economic realities
that shaped the region, it is possible not only to uncover the existing ties
that bound these two regions but to understand the implicit and explicit
ways in which political and economic policies in New Orleans impacted
lives in distant Central American enclaves.

West Indian laborers not allowed into Central American republics
sought opportunities in other parts of the Americas, most notably the
United States. Many continued to work in fruit-company subsidiaries
and related industries on the docks of New Orleans and on the countless
merchant vessels that used the city as a base of operations for trade with

ports in Central America, in the Caribbean, and on the US Gulf Coast. Relying largely on US census data, naturalization applications, and ship passenger records, in addition to fruit-company papers and other sources, this chapter delves into the lives of West Indian migrants and their Central American–born offspring who chose to make New Orleans their home. These records help situate New Orleans within the larger circum-Caribbean and Latin American cultural and economic narrative of the late nineteenth and twentieth centuries and help explain why the city attracted migrants from the region.

A Latin American Port at the Mouth of the Mississippi

During the first half of the twentieth century, the two largest fruit companies operating in Latin America and the Caribbean, Standard Fruit and United Fruit, used New Orleans as their major port of operations in the United States. In addition to being a prominent hub for trade and commerce, the city also served as a point of entry to the United States for immigrants from all over the world, rivaled only by the Northeast (New York and Boston) and San Francisco. Most of these immigrants were Irish, Italian, and Eastern European in origin, but a small number arrived from Central American and Caribbean ports. Of those arriving from Central America, the majority of passengers were black with English surnames—some with British passports—originating from the banana enclaves of Honduras, Nicaragua, Costa Rica, and Panama, all indicators of West Indian heritage. As Lara Putnam, Irma Watkins-Owens, Violet Showers-Johnson, and others demonstrate, most West Indians with experience in the banana enclaves of Central America immigrated to the Northeast and ultimately contributed to the economic, political, and artistic culture of African American communities in the region by increasing the numbers of Afro-descendants in places like New York City, Boston, and Philadelphia. These secondary and tertiary migrations also increased the diversity within an African American community dominated by rural southern migrants who settled in the area as part of the first wave of the Great Migration.[2] The Caribbean dimensions of black radicalism in organized labor, the communist and socialist movements, and growing internationalism through the African Blood Brotherhood and the UNIA in the region can be attributed in part to this population.[3]

Ira Reid noted in his seminal 1939 study on West Indian immigrants to the United States that roughly 90 percent of the 150,000 foreign-born black immigrants to the United States had arrived from the Caribbean, particularly the British possessions. Most, according to Reid, had arrived in the East and remained there.[4] Reid asserts that it was the industrial nature of the Northeast that attracted many West Indians. West Indians generally avoided the South because of the lack of economic development in the region, its antiblack racial policies, and the general anti-immigrant sentiment there.[5]

Reid's assessment of West Indian immigration to the Northeast is indisputable. An article in the *West Indian Review* in 1935 by Seaton W. Manning corroborates the established scholarly assessment of Reid and others that most West Indians residing in the United States at the time "congregated in the large cities of the North on or near the sea coast with New York City, Boston, Philadelphia, Providence, and Jersey City" being the most popular destinations.[6] Contrary to Reid's findings, however, the article further maintained that as their knowledge of the country improved, many West Indians sought opportunities in southern and western states.[7] Surprisingly, thirty years prior to Manning's assessment, an article in the *New Orleans Daily Picayune* noted that there were large British West Indian "colonies" throughout the United States, particularly in Boston, New York, Philadelphia, Newport News, New Orleans, and Baltimore, the last three of which were active southern ports.[8] The article suggested that West Indians in these areas did not stand out, because they spoke English and looked and behaved like other black Americans. And prior to traveling to the United States, they had worked and saved their money in order to buy first-class passenger tickets on steamships.

First-class passage allowed West Indians to avoid heavy scrutiny by US immigration officials, a trend Ronald Bayor documents in his study of European immigrants who passed through Ellis Island during the same period.[9] Bayor recounts the case of a Polish immigrant who noted that "when the boat landed in Ellis Island, I found that there were two types of people: the poor and the ones who looked like they had some money and were dressed that way. I was among those who looked like I had money, so I had no trouble getting off the boat, although I had only $10 in my pocket."[10] Though race was an important factor in the different experiences of European immigrants and their West Indian counterparts, higher-class immigrants maintained their privileged status while on board ships and with immigration authorities. In addition, the fact that West Indians were British subjects and often traveled with British passports would not have gone unnoticed by immigration officials unwilling to deal with the potential diplomatic fallout of harassing citizens of the country's closest ally and the world's largest empire. It is also highly plausible that combined with their familiarity with the maritime industry and its laws, West Indians were aware of US immigration policies and the unofficial practice of allowing first-class passengers to enter the country with ease owing to the continued communication between immigrants and their relatives back home.

While the established literature has enriched the scholarly debate on West Indian immigrants and their descendants in the Northeast, West Indian immigration to the South, most notably to New Orleans, has been virtually absent from the historiography. Because of its perception by many as only a port of entry from which immigrants scattered to other parts of the United States, combined with the lower numbers of immigrants to the city, New Orleans has remained on the periphery. However, as Alejandro de la Fuente asserts in his study of colonial Havana, Cuba, port cities and the ships that docked there "brought consumers, merchants, products, and business."[11] These cities stimulated local economies and ultimately linked them to markets on other continents. This chapter looks at New Orleans and its ties throughout the Americas.

The Latin American and Caribbean presence in New Orleans has a long but fragmented history that is often truncated within larger historical narratives of US political and economic expansion into Latin America and the Caribbean in the mid- to late nineteenth and early twentieth centuries. Foreign-policy debates, imperialism (most notably through the use of the city as the jumping-off point for the fili-bustering campaigns of the nineteenth century), and the aftermath of late-twentieth-century political instability in Central America dominate the historiography.[12] These discussions have focused on the influence of the United States. Very few scholars have devoted attention to the fact that while the US government and private citizens were influencing Latin American and Caribbean political, economic, and cultural reali-ties, some Latin Americans, particularly those in the banana enclaves of Central America, who were most impacted by their nations' relation-ship with the United States, were using their association with North Americans to establish stronger business and personal ties to the United States. In some cases, this involved establishing business partnerships, seeking advanced education and diplomatic positions, or using the city as a staging ground for revolutionary activity back home. In other in-stances, this relationship with the United States provided opportunities often unavailable to Central Americans of West Indian descent. Their employment in New Orleans offered economic advancement to many West Indians while they escaped the local hostilities toward them in Latin American nations. New Orleans presented an economic and cul-tural lifeline to West Indians in Central America.

For Central Americans, New Orleans occupied a unique historical position. According to the literary historian Kristen Silva Gruesz, the city served as the locus of power from which US hegemony extended over Latin America for much of the nineteenth and twentieth cen-turies.[13] New Orleans was the center of the Standard Fruit Company and a major shipping port of the United Fruit Company at the height of their Latin American dominance. The city also bridged the histori-cal and cultural legacy of the Spanish, French, and American empires, forming a connection between the Gulf Coast, Latin America, and the Caribbean that often blurred the boundaries between the regions. Silva Gruesz suggests that for many Latin Americans, New Orleans was "el París hispano," or the Hispanic Paris, of North America and served as a distant center for much of Latin American intellectual life well into the twentieth century.[14] Matthew Guterl draws a similar conclusion in his assessment of New Orleans and the Gulf Coast region. He maintains that for much of the nineteenth century the Gulf of Mexico and the Caribbean were seen as "the great point for commercial traffic, human bondage (slavery), and racial fantasy (miscegenation)."[15] He further asserts that the period from the Mexican American War to 1880 witnessed the "emergence of a shared sense of time and space across the Caribbean, binding together Spanish-speaking residents of Cuba, Honduras, Mexico, and other places along the Gulf Coast."[16] This notion of a shared past and a shared identity between the Gulf Coast, Latin America, and the Caribbean, combined with the importance of New Orleans as the major Latin American port for the United States, attracted Latin Americans to the city for business and pleasure.

Central Americans' attraction to New Orleans was not the only factor in the relationship between the city and the region. Historically, Central America also aroused a certain sense of nostalgia on the part of North Americans, particularly southerners. Marked by dreams of American empire, the expansion of slavery, and the development of new foreign markets, many in the United States saw economic potential in Latin America throughout the nineteenth century. A long history of gold and silver mining in the region, along with plantation agriculture fueled by indigenous and enslaved African labor, catapulted the Spanish Empire to economic supremacy in the early decades of the sixteenth century.[17] This history of slavery, in addition to the legacies of conquest and subjugation of the indigenous population in the region, immediately placed Latin America within the political debate on the expansion of slavery in the United States in the early nineteenth century. Because many of the countries in Central America were plagued by despotic rule after the demise of the Central American Federation in 1838, and owing to the lack of economic development and infrastructure compared with other areas in the region, many southerners felt that the incorporation of the region into the economic and social dimensions of the slavery debate was in their best interest. New Orleans existed at the center of this debate and often served as the point of departure for Americans wishing to extend their political and economic influence into the region.

Central America: The New "American" Frontier

Many North American expansionists, propagating the ideology of Manifest Destiny, saw acquiring new territories as a way of increasing their political power. Those in the northern United States understood Manifest Destiny as a means of spreading the ideals of liberty and democracy, in addition to opening new economic markets.[18] However, southern slaveholders viewed these territories as potential places for the expansion of slavery. To the southerners, these areas offered a means of gaining the political representation needed to set a proslavery agenda in the US Congress. From the US efforts to acquire Cuba from Spain for $90 million in 1848—as well as the attempts of various presidential administrations from Thomas Jefferson to William McKinley to acquire the island—to William Walker's filibustering efforts in Mexico, Nicaragua, and Honduras in the 1850s, Latin Americans, especially Central Americans, have had the misfortune of being invaded both militarily and economically by the US government and its citizenry as they sought to fulfill the dream of an American empire.[19]

Of the five Central American republics formed after the federation dismantled, Honduras was by far the weakest politically and economically throughout the second half of the nineteenth century, in part owing to the lack of infrastructure dating from the Spanish colonial period. Mexico and Guatemala to the north and Panama to the south held sizable deposits of mineral wealth. As a result, the Spanish developed these areas as centers of trade. Honduras remained on the periphery. It was not until the late nineteenth and early twentieth centuries, with the rise of the banana trade, that the country began to gain international attention.

Honduras was also the republic from which the majority of immigrants to New Orleans originated, whether they were of West Indian or Spanish American descent. One of the earliest accounts of a sizable migration of North Americans to Spanish-speaking Central America occurred in 1875. Roughly three hundred white settlers from Georgia were reported to have settled in Honduras, near San Pedro Sula on the

North Coast, to produce cotton for export. However, an insect destroyed the cotton when it was nearly ready for picking, and most of the settlers ended up penniless and returned home. According to US consular records in Honduras from the period, many also chose to remain, engaging in other ventures and becoming successful businessmen.[20] This was made possible in part by efforts by the Honduran government to promote the immigration of white North Americans and Europeans to Honduras, beginning with the immigration law of 1866.[21]

In another example from roughly the same period, African Americans from Mississippi were shipped to Honduras because a former white southern slave owner hoped to preserve his way of life following the defeat of the South in the Civil War. This was not an uncommon occurrence, as many southerners had already chosen to settle in neighboring British Honduras after the Civil War, preferring not to live in a land controlled by northerners, whom they considered foreign and exploitative.[22] An editorial in the *Washington Post* in 1902 recounts the story of Jim Dixon, the Mississippi planter mentioned above. In an effort to preserve his way of life and maintain ownership of his slaves, Dixon assembled one hundred of them before they were able to realize their freedom and sailed for Honduras. However, upon landing in Honduras, Dixon was greeted by a black Honduran soldier, and he returned to the United States disheartened. Dixon found the idea of living in a country where blacks were free and had the legal sanction and capability to bear arms and enforce the law repugnant.[23]

Perhaps more important to the Dixon story is that like so many other former Confederates, Dixon saw Central America, specifically Honduras, as a place where he could maintain his status as a planter and slave owner while recapturing his former glory. This relocation ensued even though the relatively few Africans enslaved in Central America, in comparison with the numbers in other areas in Latin America and the Caribbean, were freed in 1824, roughly forty years prior to the end of the Civil War.[24] However, the perceived weakness of the Honduran state led some North Americans to immigrate there rather than comply with US laws.

There are several accounts of white North Americans successfully immigrating to Honduras. In many cases these settlers relied on local labor sources rather than an imported enslaved population. One article in 1884 described a plantation established by a white North American from New York on the banks of an unnamed river in the Trujillo area, where he engaged in agricultural production with Honduran workers, growing mostly corn, bananas, melons, and miscellaneous crops.[25] Though some of these crops, mostly the bananas, were exported, there is no indication that this settler ever engaged in a vast agricultural enterprise on the level that would emerge in the early twentieth century with the rise of fruit corporations on Honduras's North Coast. The article also recounted the development of sugar plantations by Louisiana planters who had initially immigrated to Guatemala and Belize only to later settle in Honduras. One gentleman, E. G. Cushman, reportedly purchased a large tract of land solely for the purpose of sugar production because the Honduran variety of the sugar plant was estimated to rival the Cuban product in the amount of sugar in the stalk.[26] Honduras never became dominant in the global sugar market, but subsidiaries of many of the fruit companies that would later dominate agricultural production in the region were devoted to sugar production.

Disregard for Honduran law was not uncommon during the early period of North American settlement in the region. Honduras attracted not only former Confederate slave owners but North Americans from all backgrounds. Allison Acker maintains that in the mid- to late nineteenth century many surveyors and mercenaries, salesmen and adventurers, from North America gravitated toward Honduras. Some were fugitives from US justice anxious to take advantage of the lack of any extradition treaty between Honduras and the United States.[27] William Hair recounts the story of one politician, former New Orleans mayor Glendy Burke, under suspicion for corruption relating to a Louisiana Lottery Commission scandal, who fled New Orleans and eventually settled in Honduras in 1888. He boasted of owning more property than any other American in Honduras and claimed that the political situation in Honduras was similar to that in Louisiana, which had a notorious history of corruption.[28] In an early-twentieth-century travel account, Frederick Palmer relates an encounter in the Honduran capital of Tegucigalpa with a North American ear-and-eye specialist fleeing Chicago because of charges for which he had never stood trial. Palmer describes him as the most enterprising and active resident in the city.[29] The interactions discussed by Hair and Palmer indicate that white North Americans of all socioeconomic, geographic, and cultural backgrounds took advantage of the Honduran government's liberal immigration policies and lack of political and judicial infrastructure.

The efforts of Jim Dixon to create a semblance of the southern US slave society in Central America bear some resemblance to the efforts of former Confederate citizens from Texas, Mississippi, and Louisiana who established themselves in resettlement communities in British Honduras and Brazil. Like Dixon and the three hundred white settlers from Georgia, these former slave owners had to reevaluate their position on slavery and come to terms with the fact that African slavery had been abolished before their arrival in Honduras and that at least in theory blacks were their equals there.[30] In many instances, the Confederate settlers simply directed their antiblack sentiment toward the local nonwhite populations.

North American whites were not the only group to imagine a new existence in Latin America. There is a minor history of black immigration to Latin America, most notably among the *gens de couleur libre,* or free people of color, from southwestern Louisiana. Primarily a mixed-race group, the free people of color in Louisiana developed a culture that was often at odds with those of the masses of both blacks and whites. Maintaining a middling status built on the preservation of their distinct multiracial identity of African, European, and, in some instances, Native American descent, this group was not acknowledged by the American racial construct based on hypodescent as white (or distinct), and after the Civil War they were integrated into the newly freed African American population.

The immigration of small numbers of Creoles of color from various regions of southern Louisiana to Latin America predates the efforts of white southerners by almost thirty years. Carl Brasseaux indicates that as early as 1832 members of the St. Landry Parish, Louisiana, Donato family began to forge cultural and economic ties with Veracruz, Mexico.[31] Primarily a sugar-producing state, Veracruz allowed the Donato family and a few other Creole plantation owners to extend their resources and prepare for the inevitability of immigration in the face of white aggression and hostility to the prosperity of Creole planters. Such events actually transpired in the 1850s, when white hostility to local free blacks took the form of legal and extralegal efforts to eradicate the population from the area. As a result, a few free blacks fled the prairies of southwestern Louisiana, with a small number settling in Mexico.[32] Veracruz became a popular destination for many white Louisiana planters in later years.[33]

In the Honduran example, several instances hint at the introduction of African Americans as contract workers on the proposed industrial projects of private, white North American citizens in the country. In 1892, an American businessman by the name of Washington Valentine, founder of the Honduras and Rosario Mining Company, was given a contract to complete the Inter-Oceanic Railroad from Puerto Cortés on the Caribbean coast of Honduras to the Bay of Fonseca on the Pacific coast. Initiated in the 1860s by US and British businessmen, the project had failed to come to fruition owing to scandal and corruption.[34] According to some, the deals negotiated regarding the railroad were an example of international high financiering concocted in the banking and brokerage houses of London and Paris and negotiated between rogue diplomats and capitalists without the consent of the Honduran government.[35]

In 1897 Valentine and Henry L. Sprague requested a concession from the Honduran government in order to build an interoceanic railroad. The proposal, made in the name of the Honduras Syndicate (later the Honduran Railroad), was for Honduras Syndicate employees and settlers to be allowed to enter the country for the purpose of building the railroad. Within the first ten years of their stay in Honduras, the settlers and workers would be exempt from all forms of taxation. In this proposal, the only group specifically excluded from participating in the building of the railroad was the Chinese.[36]

In 1898, Valentine and Sprague were given the concession to build the railroad under the terms specified in their proposal of the previous March. The proposal did not specify whether blacks, from the United States or the West Indies, could take part in the project as workers and settlers. This became an issue in December 1897, when the railroad line between the cities of Cortés and Pimienta needed repair. Reflecting the racially based, eugenic thinking of the period, company officials argued that local workers, because of their "indolent nature," were unable to do the job and that blacks were best suited for the type of labor required. Therefore, the company requested that three hundred blacks from the United States be imported into the country to make the necessary railroad repairs. By all accounts, the Honduran government agreed to the request of Valentine and Sprague's company under the condition that the workers would return to the United States upon completion of their jobs, indicating a strong desire on the part of the government to prohibit permanent settlement of blacks in the country.[37]

As industry developed along Honduras's North Coast, US-owned companies and private citizens repeatedly asked that African American workers be included as part of the labor force in their business and colonization efforts. In one particular instance, J. R. Miller of Mobile, Alabama, petitioned the Honduran government to allow twenty-five families from the United States into La Mosquitia of Honduras as settlers. Miller stated that though the original plan for settlers included only whites, he was willing to bring black settlers in a number specified by the government. Miller insisted on the condition that these blacks would only have privileges as stipulated by the white settlers.[38] Though Miller's request was relatively small and his area of settlement was in a remote region of the country, the issue of African Americans as laborers in Honduras still surfaced. In the few records that exist related to this population, New Orleans remains central to the story since most of the African Americans were recruited from that city.

William Penney, a Canadian railroad contractor in Central America during the 1890s who worked for one of John Jacob Astor's companies in Guatemala, maintained that "70 to 80 Negroes weekly" were arriving from New Orleans to build railroads in Guatemala.[39] These men were recruited by agents in New Orleans whose unscrupulous methods paralleled those used by labor agents in the Caribbean to entice West Indians to the region. Penney recounts men who worked as coachmen in

New Orleans being recruited with the assurance that they would hold the same occupation in the railroad camps. In reality, the workers were tasked with clearing land and draining swamps to lay railroad tracks.[40] Each worker cost the contractor thirty-eight US dollars, which covered passage, the amount paid to the labor agent in New Orleans, the issuance of a blanket, and a mosquito bar.

The wages paid to the workers are unclear from the account, but the slavelike conditions under which the men were forced to work, the high rates of desertion, and the men's constant demands to be returned to New Orleans suggest that the situation was not favorable. Some of these African American laborers initially contracted in Guatemala (roughly 900) were also sent to Honduras to work on the railroads there. In Honduras, after these men refused to work and threatened violence if they were not allowed to return home, Astor eventually wired Penney the money to send the workers back to the United States. Astor and Penney acted out of fear that the men would disrupt the entire economic enterprise in Honduras. They were eventually sent home on a steamer bound first for Jamaica and then for the United States. However, their ultimate fate remains unclear, because New Orleans was under quarantine (for yellow fever), and Penney was on the vessel only as far as Kingston.[41] It is probable that the men were sent to New York, as that was the only other location where they expressed a willingness to debark in the United States.

While the experiences of the African American workers in Guatemala and Honduras are but minor footnotes in the larger historiographies of the respective nations, their experiences, combined with those of white American absconders from justice, former Confederates, filibusters, and businessmen, point to the centrality of New Orleans as the place where their Central American narrative began. Perhaps because of the nature of their activities in the region, very little evidence survives recounting the full extent of their time there. However, the fact that they created or tapped into existing networks from New Orleans reaffirms the importance of the city as a bridge between the United States and Latin America.

New Orleans, the Caribbean, and the Ambiguity of Race: The Caymanian and British Honduran "Exception"

While New Orleans was increasingly at the political and economic center of US activity with Latin America, the histories of both areas with regard to issues of race and identity also linked the two. Of the Central Americans and West Indians who arrived in New Orleans, the experiences of migrants from British Honduras (Belize) and, to a lesser extent, the Cayman Islands highlight the complicated ways in which racial identity, as well as British colonialism, developed among West Indians. Owing to their historical and colonial experiences, British Hondurans and Caymanians were the groups most equipped to navigate the racial and ethnic terrain of New Orleans. Belize was extremely racially diverse, with its African, European, indigenous Mayan, and mestizo populations. In the Cayman Islands, the majority of the population were of mixed African and European heritage. However, both colonies were structured within a British colonial system in which whiteness (whether real or imagined) was at the pinnacle of the racial order culturally, economically, and administratively. Citizens within these societies understood the fluidity and rigidity of race more than did most people from areas that were overwhelmingly of African or mestizo descent, in which skin color played less of a defining role in daily life.

The inhabitants of British Honduras and especially the Cayman Islands had a long history of working as seamen on fishing and merchant vessels in the Gulf of Mexico and the western Caribbean. Many English-speaking communities throughout the Caribbean littoral in Latin America (particularly the Bay Islands of Honduras and the Corn and Swan Islands of Nicaragua) trace their origins to earlier Caymanian emigrations to these areas that began in the early 1830s, just prior to the abolition of slavery in the British Caribbean colonies.[42] Many British Hondurans, particularly around Belize City, also trace their ancestry to Caymanians who settled there as well. An examination of Caymanian and British Honduran history offers insight into the experiences of these migrants and their descendants in New Orleans.

There were enslaved Africans in the Cayman Islands, though to a lesser degree than in other areas in the Caribbean. Largely owing to the islands' limited geography and the unsuitable nature of the soil for sugar production, the plantation economy that came to dominate most islands in the Caribbean never flourished in the Caymans. Instead, the islands' white settlers (British army deserters and former indentured servants, among others) made a subsistence living from the sea, as either fishermen or turtle farmers. Racial mixture was high, reflected in the population's wide ranges of colors and phenotypes. As a result, Caymanians were often whiter or lighter than most West Indians.

British Honduran immigrants to New Orleans represented a racial and ethnic spectrum that was as diverse as that in the colony. According to O. Nigel Bolland, by the end of the nineteenth century British Honduras embodied a "modally segmented plurality in which several racial stocks, languages, and cultures were incorporated as equivalent segments, though all were *de facto* dominated by the Creole group or one of its sections,"[43] which was also highly stratified along racial, ethnic, color, and class lines. The largest and most dominant group in the colony was the Creoles (the British Honduran equivalent to coloreds), who were largely a mixture of African and European descendants; they were Protestant and lived near Belize City. Their power in the country throughout the colonial period was relegated largely to the cultural sphere. The small but powerful ruling class of whites, primarily of British origin, operated as the true economic and political power brokers in the colony. They owned roughly 95 percent of all arable land in the country and monopolized the import-export trade in foodstuffs, on which most of the population depended. It was thus nearly impossible, according to anthropologist Mark Moberg, for most peasants to establish independent farms and other sources of economic independence.

Bolland maintains that those nonelites who successfully acquired land and developed it had to pay twenty-five times as much for crown land, and they ultimately were denied titles or had to relinquish their holdings to white settlers when the colonial government created the infrastructure to support and encourage European settlement to the area.[44] This in part explains the high degree of racial hostility that existed in the colony during the period. In the 1890s, US newspaper outlets reported sensationalized accounts of blacks in British Honduras rebelling against whites. While most accounts represented the white minority as victims of "violent blacks," an article in the *Cleveland (OH) Gazette* noted that whites in the colony had usurped authority and monopolized the trade and business sectors of the economy.[45] The unnamed author of the piece also maintained that whites had seized all lands and controlled the rivers and oceans (maritime industry), as well as dictated the national policies to their advantage. The unrest in the colony was represented not as racially motivated but as a fight against economic inequality and injustice.

The Maya, mestizo, and Garifuna minorities in other regions of the colony suffered a similar fate as workers in the agricultural sector. As a result, the lives of most British Hondurans outside the capital city were determined by the whims of elites, whose political and economic dominance forced the lower classes to work in industries in which they were underpaid and overworked, and they incurred enormous debt through the advanced truck system of labor.[46] For those British Hondurans who wanted a better economic future, the only option was to emigrate to other areas. The banana plantations of Guatemala and Honduras provided early opportunities for them. Once these prospects diminished, many looked to the United States for work, particularly on trade and merchant vessels operating between the Caribbean and southern US port cities.

Though agriculture and the logging industry employed the majority of British Hondurans during the period, citizens of the Belize district and elsewhere made a living in water transport and related industries. Available census data for the British colony from 1891 to 1931 reveal a consistent minority, an average of 290 men, who listed their occupation as "bargeman" or "boatsman." Roughly the same number described themselves as fishermen. The men engaged in these professions were most often aged fourteen to fifty-nine and lived in close contact with those engaged in similar professions along the Guatemalan and Honduran coasts. In fact, the census data from 1921 and 1931 indicate that by far the largest group of immigrants into the colony was Central Americans, the majority of whom were Spanish-speaking Hondurans and Guatemalans. In 1931, for example, out of a total population of 19,337 for Belize district, roughly 1,641 foreigners from the West Indies and Central America were listed. Of those, 541 were from British West Indian colonies, and the remaining 1,100 were Central Americans and Mexicans. Of the 1,100, roughly 232 were British subjects, either return migrants or their children from the neighboring Honduran and Guatemalan banana enclaves.[47] It is impossible to determine the racial breakdown of the census data because such categories were absent in the official census. The data do show that Central Americans were beginning to cross national borders in search of economic opportunity. The mechanisms that ultimately led to immigration to the United States were already in play within the region.

Despite the absence of racial categories in the official data, the gender breakdown of the figures was available. This breakdown revealed that among British subjects from other West Indian possessions, women represented 33 percent (178) of the population. Among Central Americans from the Spanish-speaking republics living in Belize, women accounted for 42 percent (459) of the population. Of the previously mentioned 232 from this population claiming British citizenship, 50 percent (117) were women.[48]

The employed West Indian women from other colonies in the British Honduran census were domestic workers, textile workers (dressmakers), sales employees at commercial establishments, students, or housewives. While the data are far from conclusive, the higher number of these women British subjects employed in Belize during the period perhaps explains why the immigrant population from the district to New Orleans was overwhelmingly male. The Creole monopoly of the male-dominated water transport industry, combined with a lack of gainful employment, increased the likelihood of migration for men, whereas women migrants to the country were able to secure more stable employment.

The period 1914–32 witnessed an expansion of British Honduran and Caymanian society to the point where international affairs such as World War I and the economic depression that ensued in the region began to have an influence on local matters. These factors, combined with the property destruction and casualties resulting from the hurricanes of 1931 and 1932, propelled many to seek further opportunities abroad.[49] These immigrants, particularly Caymanians (and Bay Islanders from Honduras of Caymanian descent), did not have the same experiences as West Indians who arrived from the banana enclaves of Honduras and Costa Rica or from the Panama Canal Zone. Their story illustrates how West Indians navigated the US racial spectrum. Because many of these immigrants were of mixed race, white, or near white, they did not fit within the traditional US black/white racial binary. Within New Orleans, there was a cultural and historical precedent for absorbing such a population, as evidenced by the experiences of the previously mentioned Creoles of color challenging this binary. Of those West Indians who were later designated as white in US census and naturalization applications, British West Indians and Caymanians are overrepresented. However, what constituted blackness on the racial spectrum in New Orleans and the larger US context gave these immigrants much to contend with.

CHAPTER TWO

Criminalizing Blackness

Liberals, Modernization, and the West Indian "Problem" in Honduras

Regardless of where their origins were in the Caribbean or Central America, the majority of West Indian immigrants in New Orleans who were employed by the United Fruit Company (UFCO) had spent some time in the banana zones of Honduras. In fact, most of these immigrants gave La Ceiba, Tela, or Puerto Cortés, on Honduras's North Coast, as their port of embarkation to New Orleans or their last known foreign address on their US applications for naturalization. In Honduras, the political establishment targeted and scapegoated West Indians as the reason for the cultural and economic decline of the nation. As a result, West Indians were subjected to violence at the hands of private citizens, the military, and the police force. Honduran historiography is limited in its analysis of this political violence during this period.

On the basis of evidence gathered from British, North American, and Honduran archives, I argue in this chapter that while the Honduran government sought to rid the nation of the growing number of West Indians, employing extreme nationalist rhetoric to incite popular violence against them, West Indians in the banana enclaves used these violent altercations to challenge the British government to fulfill its (real and perceived) obligations to its subjects abroad. The violence also forced American employers to reconcile their complicity in the deterioration of race and ethnic relations on the Caribbean coast and reassess their business practices related to hiring and compensation. Unfortunately, many

West Indians employed by the American fruit companies discovered that they were expendable to the corporations. However, the fruit companies did allow for their safe passage to the United States. The events in Honduras and their treatment by the previously mentioned interests compelled West Indians to acknowledge a black racial identity that in the face of mob violence superseded class distinctions. Their blackness also aided in their transition into the New Orleans racial dynamic, surpassing ethnicity as the most defining feature of their community.

The Hondurans, British, and Americans in the banana enclaves fostered an environment that ultimately scapegoated West Indians and forced them to repatriate to their home colonies or emigrate to the United States. Because West Indians had been a presence in Honduras since the 1890s (earlier in the Bay Islands), their children born in Honduras represented an additional political and diplomatic challenge. Unlike in Costa Rica, where citizenship was not granted to West Indians and their descendants until 1948, or Panama, where the citizenship issue was not resolved until 1946,[1] in Honduras West Indians and their descendants were legally Honduran citizens by birth despite being raised culturally as "British" and "West Indian" and educated in English-speaking schools that promoted the values of the British Empire. The status of these Honduran-born "British" West Indians challenged the fundamental principles of citizenship for both Hondurans and West Indians and forced both to come to terms with the nation's changing demographics and multicultural dimensions.

When West Indians began to leave Honduras and emigrate to the United States, questions arose about their racial, ethnic, and national identity. US immigration authorities questioned whether they were black and West Indian, and therefore subject to the racial politics of the Jim Crow South, or British or Latin American, and therefore excluded. The ways in which this complex identity built in the banana enclaves of Honduras over decades of transnational migration translated in the rigid and limited racial structure of the United States is best understood within the context of the banana enclaves of Central America. In the banana enclaves, Honduran detractors stereotyped West Indians as a political and racial "problem," associating them with criminality, degeneracy,

and an unfit citizenry. As they confronted political violence in Honduras, West Indians developed diplomatic and community-organizing skills
pivotal to combating the unyielding racial antagonism in Honduras that
would later serve them well in New Orleans.

Much of the discourse on race and crime in Latin America surfaced
during the rise of liberal ideology in the aftermath of Latin American
independence from Spain. The anthropologist Adrienne Pine suggests
that in the past as in contemporary times, Hondurans' perceptions of
themselves were defined "largely in opposition to what they were not."[2]
During the late nineteenth and early twentieth centuries, Honduran
intellectuals and politicians attempted to construct a homogenous national identity in a historically multiracial and multiethnic nation. Such
efforts mimicked those of elites in other nations across the region, particularly those into which US business interests expanded. According to
Richard Graham, Latin Americans during the period aspired to an even
closer connection to Europe and the United States and sought to follow
their leadership in every realm.[3] This ultimately meant developing a ra-
tionale for excluding undesirable elements of the population through
the adoption of racist policies. This attempt at modernization, according
to Robert Buffington, strengthened state power in Latin America but did
not result in more open societies.[4] In fact, the desire for control of different social groups undoubtedly influenced the formation of state policies that led to negative perceptions of certain elements within society.

Anti–West Indian sentiment throughout Central America progressed
within this trend and coincided with a growing sense of Honduran nationalism organized around a mestizo (Spanish and indigenous) identity.
At the same time, there was a heightened political instability within the
country, most observable in the numerous revolutions, military coups
d'état, and cases of government corruption. In the Caribbean coastal
towns of Honduras, this nationalism was centralized and voiced most
effectively by nativists in relation to labor and worker solidarity. The
nativists believed that Central American leaders who sacrificed national
sovereignty and the needs of their fellow citizenry for individual wealth
and short-term political gain had abandoned nationalist aspirations for
political, economic, and cultural autonomy.[5]

Nationalist sentiments in the country had some merit in that the economic and political influence of the American-owned fruit companies enabled them to circumvent Honduran law and allowed these foreign companies to maintain a sizable West Indian contingent in skilled labor positions, despite Honduran officials' success in eradicating the majority of West Indian laborers in other parts of the country. The fruit companies could not import more West Indian labor into the country, but those who were already in Honduras continued to advance within the companies and served as a reminder to many Honduran nationalists that they were not in full control of their nation.

Brought over primarily as laborers to work in the banana industry, West Indians (the majority of whom were Jamaican and British Honduran subjects of the British Empire) often competed with native Hondurans and other Spanish-speaking Central Americans for employment. More importantly, they represented a population that was black, English-speaking, Protestant, foreign, and tied to the US corporate interests that many Hondurans felt threatened national sovereignty and hindered the economic development and political stability of the nation, as well as its racial and cultural integrity.

Such sentiments were precursors to more contemporary notions of modern imperialism. According to Stephen Streeter, John Weaver, and William Coleman, formal collective autonomy coexisted with economic dependency; nations relinquished some local political control to US interests in exchange for access to US markets and trade.[6] However, in the Honduran example, because US corporations monopolized the majority of economic activity on the North Coast, their influence extended into every facet of Honduran life, and politicians were easily swayed through bribes and other incentives to appease the fruit companies.

The Honduran politicians responded to the growing local discontent with foreign dominance of the nation and the conclusion of the masses that immigration was to blame for their economic uncertainty by developing an immigration policy that by 1929 had become increasingly anti–West Indian and by 1934 was outright exclusionary. Though West Indians made up a significant portion of the immigrant population on the Caribbean coast, their numbers were miniscule in comparison with other Central Americans (mainly Spanish-speaking Salvadorans, Guatemalans, and Nicaraguans) working for American fruit companies as day laborers and seasonal employees. West Indians, with their privileged status in the fruit companies, were targeted largely because they were the most vulnerable within the banana enclaves. A direct attack on the American fruit companies could result in US military intervention and certain failure, as US warships were permanently in close proximity to protect government interests in the Caribbean and the Panama Canal Zone. However, West Indians were considered expendable by all parties involved. Attacks on them or other non-Hispanic workers gained the attention of the American employers and created opportunities to negotiate for better pay and working conditions. In addition, the attacks on West Indians forced the Honduran government to address citizens' demands or risk further alienating constituents and potentially inciting a revolution.

West Indians, more than any other immigrant population in Central America, represented US interests. There was an abundant local labor supply for unskilled positions in the banana fields. For skilled positions, the fruit companies preferred West Indians. American employers often justified their preference for West Indian labor through the disparagement of natives. Native workers, according to many Americans, "had no knowledge of construction, field surveying, or wharf, motor, fireman, and stevedoring work," which was essential for business operations.[7] One US diplomatic official argued that "if companies were compelled to rely on local labor . . . they would soon have to close down operations" owing to the ineptitude of local workers.[8] American merchants also expressed their desire for West Indian laborers in Honduras. "If the colored people (West Indians)," according to the merchants, "were to leave, their [merchants'] businesses would end because they are the only ones who put money into circulation."[9] Hondurans, on the other hand, were described as drunks who spent their pay as soon as they received it and then blamed their employers for their misfortunes.[10] Such observations suggest that for American employers and business owners, West Indians' value centered as much on their role as consumers of US products and contributors to the local economy as on their skills as workers.

The American fruit companies practiced a form of welfare capitalism in the banana enclaves that benefited North American and West
Indian employees to the exclusion of all others. This approach unwit-
tingly encouraged Honduran animosity toward West Indian labor. The
fruit companies imported various aspects of the company town model,
which had been a part of the American industrial fabric since the early
nineteenth century, to the North Coast of Honduras. Welfare capitalism
arose out of the Progressive Era of the 1890s and the first decade of the
twentieth century. The term was defined as any service that provided
for the comfort or improvement of employees that was neither a neces-
sity of industry nor required by law.[11] Some of the unique attributes of
this model, according to Arnold Alanen, included innovative physical
designs that utilized the talents of professional architects, landscape
architects, planners, and engineers; and social programs that provided
benefits for workers and their families.[12] This approach was intended to
attract skilled and dependable workers who would be contented, effi-
cient, and less likely to engage in strikes and labor disruption.[13]

Welfare capitalism aimed at paternalistically controlling employee
behavior in the workplace and at home. Home-ownership programs,
health-care and life-insurance plans, stock-investment options, limited retirement benefits, workplace-safety improvements, and even
home-economics classes for wives and daughters of workers were some
of the most common benefits of employees who worked for major companies during this period and maintained amicable relations with them.

Kenneth Warren, in his study of the Bethlehem Steel Company,
paints a picture very similar to Alanen's of US Steel. The owner of Bethlehem paid bonuses (often quarterly) to those in management, believing that they would work harder if they knew their families were well
provided for. The company also filled key positions by promoting from
within rather than hiring from outside. Warren maintains that in some
cases the company's bonuses and other incentives reached as high as 7.31
percent of the net annual income.[14] Despite the numerous benefits afforded management and other workers in key positions, for the majority
of laborers wages were stagnant, work was inconsistent, job-related inju-
ries because of substandard safety conditions were high, and organized

labor and collective bargaining were strictly prohibited, punishable by termination and blacklisting.[15]

Though the methods employed by large industrial companies in the United States developed in different political, economic, geographic, and historical contexts than those of fruit-company operations in Honduras, the fruit-company towns there were extensions of much larger multinational corporations based in the United States (Boston and New Orleans). Therefore, some of the operational methods employed by these companies in Honduras mirrored practices employed by other industries in the United States during the period, especially the ways in which they dealt with employees. In the Honduran banana towns of Omoa, La Ceiba, Tela, Trujillo, and Puerto Castilla, the majority of the design and architectural details, living quarters, and recreational activities for company officials (including West Indians) were developed in New Orleans or Boston. Neighborhoods in La Ceiba such as Barrio Inglés or Watertank and the White Zone (later the American Zone) in Tela are a few examples of communities built by the fruit companies to house their West Indian employees and their families in Honduras. These neighborhoods continue to exist, offering a testament to the comprehensive planning and sustainability of these projects. Ronald Harpelle notes that while these communities were segregated, with black and white neighborhoods for workers and their families, most locals were excluded from residing in these spaces. More importantly, the companies owned the communities and all of their resources, which were designed to maximize profits and give the companies complete control.[16]

Though the fruit companies' efforts to control the West Indian workers were relatively successful, they could not control local perceptions of the mostly black workers. Despite the stereotyping of both West Indian and Honduran workers, job competition was a common justification for increased efforts to pass anti–West Indian immigration legislation. To make this case, many Honduran intellectuals and government officials constructed a link between increased criminality along the coast and the growing West Indian population. Such discourse granted local police forces and the military on the North Coast carte blanche to exercise a level of violence against blacks that was unparalleled in the region. The intellectual arguments and police violence, combined with a Honduran labor force scapegoating West Indians as an obstacle to Honduran nationalism, led to most West Indians' leaving the country by 1934, the year in which the most restrictive antiblack immigration legislation was passed.[17] Because Honduras had become increasingly hostile to West Indians throughout the 1920s, those British Hondurans, Caymanians, and Jamaicans who in previous years had considered migrating to the country had to seek other opportunities.

While many Hondurans and other Central Americans felt that West Indians were a significant obstacle to national political and economic success, the treatment experienced by them at the hands of both the government and the private citizenry was only a symptom of a much larger problem, the populace's discontent with a failing state and their inability to save it and themselves from being swallowed up by global US political, economic, and cultural influences. Nancy Appelbaum maintains that the historically liberal ideologies of the elites presumed an unmarked, raceless, even genderless citizenry but described the ideal qualities of citizens and nations in implicitly racial and gendered terms.[18] Literacy, property ownership, and individual autonomy were associated with whiteness and masculinity by the elite.[19] Appelbaum asserts that in addition to blaming the ills of Latin American societies on politics, dictators, conservative plots, the church, and various other institutions, liberals adopted the views of conservative social Darwinists, who blamed the high level of poverty and the lack of industrial growth in many Latin American countries on the inherently inferior racial and genetic makeup of their multiracial populations.[20] Carlos Aguirre and Robert Buffington argue that the adverse effect of this was that blacks, women, street vendors, prostitutes, political dissidents, foreigners, and others who went against societal norms were designated as criminal.[21]

In the banana enclaves on the Caribbean coast with significant West Indian populations, labor organizations and private citizens who resented the West Indian presence took their cues in part from Honduran intellectuals and government officials. By the 1920s, the Honduran ruling class had established a precedent of exploiting the issue of West Indian labor on the North Coast for political gain through race-baiting tactics cloaked in Honduran nationalist rhetoric. These politicians and intellectuals positioned West Indians as the consummate other by emphasizing the racial, linguistic, religious, and cultural differences between them and other Hondurans. Elizet Payne Iglesias notes that during this period, the rhetoric, particularly on the North Coast, presented all other Hondurans as *del país* (of the nation), while West Indians were referred to as *los ingleses* (Englishmen), an allusion to their real or perceived status as British subjects and therefore foreigners.[22] This rhetoric, according to British officials in Honduras, was used most often by recently elected political officials, who successfully played both sides of the political divide to maintain power. On the one hand, politicians successfully depicted the West Indian as the "other." On the other hand, they collected customary graft for "protection" of the West Indians through threats of deportation.[23] Such policies underscored the immense political corruption on the North Coast.

Nationalizing Antiblackness and Localizing Violence

On many levels taking their lead from the politicians, the local population on the North Coast took out their frustrations through violence toward the West Indian population. The development of anti–West Indian sentiment in Honduras had far-reaching implications for other areas in Central America. Through an analysis of Honduran discourse on black criminality, combined with the massive labor strikes of 1924, in which the rhetoric coming from both elites and nonelites clearly positioned the West Indian (and by extension all Hondurans of African descent) as the antithesis of Honduran national identity, it is possible to discern the culture of antiblack violence in Honduras and the West Indian reaction to it. The failed West Indian response to this violence, most often through diplomatic channels but also through a reassessment and revitalization of a strong West Indian cultural identity, made it difficult for subsequent generations of Afro-descended populations in Honduras to be integrated into the nation. The labor strikes throughout the 1920s led to the mass migration of West Indians and their descendants to other locales, most notably the United States.

Political corruption on Honduras's North Coast has a long history. Reports from La Ceiba as early as 1895 maintained that the number of crimes committed by police in the city and along the coast was high.[24] In the Trujillo–Puerto Castilla area, the eventual seat of the Truxillo Railroad Company (a UFCO subsidiary) and site of the most intense and violent anti–West Indian sentiment, much of the crime could be attributed to corruption within the city's leadership. The chief of police was arrested for his involvement in the illegal contraband trade that both fueled and plagued the region.[25] The police chief claimed that he had been incarcerated solely for political reasons. However, an investigation revealed his culpability. Because corruption was rampant among officials in the region, the government faced considerable difficulty appointing a replacement within the existing leadership. As a result, the area experienced widespread disorder and increased lawlessness, a point that local citizens voiced candidly to officials in the capital, Tegucigalpa.[26] The chief was incarcerated in June 1895, but his replacement was not appointed until October, so that there were months of instability in the city during which police and other officials continued to commit crimes and abuses (notably theft and extortion) on the local population without fear of retribution.

The situation with the police chief offers one example of corruption among Honduran political officials. US diplomatic officials in the region documented numerous other instances in which Honduran officials, mostly soldiers and policemen, contributed to crimes and public disorder on the North Coast.[27]

Though anti–West Indian sentiment in Honduras started to develop as increasing numbers of them arrived on the North Coast in the early twentieth century, the first organized attack on West Indian labor as a political strategy at all levels of Honduran society emerged in the 1920s. Prior to that time, the bulk of the anti–West Indian sentiment was reactionary and limited to random protests by small groups of dissatisfied workers and the rants of a few intellectuals and minor politicians seeking votes during national elections. However, in the years leading up to the 1924 revolution, West Indians were increasingly identified as the primary obstacle to Honduran sovereignty. In the Honduran press, contradictory reports on the West Indian presence on the North Coast by journalists and intellectuals depicted them both as poor criminals responsible for many of the social ills degrading the national culture and as the wealthy beneficiaries of fruit-industry capital and thus, exploiters of the Honduran masses. Either scenario justified the removal of this population from Honduras.

Honduras for the Hondurans: Nativism, Xenophobia, and the West Indian Worker

Honduran intellectuals who opposed nonwhite immigration also portrayed West Indians as a criminal element on the North Coast.[28] Most of the attacks on West Indian immigration occurred from 1915 to 1918 and from 1929 to 1934, periods in which new immigration legislation was formulated to restrict West Indians. According to Darío Euraque, the expansion of the banana industry in Honduras through foreign capital motivated Honduran intellectuals to mobilize the masses around the concept of mestizo national identity.[29] Peter Lambert maintains that for weak states confronted by powerful opposition, "arguments of national identity offer a degree of political legitimacy and are seen to legitimate and justify the use of coercion, repression and violence."[30] This nationalism, according to Lambert, associated with xenophobia, authoritarianism, domestic repression, subordination of separatist regions, and a militarized confrontation with other sovereign states, defined much of Central American history from the late nineteenth to the mid-twentieth century.[31]

Froylán Turcios, a noted Honduran poet, intellectual, and prolific commentator on the state of Honduran society, and other prominent figures galvanized the nation around immigration reform through the language of xenophobic nationalism. Euraque asserts that in response to the withering of Honduran national sentiment as a result of increased foreign investments and involvement in the political and economic affairs of the country, intellectuals sought to recover national sovereignty without alienating foreign investors by "waging a battle against immigrant workers."[32] Turcios claimed that "black labor, particularly from the

Anglo-Saxon countries such as the West Indies, constituted a source of unease and neighboring danger."[33] "Black workers," he further insisted, were "less intelligent, less apt for agricultural work, and . . . more prone to violence and crime due to their physiological makeup."[34] Turcios offered widely held notions of black inferiority and degeneracy as a justification for a race-based immigration policy. His remarks represented some of the few instances within the national debate centering on immigration when an influential figure specifically labeled English-speaking black labor as a danger to Honduras.

Other comments in the press appeared largely in editorials anonymously written by concerned citizens, most often from locales far away from the banana zones of the North Coast, in regions where there were no West Indians. One editorial from Tegucigalpa reprinted in a La Ceiba newspaper stated that blacks brought an "unpleasant diagnosis" for Honduran society by importing their "disgusting culture" to the country.[35]

Attributing criminal activity to the West Indian population served multiple purposes for Honduran officials. The arrival of substantial numbers of West Indians in the late nineteenth and early twentieth centuries threatened the validity of Honduras's claims to having a racially mixed society.[36] As previously discussed, the early decades of the twentieth century witnessed a concerted effort by the government to promote a mestizo identity with an emphasis on the Iberian and indigenous cultural heritage of the nation. The term *mestizo* later incorporated other mixed-race groups, such as mulattoes, to create a broad interpretation of *mestizaje* that served the purpose of uniting the nation under one racial paradigm. However, while this broad definition recognized the validity of a large segment of the Honduran population, the term excluded people who chose to culturally and racially identify with African or Indian descent. Breny Mendoza maintains that the tendency in Honduran historiography to focus on the myth of a harmonious relationship between the Spanish and the indigenous peoples that created the mestizo during the colonial period and to overemphasize the importance of these two groups to the development of the national culture has created a situation in which the immigration histories of groups like West Indians in the postcolonial era are rendered "insignificant and non-existent to Honduran nationalism."[37] Because of their "blackness," West Indians were regarded by many in Honduras as a threat to the mestizo national identity, despite a long history of racial and cultural mixture on the North Coast between the African, indigenous, and European elements of Honduran society.

In addition to their African ancestry, West Indians also held coveted skilled positions in the growing banana industry in Honduras. British officials in Guatemala and British Honduras often commented on the internal dynamics of the banana enclaves. While most West Indians worked as agricultural laborers, some secured employment as maintenance men, artisans, and mechanics.[38] Sir Harold Kittermaster, governor of British Honduras, noted that American employers exacerbated tensions between Hondurans and West Indians on numerous occasions by arguing that West Indians possessed a greater "aptitude for work as compared to the natives of Honduras."[39] The preference for West Indians and the racialization of the labor force by the fruit companies created a situation that led one British observer from the British Consulate in Guatemala City to state that the people of Honduras's North Coast felt "more against people of the Negro race than elsewhere in the region."[40] The North Coast, he continued, was "more dangerous as conditions were lawless and local jealousy against foreigners was fueled by economic depressions."[41] Most Hondurans and other Spanish-speaking Central Americans were relegated to seasonal labor, cutting and packaging bananas. Honduran politicians used the overrepresentation of West Indian labor in permanent, skilled positions as evidence of the displacement of Honduran workers from jobs within the banana zones by black immigration. According to some, West Indians were "taking the bread out of the mouths of native workmen."[42]

In order to rid the nation of this population, manufactured literature such as the previous examples written by Froylán Turcios associating the West Indian population with high rates of crime and violence was used as a vehicle to nationalize the Honduran labor force and eliminate job competition for Hondurans.[43] This strategy worked in that the rise in antiblack immigration legislation coincided with increased journalistic coverage of black criminality on the North Coast. The 1929 and

1934 immigration laws, which restricted and banned black immigration to Honduras, respectively, were fueled largely by the growing antiblack sentiment in the banana zones. These laws represented the culmination of a long and arduous legislative campaign to limit the arrival of non-white immigrants to the nation.

Police and Thieves: State-Sanctioned Violence on the North Coast

While Honduran immigration laws fueled anti West Indian sentiment and increased the level of violence committed against blacks on the North Coast, the origins of this violence can be traced largely to the liberties granted to the Honduran police in the legislative reforms of 1906. Though meant to restructure immigration policy, the reforms also consolidated laws concerning the authority of the national police force and foreign consulates, two government agencies that were potential impediments to settlement and sources of assistance to the burgeoning West Indian population on the North Coast.

The initial intent of the legislation was to codify Honduran police practices and uniformly enforce the law throughout the country. In subsequent decades, authorities selectively cited portions of the law as justification for targeting West Indians. Interpretations of what consti-tuted a violation of the law were often left to the arresting officials, and subsequent penalties were rendered through the courts. Police officials often referenced chapter 3, article 43, of the police law, which strictly prohibited gambling, including dice games, roulette, and all other games of chance, raffles, and drawing of lots.[44] Another often-mentioned sec-tion of the law, chapter 2, article 38, targeted public drunkenness.[45] Fines and/or imprisonment were frequently the punishment for these offenses. Not surprisingly, the police used crimes stereotypically at-tributed to West Indians in the Honduran press, such as public scandal, inebriation, and conduct leading to the decline of the moral fabric of Honduran society (gambling and prostitution), to harass West Indians. All of these crimes were deportable offenses.

British officials in La Ceiba often noted the heavy-handed manner in which Honduran authorities treated British West Indian subjects resident in the city. Force was the primary tactic employed by the police and military authorities when imposing their interpretation of the law. Local authorities targeted West Indians and made examples of them in order to demonstrate their dominance. They impressed British subjects to perform duties such as digging paupers' graves, heavy moving and lifting, and other forms of manual labor from which foreigners were exempted. Penalties for failing to comply ranged from stiff fines to imprisonment, as in the 1912 case of one Roach White, who was held in jail for four months without trial for refusing to dig a grave.[46] Charles Manning, a Jamaican living in the Bay Islands, told British officials that he had been arrested and fined five US dollars by local authorities for refusing to do police patrol duty in the town of Coxen Hole.[47] By virtue of his status as a foreigner, Manning was exempt from conscription, but the Bay Islands represented a distinct reality from the mainland. Most residents of the islands were Honduran citizens who were the English-speaking descendants of Jamaican and Caymanian immigrants who had begun to arrive on the islands in the 1830s. While officially Honduran citizens since 1859, Bay Islanders retained strong cultural ties to the British Caribbean, and many continued to claim British citizenship unsuccessfully well into the 1930s. While at first it might appear difficult to determine Manning's citizenship simply on the basis of his claim, the presentation of a legitimate British passport should have cleared him from any obligation to comply with the police orders. Instead, it took an intervention by the British consular delegation to achieve Manning's release.

Conscription proved to be common in areas with a large West Indian population. As late as 1931, during the period in which West Indian immigration to Honduras declined as a result of the 1929 immigration law and the Honduran government's success in forcing fruit companies to hire Honduran nationals, a British consular report from Trujillo maintained that seventy-five British subjects (mostly Jamaicans) had been compelled to join the local police force. The consular agent obtained the release of the Jamaicans from service, but only after negotiating with the Honduran minister of foreign affairs.[48] In most cases in which West Indians were either conscripted by the Honduran authorities or imprisoned for refusal to comply with conscription orders, they successfully achieved release by going through diplomatic channels. However, the reliance on diplomacy indicated a disconnect between the interpretation of Honduran law and its enforcement on the North Coast. The minister of foreign affairs often interceded to rectify misinterpretations of the law by local Honduran authorities. Honduran legislation covering foreign consulates strictly stated that the government recognized the right of consulates to represent and protect their citizens within their jurisdiction.[49] Still, local authorities often questioned the jurisdiction of the British consular officials on the North Coast because the British Legation was housed at Guatemala City, with only a satellite office in Tegucigalpa. There was never a permanent consulate on the North Coast.

Forced conscription was also used to test the loyalties of West Indian workers on the North Coast, especially during periods of civil and political strife. Following the La Masica incident of 1911, in which three unarmed West Indian employees of the Standard Fruit Company were violently assaulted by police (one employee was beaten, and another was shot to death),[50] there was an increase in the number of claims filed by West Indian residents in La Ceiba and nearby areas in which West Indians reported being victims of police violence. One Samuel Devine insisted that he had been conscripted by local authorities to carry a corpse to a cemetery for interment and that upon his refusal he had been severely beaten by police. He alleged that eventually the corpse had been tied to his neck, forcing him to comply with the order. He had subsequently been jailed. According to the British vice consulate, the police tried to prevent Devine from seeking consular assistance.[51] Devine's case demonstrated the tenuous relationship between West Indians, Honduran authorities, and British consuls.

British sources revealed a similar incident in which police in La Ceiba assaulted Samuel Joseph Banner, a West Indian subject, around the same time as the incident involving Devine. Banner sustained five wounds to the head and neck and bruises on the shoulders and arms after being beaten with clubs and machetes by police officers following an altercation with a store owner. Two witnesses corroborated the incident, and a medical examiner's report documented the wounds.[52] It was unclear from the available records why the incident occurred.

Banner claimed that the store owner had assaulted him after a dispute over change, while the store owner claimed that Banner had committed theft. Whatever the reason for police involvement, British authorities in Honduras agreed that the treatment was excessive.[53]

West Indian observers in La Ceiba noted that there had been ten to twelve other cases of violence committed against West Indians similar to those of Devine and Banner in 1912. Unfortunately, no record of the incidents exists in the available sources. British officials corroborated a few cases of arrest involving subjects being beaten for resisting arrest. However, the British were typically unsympathetic to the plight of West Indians and demonstrated their own racist sentiment toward them in official correspondence. Most of the British subjects in Honduras were Jamaican; according to British authorities, they were of a "turbulent character" and prone to drink in excess. Some British officials even maintained that West Indians were filing false claims in hopes of receiving an indemnity from the Honduran government if the claims of abuse were found to be true.[54] Except in relation to the La Masica incident, there is no existing evidence in British or Honduran records of an indemnity claim ever being filed by West Indians or their descendants against the Honduran authorities for acts of abuse.

The Outrage of the Masses:
The 1923 Presidential Election and Public Acts of Violence

Despite the established record of violence by Honduran authorities against West Indians in the early decades of the twentieth century, the events leading up to the 1924 revolution are pivotal to understanding the outgrowth of violence against West Indians committed by ordinary citizens. In October 1923 the results of the Honduran presidential elections divided the country politically. The political conservatives united under the National Party of Honduras (PNH) ran Tiburcio Carías Andino as their presidential candidate. The Liberal Party was unable to unite around a single candidate, so the party's votes were split between former president Policarpo Bonilla and Juan Angel Arias. Carías received the greatest number of votes in the general election but not enough to declare a political majority and all-out victory. Constitutionally, this placed the election of the president in the hands of the national legislature, which was also split along party lines, and the split hindered a decision on a clear victor. As a result, the incumbent president, Rafael López Gutiérrez (who many perceived as a tool of the fruit companies and the United States), announced his intention to stay in office, which was unconstitutional. In January 1924, Carías declared himself president, and violence exploded throughout the nation, intensifying on the North Coast. Many suspected the UFCO of instigating the revolution and backing Carías, an accusation that made those in the North Coast banana enclaves subject to violence from the opposing side. In March, General Vicente Tosta, the eventual provisional president, occupied the North Coast cities of Tela, La Ceiba, and Puerto Cortés, and peace was soon achieved with the assistance of international negotiations involving the United States.[55]

In addition to the political unrest, the simultaneous labor strikes on the North Coast took on a distinctly antiforeign and antiblack character. US Department of State correspondence from August 1923 originating in Puerto Castilla included a transcription of a newspaper article in the paper *El Precursor* entitled "The Negro Problem." US officials found that most Hondurans were sympathetic to the article's premise that blacks enjoyed greater (economic) privileges than Hondurans. For the authors, the unfortunate superiority over them of what they considered an inferior race (blacks) "embittered the soul of Hondurans."[56] The authors alleged that blacks lived in better areas (company housing), were well paid, held better jobs, and were employed more frequently and more gainfully than Hondurans. The crux of the argument centered on the lack of national sovereignty in Honduras. The authors blamed the former president, Rafael López Gutiérrez, whom they accused of being a pawn of the fruit companies, and the presence of blacks, who were specifically mentioned as "depriving Hondurans of their right to national sovereignty."[57]

Antiblack sentiment on the North Coast continued into September. While previously US government and fruit-company officials had dismissed the actions of protesters and demonstrators as the rants of misguided workers, the events in September suggested the possibility of real danger. Unlike in previous incidents, *El Precursor* was instrumental in organizing demonstrations and had a wide distribution to spread its message. As a result of the propaganda, an anonymous posting was later placed at the Balsamo camp (banana farm), near Puerto Castilla, that read: "With morality and civility and assurances of true gentlemanliness, we beg the people of Jamaica and Belize to please leave Balsamo camp by the tenth day of September, failing which we are not responsible for your lives."[58]

Despite the threats, there were no reports of violence against West Indians as a result of "The Negro Problem" and the protest the article instigated. Though this protest appeared to be like the earlier ones, the sentiment in the article mobilized the masses and added fuel to a fragile situation. The harassment of West Indians continued, and threats against their lives persisted. Politicians such as Carías and López perpetuated some of harassment in their bids for the presidency and afterwards by insisting that if they were elected, they would work to end the importation of West Indians to Honduras and diminish the fruit companies' hold on the Honduran economy. Such rhetoric endured even amid the rumors that both politicians were in the pocket of the fruit companies.[59]

The political unrest of 1924 ended with Vicente Tosta serving as provisional president of Honduras for a year. During this period, labor unrest continued on the North Coast as a decline in productivity and profits within the banana industry—resulting from widespread droughts and ensuing fires (possible arson) and plant diseases that ruined crops— caused many seasonal workers and day laborers to be laid off. The majority of these workers were Hondurans. Since West Indians were contract employees recruited to Honduras by the companies, they were more likely to be retained. The fruit companies even brought in West Indians as strikebreakers, which only added to the racial and ethnic hostility. This strategy of creating social divisions was often employed by fruit companies throughout Central America to control their workforce.

Rather than viewing their employment situation within the context of the larger economic and environmental issues impacting the banana industry, Honduran workers blamed the West Indians for their inability to make a living. In July 1924, spontaneous labor protests, led by Honduran workers at the Truxillo Railroad Company, erupted on the North Coast in Trujillo and Puerto Castilla. At first it appeared that the protests were a reaction to an earlier incident in which a Honduran had been killed by a Jamaican night watchman employed at the Truxillo Railroad Company. However, Honduran, British, and US accounts of the strike report no direct references to that event as the catalyst for what unfolded. Leaders of the protests stated that their primary objective was the expulsion of blacks from the company. They made this demand to the fruit company and to the local and regional governments, none of which complied with their requests. When government officials explained to the workers that the West Indians were in Honduras in accordance with a treaty between Honduras and Great Britain, which the officials in turn read to the workers, they said they were "not concerned with laws and intended that the will of the people should reign supreme." According to one account, some laborers stated that the protesters should kill the blacks. Specifically, some were witnessed as saying, "Let's do the same to the Negroes in Honduras as was done to them in Guatemala, chop off their heads."[60]

The reference to Guatemala demonstrates that the workers saw their experiences in the banana enclaves as part of a much larger political and economic phenomenon involving West Indians, Spanish-speaking Central Americans, and their US employers. The banana enclaves near Puerto Barrios, Guatemala, had long been a hotbed of labor activity and racial and ethnic conflict between blacks (Jamaican and African American) and ladinos. As Paul Dosal writes, racially motivated violence had been a reality in the Caribbean coastal areas of Guatemala since the construction of railroads and the development of the banana industry beginning in the 1880s.[61] Frederick Douglass Opie notes in his assessment of the 1923 dock strike in Puerto Barrios that Guatemalan laborers, in their efforts to advance their plea for higher wages, gradually came to frame their arguments in a way that was at the expense of English-speaking, mostly black workers.[62]

Though no deaths were reported in the 1923 strike in Guatemala, it is plausible that rumors of Guatemalan workers killing blacks spread to

Honduras. The American vice consul at Puerto Castilla, Willard Beaulac, a witness to the events, gave a more plausible explanation for the intensity of the violent rhetoric against the West Indians. Beaulac linked the increased violence against blacks to a speech on the eve of the strike by Dr. Giron Aguilar, a nephew of a government official during the Gutiérrez administration, who had recently returned to the country and was trying to win favor with the Carías supporters. Aguilar was respected in Trujillo and self-described as an anti-American agitator. US diplomatic correspondence reported that Aguilar had made a speech in Puerto Castilla in which he called upon all "loyal Hondurans to expel the Negroes from the country." He had also referenced the practice of lynching in the United States and given statistics for an unnamed state in which thirty-five blacks were lynched in one year. He had insinuated to the crowd that "there were 48 states in the United States and asked his audience to draw its own inferences."[63]

Most labor strikes and protests were responses to direct fruit-company policies related to work shortages, low wages, or the actions of individual company officials. Organized labor did not play a major role in Honduran politics until at least 1926.[64] Even then, such efforts were attributed to outside forces such as "communists" from neighboring Guatemala and Nicaragua or American labor unions, whose ideas reached Honduras from New Orleans.

Flyers, graffiti, and other postings from the 1924 strike reveal the level of antagonism exhibited toward black workers in particular. Some Honduran workers organized themselves loosely as the North Coast National Labor Party and distributed makeshift flyers calling for the murder of blacks. One image showing a crucifix, a skull and crossbones, and a graveyard (fig. 2.1) bore the following caption: "Blacks are given free passage to this rural area [cemetery]. If you need it explained to you [talk] with any Latin American."[65] While the reference to the cemetery is obvious, the strikers' use of the word *campo*, alluding to the countryside, is a clear reference to the failed negotiations between the Truxillo Railroad Company and the Honduran workers at the initiation of the strike, when the company refused to remove West Indian workers but promised the Honduran workers employment in the rural areas (for less

FIG. 2.1. *"Blacks Are Given Free Passage."* From Willard L. Beaulac, American Vice Consul at Puerto Castilla to US Department of State, 19 July 1924, US Department of State Records Relating to the Internal Affairs of Honduras, 1910–1929.

money) in exchange for an end to the unrest. The workers emphatically refused and continued to push the company on its hiring practices. A second flyer, with an image of a skull and crossbones, depicting death, was also distributed. Its simple caption, "Dedicated to the Blacks," was meant to strike fear in West Indian workers.

While the two abovementioned flyers were written in Spanish, the final flyer, which was the only one written in English, attributed to the North Coast National Labor Party, stated: "Go all Negroes. We hereby notify all Negroes residing at the North Coast of Honduras to leave the country immediately under the penalty of death."[66] The intensity of the situation and the threat of racial violence did not go unnoticed by the UFCO and US diplomats. Both were in communication with the Honduran government and actively pursued a peaceful resolution to the situation. The available evidence suggests that the Honduran government played the two sides against each other during the strike. On the one hand, the government assured the UFCO and US officials that their property and foreign workers would be protected. On the other hand, it did very little to ensure the safety of black workers and their families or to bring strike leaders and perpetrators of the violence to justice.

Intensifying Violence and the Beginnings of West Indians' Departure from Honduras

At the height of the strike, roughly 200 protesters stole a train in a failed effort to extend their cause to the cities of Tela, La Ceiba, and Puerto Cortés, all major centers of the banana industry on the North Coast and in the West Indian settlement in Honduras. They saw their efforts in national terms, but the train they appropriated operated on a short track that did not connect to the other major cities along the coast. The government sent troops after the protesters and encouraged West Indians in the area to board a Norwegian steamer for safety. Some 900 people (400 men and 500 women and children) took shelter on the ship for several hours. Some 100 others sought safety in La Ceiba, and another 300 reportedly left for the safety of neighboring British Honduras.[67]

The Honduran government reassured the 900 West Indians on the Norwegian ship that they were free from danger, and the West Indians disembarked and returned to their homes. Not long after, however, West Indians in the area were attacked; one man, Levi Gooding, was severely stabbed, and another, Amos Rich, was beaten over the head with a machete. Neither died as a result of the attacks. Both men identified their attackers as Honduran employees of the Truxillo Railroad Company whom they did not know personally but whom they had seen occasionally at work.[68] After these incidents, a heavy Honduran police presence arrived in Puerto Castilla, an area populated by West Indian employees and referred to as "Labor Town." However, many West Indians reported to US authorities that the Honduran soldiers and policemen instigated or were at least complicit in many of the threats and attacks on West Indians. Eventually seven West Indian men were arrested and sent to Tegucigalpa to face charges for their role in the violence. None were ever tried, despite the efforts of the fruit companies.

The British government took no serious action during the strike and the ensuing violence. British representation in Honduras was sporadic at best and declined at the end of the second decade of the twentieth century. Because the British Legation was based in Guatemala City, and because the British government historically held a negative view toward its West Indian subjects (based largely on racial and ethnic stereotypes), West Indians in Honduras relied heavily on their American employers for protection. The Americans, in turn, concerned themselves more with property damage and the loss of profits than with the lives of their foreign employees.[69]

In the few instances in which West Indians reported incidences of violence to the British authorities, the reasons given for the altercations were very similar to those given in the American records. British records from 1922 to 1924, which included the labor strikes in Puerto Castilla and Trujillo, largely corroborated the American reports. However, the British reports revealed that the violence against West Indians did not cease after the strike ended. In the period following the strike, six British subjects were shot, stabbed, or beaten by Honduran private citizens or members of the military or police. The violence was now happening at all levels of Honduran society. These violent acts were a result of the abuses stemming from the 1906 reforms. However, in the wake of the 1924 revolution and labor strike, West Indians became perpetual targets of all segments of Honduran society. The year 1924 proved especially brutal for West Indians.

British reports substantiated American interpretations of the labor strikes in Puerto Castilla and Trujillo, stating that the protests had been directed specifically at the "coloured" population and that several British West Indian subjects had been seriously wounded.[70] In addition to the violence, it was reported that more than four hundred West Indians were forced to flee the country. The British diplomats maintained that the Honduran authorities had been absent, and they attributed the British lack of response to limited resources in the country to assist British citizens. They did send pleas for British warships to protect the West Indians, but these appeals fell on deaf ears in London.[71]

The 1924 labor strike and the increased hostility toward West Indians that it fostered forced West Indians to reevaluate their ties to Honduras. Britain's failure to protect its West Indian citizens abroad also caused them to reassess their status within the British Empire. Despite the considerable level of violence rendered against them, West Indians on the North Coast did not respond in kind. Most expressed their complaints to their American employers and to British diplomatic representatives. When these channels failed, most chose to return to their native lands or to seek opportunities in other Latin American countries or the United States.[72]

The Honduran perception of West Indians as a threat to the nation temporarily fostered political and cultural solidarity on the North Coast. The violence committed against West Indians on the North Coast by Honduran workers offers a glimpse into the competing notions of nationalism and race in the construction of Honduran identity. West Indians were an inassimilable group within Honduran society; they were black, foreign, and attached to US capitalist ventures in Honduras that excluded or derided the local population. The legislative policies of the Honduran government defined the West Indian presence in the country as a threat to the social and cultural fabric of the nation. The legislative history of immigration demonstrated a varying degree of acceptance of West Indians. When the fruit companies exerted influence, the status of the West Indian in Honduras was favorable. When foreign businesses and investment were under attack, the West Indian community became the target of intellectual and political attack. By representing this group as the "other" and pandering to nationalists and xenophobes, politicians and intellectuals ensured that even when government policies of immigration reform failed, violence was a viable option for eradicating the West Indian presence from the country. Equally important, the fact that blackness was ultimately synonymous with West Indian immigration and the foreign exploitation of the banana industry created a political and cultural obstacle for other Afro-descended populations on the North Coast who were attempting to exert their full rights as citizens of the nation without compromising their black identity by succumbing to the racial ambiguity of *mestizaje*.

There is no significant evidence to support Honduran claims regarding the criminality of West Indians and their being a threat to the cultural fabric of society. Very few Honduran police records from the period survive. The only noteworthy police arrest records from the North Coast that exist are from 1933 and 1934, by which time the West Indian population in the country had waned significantly. In these years, of the 210 arrests for drunkenness reported in all three North Coast departments (Atlántida, Cortés, and Colón), only 3 were attributed to West Indians.[73] All the other offenders were Hondurans, indicating that West Indians were no longer a noteworthy criminal element.

The violence that was prevalent in the 1920s, however, did persist into the 1930s and continued to coincide with other political events. Following an uprising in February 1937, British officials in Honduras noted that harsh, oppressive measures were taken against elements of the civil population suspected of harboring or sympathizing with the antigovernment rebels.[74] A number of West Indians remaining in Honduras received brutal treatment at the hands of government soldiers. British authorities quelled the violence by pressuring the Honduran government to take action against the perpetrators.

Though the majority of the soldiers in the Honduran army had enlisted, the conscription of additional soldiers during times of conflict, particularly in the North Coast banana zones, was common. A photo on a postcard from the period shows Honduran soldiers receiving their weekly pay of fifty cents in US currency (fig. 2.2). As the men are all dressed in plain clothes, it is impossible to distinguish soldiers from civilians. And because of the speed with which citizens were conscripted into the Honduran army, it is unlikely that new soldiers ever received proper military training. In such circumstances, the likelihood of antiblack and xenophobic sentiments infiltrating the Honduran military increased.

Just as in earlier cases, when British diplomatic channels failed, West Indians resorted to seeking assistance from their American em-

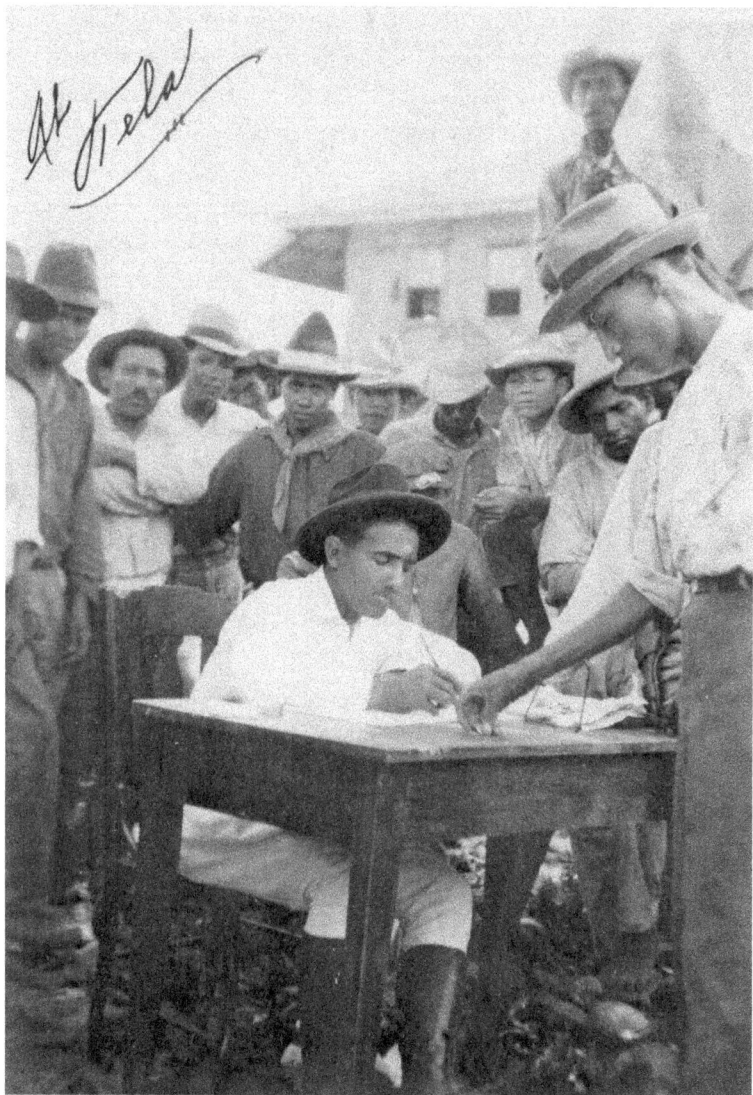

FIG. 2.2. *Payday in the Army.* Panama and Central America Postcard Collection. Courtesy of the Image Archive, The Latin American Library at Tulane University.

ployers in the fruit companies and US diplomats, but both could only offer limited protection. The fruit companies could only protect West Indians within the confines of their places of employment, while US diplomats could offer no legal protections because West Indians were not American citizens.

By the mid-1930s, West Indians who remained in Honduras were technically not West Indians at all but rather Bay Islanders and the Honduran-born children of West Indians clinging to an imagined sense of British nationality. It was within these two groups that the reconciliation between a Honduran identity and British West Indian culture emerged on the North Coast. Throughout their time in Honduras, West Indians exerted their "rights" as British subjects when faced with legal problems or when seeking to extricate themselves from political situations. However, the West Indian population was a migrant one. Because the West Indies were no longer central to the economic livelihood of the British Empire, and owing to the legacy of British racism and discrimination against non-Anglo-Saxon colonial subjects, West Indians were often treated as second-class citizens by the British. West Indians in Honduras who made claims against the Honduran government were completely dependent on British diplomats not only to defend them politically but also, as witnessed in the case of Charles Manning, to prove their West Indian nationality. Failure on the part of the British government to validate the authenticity of their citizenship claims left West Indians in a state of diplomatic ambiguity.

The fate of West Indian children born in Honduras was more uncertain than that of their parents. They spoke English at home, it was the primary language of instruction in the private religious or company schools they attended, it was the liturgical language in the various Protestant churches to which they belonged, and many of the children were raised in English-speaking West Indian neighborhoods such as Barrio Inglés in La Ceiba. West Indian parents created a completely Anglophone existence for their children and promoted the superiority of West Indian and British cultures over that of Honduras.[75] Perhaps this was a response to the antagonism West Indians experienced at the hands of local authorities and anti–West Indian Hondurans. It is more likely that West

Indian immigrants in Honduras re-created a British identity that had never truly existed for them.

Though Honduras was the country of birth for the children of West Indian migrants, their upbringing was such that the nation was culturally and politically foreign. In Honduras, children of West Indians born in the country acquired Honduran citizenship as a birthright. Yet, their parents instilled in them the conviction that they were West Indian subjects of the British Empire. Caught between nations and cultures and confronted with a North Coast society in which debates over race and ethnicity continued to stratify not only the Afro-descended population but also the nation as a whole, the West Indian community was in constant flux.

Ironically, though West Indian children born and raised in Honduras were "foreigners" in the land of their birth, many discovered on returning to the West Indies to visit family or attend school that they had a similar status in the West Indies. They experienced difficulty adjusting to Caribbean life. Caribbean culture was familiar on the surface, but the culture in their Honduran communities existed within a vacuum and proved equally foreign. The Caribbean region had undergone enormous political, cultural, and economic shifts since their parents emigrated, most notably a growing sense of regional nationalism and disenchantment with the British colonial system. In Honduras, British culture was a source of pride for West Indians. However, in the British Caribbean, citizens began to challenge the primacy of the British. Caribbean trade unionism emerged in the 1930s as the mechanism by which political organizations would form and press the British government for more autonomy.[76]

According to Honduran law, anyone born in Honduras was a Honduran citizen. However, under British law, a Honduran of West Indian parentage could claim the right to British nationality and petition for dual citizenship, though acceptance was not guaranteed. In practice, dual status had little bearing on the children of West Indian workers in Honduras because the British government offered no legal protection as long as they resided outside Great Britain and its possessions.[77] Many Hondurans of West Indian descent eventually left the country for the Caribbean, the United States, or Britain. Others chose to remain in Honduras and embraced the nation by integrating into the larger society, though claims of British citizenship persisted in the Bay Islands well into the 1940s.

In the Bay Islands, police violence, anti–West Indian sentiment, Honduran nationalism, and citizenship converged to challenge both West Indian and Honduran interpretations of the nation. In 1939, several Bay Islanders complained to the British government that their rights as British subjects had been violated. They maintained that some Bay Islanders had been shot for failing to appear at weekly military parades. Others reported that innocent people had been incarcerated. Reports also surfaced that taxation was higher for British subjects than for Hondurans and that Bay Islanders were barred from having English as the primary language of instruction in their schools.[78] The complainants contended that of the twelve thousand or so inhabitants of the Bay Islands, only two hundred were native to Honduras; all others were British subjects or children of British subjects (dual citizens). The Bay Islanders believed that the British would come to their rescue, and they hoped the British would take the Bay Islands and "fly the Union Jack over their heads" again.[79]

The British Foreign Office never responded to the requests of the Bay Islanders. There was little likelihood that any significant population of British who had been alive when the islands were ceded to Honduras in 1859 were still alive in 1939. Most residents of the island were in fact Honduran and subject to Honduran law. The British government's decision to ignore the zealous and patriotic appeal for aid from Bay Island residents represented a turning point not only for Bay Islanders but for Hondurans of West Indian descent on the North Coast. While there may have been historical and cultural ties to the British Empire, the "British subjects" were in fact Hondurans, subject to the laws of the land. In British and US diplomatic correspondence filed by West Indians in Honduras after 1940, there are no complaints related to issues of police or military violence or citizenship. Most West Indians had left the country by then, forced out by violence and the realization that they were politically and economically on their own.

CHAPTER THREE

West Indians and the Call to Citizenship in Early-Twentieth-Century New Orleans

Forced out of Central America, those West Indians who chose to immigrate to New Orleans encountered others from the region in similar circumstances. The reasons for their immigration to the city were rooted in ideological and violent struggles involving race, immigration, religion, and labor in Central America. Caught between nations struggling to make sense of their political and cultural identity, West Indians desperately tried to curb the barrage of US influences in every aspect of their lives. The story of these West Indian immigrants from Central America—abandoned by the British Empire, betrayed by their North American employers, and terrorized by their neighbors and fellow citizens in their respective nations—is part of the larger history of race relations that goes beyond the black-white binary.

While most Central Americans who came to New Orleans were of West Indian descent, their racial and ethnic backgrounds were diverse, reflecting the complexities of their home countries. Those self-described as white, black, mestizo, West Indian, Garifuna, and indigenous were all represented throughout Central America. In keeping with the common practices of the period, US immigration records conflated race, nationality, and ethnicity. However, for those of African descent, in addition to giving their nationality, the documents racially identify them as "African."[1]

The rigidity of the Jim Crow racial structure that these immigrants encountered in New Orleans compelled those who were discernibly of African descent to ultimately embrace a black American identity. New Orleans was the site of *Plessy v. Ferguson*, the 1896 Supreme Court case that institutionalized legal segregation in the United States. As Blair Kelley writes, segregation began long before the *Plessy* decision and was not limited to the South.[2] Because of New Orleans's unique cultural and racial hierarchy, there was no evident racial solidarity between the Afro-Creole (*gens de couleur*) and African American populations.

While West Indians had trickled into New Orleans throughout the nineteenth century, they became a visible and distinguishable group during the banana boom of the early twentieth century. Those who were either white or light enough to pass for white assimilated into the dominant society, forgoing their West Indian identity to embrace a British or English one. Central Americans who were mestizo and/or Spanish speaking embraced their Iberian heritage whenever possible and used the ambiguity within the federal racial-classification system to become "white." This chapter examines the ways in which the identities of West Indians and Spanish-speaking Central Americans shifted from the banana zones to New Orleans as they confronted the challenges of the US racial system. These immigrants' stories demonstrate how place and space shaped immigrant experiences. Moreover, the ways in which these immigrants negotiated their new realities speak to the arbitrary ways in which racial identities were shaped in the United States.

For those immigrants of visible African descent, incorporation into a US-centered "black American" identity complicates the ways in which notions of diaspora are created. The richness and distinctiveness of their historical and cultural experiences are overshadowed by the political and economic realities of living in a racially hostile environment. For those immigrants arriving from Central America, to be Central American or West Indian meant very little in a racially segregated New Orleans. However, their international experience and foreign origins benefited them economically.

Many native-born blacks in New Orleans worked as day laborers on the docks and wharves of the Mississippi River, unloading banana boats from Central America for as little as twenty-five cents a day.[3] This life, with its racial overtones, was depicted in an article in the *New Orleans Times-Picayune* in 1920. The article described the laborers on the wharf as the "typical Southern darkies" and said that the sorting and counting of the fruit was done by Sicilian immigrants.[4] Eric Arnesen argues that even where there was interracial cooperation, such as in the unionization of these waterfront workers in New Orleans, there was little understanding or sympathy for the plight of blacks.[5] Arnesen maintains that this lack of understanding stemmed from the aftermath of Reconstruction, when white disdain for the former institutions of slavery and the slaveholding class, combined with the increased exploitation of racial divisions within the lower classes by ruling elites, created a hostile environment for blacks.[6] This environment, combined with the legal codification of inequality through Jim Crow laws, limited opportunities for blacks in New Orleans.

These limited opportunities compelled many blacks in the city to migrate to other locations throughout the United States in search of better economic prospects and a reprieve from the racial hostility.[7] There is evidence that a smaller minority chose to migrate to other countries, particularly in Central America.[8] Black Americans exposed to the life of the merchant seaman through their experiences on the wharves and docks chose to enter that profession. Life as a seaman, even if one were relegated to the steward's (service) department, provided an opportunity to earn a better wage and travel to places where Jim Crow racism was potentially less inhibiting.

The turn to the sea by blacks in search of better opportunities is as old as the history of African peoples in the Americas. W. Jeffrey Bolster documents that by the early nineteenth century one-fifth of the one hundred thousand men employed yearly in the United States as sailors were black. Notable African Americans such as Paul Cuffee, Denmark Vesey, Frederick Douglass, and countless other enslaved and free blacks made a living from the sea.[9] Some blacks were able to achieve their freedom through their work as seamen. While many whites during the period loathed the life of a seaman, Bolster emphasizes that for many blacks in the southern and Caribbean plantation zones, the life of a seaman provided access to freedom and refuge from enslavement as well

as mobility otherwise prohibited.[10] Travel throughout the Atlantic world
and exposure to different peoples, cultures, and ideas made black sailors some of the most aware and connected of citizens in the Americas
during the period. This mobility and "worldliness" help explain the Denmark Vesey revolt of 1822 in South Carolina, in which Vesey galvanized
the enslaved population in part by suggesting that blacks in other parts
of the diaspora, particularly Haiti, would come to their aid in Charleston
once they initiated the revolt. Vesey was aware of the Saint Domingue
revolution and other revolts within the plantation zones largely because
of his travels in the region as a seaman.

Vesey's failed revolt led to South Carolina's passage of the Negro
Seaman's Act of 1822, which legally sanctioned the quarantining of free
black crew members upon docking in South Carolina ports. This policy
created national debate in Congress and caused diplomatic conflict with
Britain and France because several of their black citizens were imprisoned under the law. Nevertheless, the state persisted in implementing
the law until after the Civil War. Leon Fink writes that Louisiana was
the only other state that was equally persistent in enforcing the law.[11]
Opportunities to work as sailors resumed throughout the South after
the Civil War, with Louisiana and its port of New Orleans emerging as
a vital organ for trade between the United States and all major ports in
Latin America and the Caribbean.

In the early 1880s, officials in New Orleans struggled to persuade
national companies to establish large-scale trade with the Caribbean
and Latin America from a southern port city prone to outbreaks of yellow fever and other tropical, mosquito-borne diseases. There was also a
shortage of white men willing to work as sailors in the region, as it was
widely believed that whites were more susceptible to contracting these
diseases. One solution to this impasse was to hire African Americans
from across the nation as sailors on oceangoing vessels. African Americans were already well represented on riverboats and in the "lake trade"
throughout the United States, particularly in the South. Pseudoscientific
research also argued that African-descended peoples were immune to
yellow fever. As a result, the city of New Orleans directly petitioned the
secretary of the navy to allow merchant ships to be manned by African

Americans.[12] Additionally, it requested that the navy station a ship at either New Orleans or Savannah, Georgia, so that African American youth could learn navigation prior to working on vessels.[13]

When African Americans entered the merchant service in the early decades of the twentieth century, they were reclaiming a role that had deep historical roots. However, they were often minorities within a minority on board. Most of the black crew members on merchant vessels in and out of New Orleans were either West Indian or Central American, with significant experience navigating the racial and political dynamics of life as a sailor on UFCO vessels. The experiences of these seamen and their fellow citizens of various occupations are the subject of this chapter.

A Diverse and Scattered Lot

Wilfred Levy, a black merchant seaman born in 1901 in Kingston, Jamaica, immigrated to New Orleans from Cristóbal, Panama, in 1928. He gave his last address as Tela, Honduras, which he had left a few years before filing his application for US citizenship in 1935 at the East District Federal Court in New Orleans.[14] Tela was a UFCO town that since 1911 had specifically imported British West Indians, primarily from neighboring British Honduras and Jamaica, to work at the Tela Railroad Company, a UFCO subsidiary and major producer of bananas. A citizen of the British Empire like many of his fellow workers born in the British West Indies, Levy had traveled up and down the Central American coast in search of economic opportunities. When work in the banana industry declined in the 1920s and early 1930s, Levy sought other means of employment.[15] Like many others tied to the fruit companies, Levy served as a merchant seaman on a UFCO merchant vessel—the *Coppename,* based in New Orleans—that transported tropical goods (bananas) from Central America to New Orleans. In New Orleans in 1931, Levy met and married Beatrice, an African American native New Orleanian who, according to Levy's US naturalization application, had never resided outside the city. From that point, Levy chose to settle in New Orleans, and in 1935 he applied for and received US citizenship.

Born in Puerto Cortés, Honduras, in 1893, Burnis Emmanuel Davis identified himself as a carpenter on his 1941 US citizenship application. He first arrived in New Orleans at the age of 25 in 1918 and married an African American native of the city in 1921. Together they had six children, all of whom were born in New Orleans and resided there at the time of Davis's application.[16] US passenger lists from 1923 indicate that Davis was once employed on the Cuyamel Fruit Company merchant vessel *Omoa* as a fireman. The ship traveled back and forth between Puerto Cortés, Honduras, and New Orleans with a crew of Europeans, West Indians, Latin Americans, and North Americans. No record of Davis's declaration of intent to apply for citizenship exists in the available records. Therefore, apart from his initial arrival in the city in 1918 and his work for the Cuyamel Fruit Company, the details of Burnis Davis's life are unknown.[17] Perhaps his failure to apply for US citizenship (or even to declare his intent) prior to 1941 was tied to the transition of fruit-company merchant vessels from commercial liners shipping bananas to military supply vessels for the US effort during the Second World War. No longer employed by the Cuyamel Fruit Company, Davis would not have had the freedom or security afforded company employees to enter the United States at will. Perhaps Davis's age (48) warranted a change in career or even a desire to spend more time with his family. In any event, Burnis Davis had established roots in New Orleans through his wife and children and made a life for himself in the city. His 1942 draft registration listed his address in the African American uptown section of the city.[18]

Amy Agnes Nash, a Jamaican housewife who identified herself as white and English, applied for US citizenship in the same New Orleans federal court as the others in 1935. Born in 1883 at Rio Bueno, Jamaica, Nash was a widow; her husband, William, also a white Jamaican, had died in 1923, just prior to her immigration to the United States. Perhaps his death facilitated her immigration and that of her five children. Prior to arriving in New Orleans, Nash lived in Cuyamel, one of the first major fruit-company towns in Honduras, founded by the Russian-born, American entrepreneur Samuel Zemurray and his Cuyamel Fruit Company, which served as the model for many future company towns in the region. Four of Nash's five children were also born in Jamaica; the

FIG. 3.1. *Corps of Waiters, SS Anselm—Costa Rica*. John N. Teunisson United Fruit Company Collection. Courtesy of the Image Archive, The Latin American Library at Tulane University.

youngest was born in Costa Rica, indicating that perhaps the family resided there briefly while her husband worked for the UFCO. She lived permanently in New Orleans beginning in 1930 and received citizenship in 1936 along with three of her children.[19]

As different as Levy's, Davis's, and Nash's circumstances were in New Orleans, in Central America (with the exception of British Honduras) all would have been seen as foreigners (despite Burnis Davis's birth in Honduras), referred to by Spanish-speaking Hondurans as *ingleses,* or English, because of their shared West Indian cultural heritage, island of birth, British citizenship, or affiliation with the UFCO. Though the de facto Jim Crow racial climate imported into the banana zones by American employers favored whites over blacks and would have placed Levy and Davis in a position subordinate to Nash's, their West Indian heritage (because all on some level embraced their colonial realities) would have served as a unifier in times of violent anti–West Indian protests. However, the race, class, and gender hierarchy in New Orleans would take them in completely different directions.

The bits and pieces of their lives retrievable in the archives speak to the experiences of many West Indians who came to New Orleans from Central America. Most of the men arriving in New Orleans at some point worked as stewards on intercoastal merchant vessels owned and operated by the UFCO or the Standard Fruit and Steamship Company and based in either Central America or New Orleans. The crews on these vessels were recruited from seaports all over the Caribbean, Latin America, and Europe, with an overrepresentation of workers from Central America. As illustrated by a photograph taken in 1906 on the UFCO's SS *Anselm* in Costa Rica, the diverse crew of workers represented a dignified and capable segment of the UFCO workforce (fig. 3.1).

Gerald Horne notes in his assessment of the communist influence on sailors in the United States that blacks, particularly West Indians, often worked as seamen in southern ports during the period.[20] Most were employed in positions reserved for blacks, such as cooks, mess men, waiters, or other service jobs in the steward's department.[21] Because they were on the margins of society, most sailors placed little stock in traditions that historically had created a sense of community among blacks. Horne observes that on these vessels the course "was not determined by religious beliefs, race worship, personal inclination, or utopian dreams, but rather by the navigator's scientific knowledge of nature."[22] Sailors were practical and relied on their wits. Many used their position to their benefit whenever possible. For instance, in their naturalization applications, they successfully used their records of merchant and military service—UFCO and Standard Fruit vessels and their crews were commissioned by the US government to assist in both world wars—to petition for US citizenship. The conditions on merchant vessels, combined with the severity of the work, also fostered a strong sense of group solidarity.[23] This alliance based on occupation also translated into ethnic solidarity among West Indians.

Overwhelmingly, women like Agnes Nash journeyed directly from British colonial possessions such as Jamaica, British Honduras, and the

Cayman Islands. Most who gave their racial and ethnic background as white, English, and/or British were housewives (married to white Americans), clerks, stenographers, nurses, or students. The few women who identified as black came from the same locations as their white counterparts but were employed primarily as domestic workers.

Some of the women attended the numerous universities in the area. Others, such as Dorothy Davis, whose life embodied the connection between New Orleans, the Greater Caribbean, and Honduras, were nurses at area hospitals. A photo of nurses taken in Belize City during the early twentieth century illustrates the multiracial and multiethnic makeup of many of the women who arrived in New Orleans (fig. 3.2). Born in Jamaica, Davis was single and twenty years of age when she requested a visa from the Honduran consulate in New Orleans in 1934 to visit her parents in Honduras for two weeks. Her father, R. H. Davis, was a longtime Truxillo Railroad Company employee in Puerto Castilla, on the North Coast. Dorothy requested permission from the Honduran government to visit the country because she was not a Honduran citizen. Though it appears that Davis was white, her Jamaican identity, regardless of her racial background, raised red flags for Honduran officials since most of the black immigrant workers in the country historically had come from Jamaica. In 1934, antiblack immigration laws were passed in Honduras that explicitly forbade the entrance of blacks into the country as either immigrants or tourists. Davis retained her British citizenship as a Jamaican subject of the British Empire and was traveling to Honduras on a British passport. In a letter accompanying her visa request, the assistant to the vice president of the UFCO, of which the Truxillo Railroad Company was a subsidiary, maintained that Davis's travel would be exclusively on UFCO steamships, with an itinerary from her home in New Orleans to Tela, Honduras, and then on to Puerto Castilla.[24] She ultimately received a visa to travel.

The 1934 trip was not Davis's first on a fruit-company vessel. In 1930, when she was sixteen, she had arrived in New Orleans from Tela, Honduras; her last address was given as Jamaica, indicating a brief stay in Honduras. From 1930 on, she made an annual trip from her home in New Orleans to Puerto Castilla. There was no evidence over the years

FIG. 3.2. *Belize. Hospital Nurses.* John N. Teunisson United Fruit Company Collection. Courtesy of the Image Archive, The Latin American Library at Tulane University.

that Davis ever applied for US citizenship or had a desire to. There is also no indication in the visa application that she had ever lived in Honduras with her parents. Unlike other British West Indian residents of Honduras seeking to be reunited with their families, Davis applied for a visa not as a resident seeking reentry but as a tourist, which was an acceptable category on visa-application forms issued by the Honduran government. In New Orleans, Davis worked as a nurse at Charity Hospital and was also a student.[25] By 1936, Davis appeared on passenger lists in Boston. She identified herself as a nurse and gave her home address as Puerto Castilla, indicating that at some point between 1934 and 1936 she had relocated permanently to Honduras.[26] For Davis, like other West Indian women, New Orleans was a place to acquire an education and gain practical experience that translated to a career elsewhere. Thus,

Davis's life reveals another characteristic of West Indian settlement in New Orleans: men were much more likely to permanently settle in the city, especially if they first encountered the city as merchant seamen. The power of the fruit companies to bypass immigration and tourist restrictions on its employees and children allowed men to settle more easily in New Orleans. On the other hand, most West Indian women did not intend to make New Orleans their permanent home.

The internationalization of the Central American coast as a result of the banana industry also served as the catalyst for the migrations of Spanish-speaking populations from the interior of the region to major company towns in search of work. Central Americans from the interior of Guatemala, Nicaragua, and El Salvador arrived in coastal ports such as Puerto Barrios, Bluefields, and the Honduran ports of La Ceiba, Tela, Puerto Cortés, and Trujillo. Their presence added to the cultural and ethnic diversity of the increasingly international zone. For rural Hondurans like José Tomás Idiáquez, this rapid internationalization provided an opportunity to improve their economic circumstances.

José Idiáquez's experience was distinct from those of his West Indian contemporaries. Born in 1905 in the southern town of Danlí, Honduras, roughly 175 miles from the Caribbean coast, Idiáquez identified himself at the time of his US citizenship application as an assistant steward on a merchant vessel that traveled frequently to New Orleans. José initially emigrated from his rural town to the booming North Coast city of San Pedro Sula, a city that owed much of its economic success to the import-export trade controlled by the banana industry, situated in the nearby towns of La Lima, Omoa, and Cuyamel. He immigrated to New Orleans in 1924 and married Minnie, a native of Mechanicsburg, Mississippi, who had migrated to New Orleans prior to the marriage. On his declaration of intent and his naturalization application, José listed his race as white and his nationality as Spanish American, which was not uncommon at the time, as many Latin Americans without a discernible African or Native American ancestry were legally classified as white in the United States. More importantly, he legally changed his name to Joseph Thomas Idiaguez and had three children, all born in New Orleans. Both of his witnesses at his citizenship interview were white New Orleanians, and by all accounts José, or rather Joseph, used his experiences as a seaman, his marriage, and his peer associations to become white.[27]

Idiáguez's fellow countryman from the coastal town of Trujillo, Francisco Javier Herrera, a black Honduran, most likely Garifuna, experienced a different outcome. Born in 1897, he immigrated permanently to New Orleans in 1929 from the Honduran port city of Puerto Cortés. His previous address was La Ceiba, Honduras, the seat of the Standard Fruit and Steamship Company. Herrera worked in the steward's department as a cook on a merchant vessel that traveled between Puerto Cortés and New Orleans. In 1921 he met and married Hattie, an African American migrant originally from Wakefield, Louisiana. They had six children, all born in New Orleans, where they had settled into the local black community. Herrera received his US citizenship in 1937.[28]

Of the historical records for the abovementioned immigrants to New Orleans, Herrera's is one of the most abundant. He surfaces on crew lists for passenger and merchant vessels for the period between 1918 and 1953 in various ports of call throughout the United States. In 1918 Herrera was listed as a twenty-one-year-old, third-rank steward on the Honduran steamship *Ceiba*, which was owned and operated by the Standard Fruit Company and based at La Ceiba, Honduras. The ship departed La Ceiba on October 17 and arrived at New Orleans on November 9. None of the crew, including Herrera, remained in New Orleans after this date, and the international crew returned to Honduras.[29] By 1925 Herrera was a chief cook on the Honduran SS *Nicarao,* another Standard Fruit Company vessel that arrived in New Orleans from Puerto Cortés. However, unlike in 1918, Herrera signed up for the *Nicarao* in New Orleans, the original port of embarkation for the vessel, indicating that he had settled in New Orleans during the intervening years. Though his nationality was still listed as Honduran, he was residing in New Orleans at the time of his service on the vessel.[30] Herrera made numerous voyages throughout the 1920s and early 1930s as a Honduran national on fruit-company vessels, perhaps as a contract employee. At times, he was listed as a Honduran of the Spanish American race; at other times he identified as a Honduran of the African, or black, race. The varied racial classifications appear to have been arbitrary, more the product of who was keeping records of the crew at the port of call than of self-identification. Following his naturalization as an American in 1937, Herrera's racial and occupational status was solidified; all further documentation from the shipping companies and US federal documents listed him as a "Honduran Negro" with American nationality who worked only for private companies.

In 1945 Herrera was listed as a steward on the merchant ship *Elizabeth Lykes,* which was owned and operated by the Lykes Brothers Steamship Company, based at New Orleans. The ship arrived in New York City in August, after a two-week voyage from Montevideo, Uruguay, with Herrera as a crew member. He had originally signed on to the vessel in Philadelphia in May. It is unclear from the documents where the ship traveled between Herrera's joining it in Philadelphia and its arrival in Montevideo or how he came to be in Philadelphia.[31] According to the documents, New Orleans was still his home, and at the age of forty-seven he was recorded as having spent twenty-seven years at sea on merchant vessels. Almost nine years later, in 1953, Herrera was still working as a seaman on Lykes Brothers merchant vessels. At fifty-six years of age he was listed as a steward on the SS *Gretna Victory* as it left the port of San Francisco for an undisclosed foreign location. This particular manifest revealed some aspects of Herrera's personal life. His contact information named his next of kin as his wife of thirty-two years, Hattie, and gave a home address in the Seventh Ward of New Orleans.[32] A journey that began in La Ceiba, Honduras, in 1918 took Francisco Herrera from his native Honduras to New Orleans, Philadelphia, San Francisco, Uruguay, New York City, and undoubtedly numerous other ports. His identity shifted from Honduran to Spanish American, Negro, black, and American throughout this period. Despite his travels, he remained married to the same woman, raised a family, and maintained a residence in the city of New Orleans, where his American journey had begun.

Organized Labor as a Path to Racial "Equality"

Though there is no record of the events Herrera may have witnessed or experienced on the numerous merchant vessels he worked on throughout his career, the fact that he dedicated his life to the profession and rarely dwelled in the city in which he established a family and residence says more about New Orleans during the period than it does about Herrera. Life in the Mississippi River port city was difficult for everyone, but especially for black residents. A turn-of-the-century US Merchant Marine Commission report indicates that the average salary for a steward on a US merchant vessel was thirty US dollars a month. Wages for stewards on foreign-owned vessels, particularly Norwegian, German, and Swedish ships (the United States' major competition at the time), were roughly fifteen US dollars a month.[33] By the 1940s the salaries for stewards had increased, but the salaries for black sailors were still below those of their white counterparts. Such wage discrepancies also existed for related professions that employed black labor.

According to Merl E. Reed, black dockworkers at New Orleans earned a meager 25¢ per ship, or 10¢ an hour for two and a half hours of work. Because the number of workers far exceeded the number of ships coming into port, most dockworkers unloaded only one ship per day. Of those earnings, 10¢ went to lodging expenses, leaving very little for the workers to sustain themselves and their families.[34] When the dockworkers affiliated with the Industrial Workers of the World (IWW) went on strike for an increase in wages of $0.90 an hour, $1.20 for overtime, and $2.00 on weekends, the banana companies rejected the strikers' demands and nonunion blacks and Chinese were brought in as strikebreakers. The presence of these workers undermined the fragile interracial cooperation that the IWW sought to foster, as the presence of nonwhite strikebreakers in Jim Crow New Orleans exacerbated racial tensions.[35] Under such constraints, employment on merchant vessels in any capacity proved attractive to those who could get it.

The report of the Merchant Marine Commission also noted that at the turn of the twentieth century "nearly half of American sailors on Atlantic seaboard vessels were Negroes." Most of these sailors were recruited directly by the shipping lines. Owners of shipping companies said that if they wanted to build a sustainable American merchant marine and hire American sailors (which was the aim of the federal government), then "they had to go down South and get Negroes."[36] With the exception of the officer ranks, the difficult life of a sailor did not attract many native-born white Americans, who viewed the work as unprofit-able and without prestige. Merchant vessels supplemented their work-force with foreign-born crew members. Norwegians, Swedes, Italians, Germans, Latin Americans, and West Indians made up the majority of foreign workers on US merchant vessels, where they worked alongside African Americans, creating a multicultural, multinational, and polyglot crew. Though New York was the largest port in the United States at the time and therefore attracted the largest number of workers, New Or-leans operated as the second largest port in the country and attracted a similar combination of workers.

Employment on merchant vessels was advantageous to those who could obtain work. However, conditions on the ships were less than ideal, so merchant seamen based in the United States joined multiracial and multiethnic unions to lobby their employers for improved working conditions and other benefits. Unions such as the IWW (through its affil-iated Marine Transport Workers) and the International Seamen's Union (ISU) competed for members. The ISU successfully lobbied for passage of the Seamen's Act of 1915, which improved food rations, work hours, and wages for seamen, among other advances. Both unions were based in the United States. However, because most of the shipping lines along the Gulf Coast worked extensively with Latin American and Caribbean ports, large portions of their crews were from those areas. Prior to their experiences in the United States, Latin American and Caribbean seamen had little success organizing collectively despite numerous attempts.

In the late 1920s, the Honduran communist revolutionary and labor organizer Juan Pablo Wainwright unsuccessfully attempted to organize UFCO workers on Honduras's North Coast under the Federación Sindi-cal Hondureña (Honduran Trade Union Federation). Through the in-tervention of authorities in Guatemala and Honduras, combined with the efforts of the UFCO, Wainwright was ultimately tried, convicted, and executed in Guatemala by the government of Jorge Ubico in 1932. Though Wainwright was officially jailed for plotting a revolt against the government, some argue that his real crime was spitting in President Ubico's face during a heated argument at the prison where Wainwright was being held. Shortly thereafter, Wainwright was killed by a firing squad. Organized labor was virtually nonexistent in Honduras before Wainwright and continued so after his execution.[37]

During this same period, the IWW, at the behest of Honduran workers, attempted to organize Honduran workers and fill the void left by the failed efforts of Wainwright and others. In 1927, only a year after Wainwright's initial efforts, the Supreme Council of the Central American Labor Federation (Confederación Obrera Centroamericana) wrote to the IWW expressing an interest in cultivating a relationship with the US-based labor union.[38] The IWW reciprocated the Honduran efforts and sought to formalize ties with the Central American organization, but such efforts did not go beyond disseminating literature translated into Spanish from New York to the region.[39] However, IWW-affiliated publications had always reported on worker abuses committed by the UFCO and the Standard Fruit Company both in Central America and aboard their vessels at sea and continued to do so throughout the 1920s and 1930s.

A 1920s article from the *Marine Worker*, a publication of the Marine Transport Workers Industrial Union, entitled "The Great White Graft" (a play on the moniker of the UFCO shipping line, "The Great White Fleet"), reported that three workers had been killed aboard a company ship when a steam boiler burst. Rather than allowing the crew to attend to the wounded and dispose of the dead workers' bodies, the company officials forced the crew to carry on and leave the dead exposed to the elements so that they would not miss their scheduled arrival time.[40] Unfortunately no other accounts of the incident exist, so the response to the report is unknown. Still, the union continued to push for change within the companies. Efforts intensified at the 1st International Conference of Workers in New Orleans in March 1925. Conference participants agreed that the strategy of coordinating isolated strikes in the various ports throughout the region was not successful and that there needed to be a "united front in order to beat capitalism."[41] The conference report, which was translated into Spanish, also stated that the conference the following year would be held in Havana, Cuba—perhaps an effort to engage the numerous Cuban-based workers on fruit-company vessels.

Though these efforts to unionize workers in Latin America during

the 1920s were notable, the efforts of the IWW had little long-term success. In Honduras, where most of the merchant seamen who arrived
in New Orleans were either based or had significant prior work experience, organized labor unions were not sanctioned by the Honduran
government and endorsed by American employers until the early 1940s.
According to a confidential US State Department report from 1943, the
only official labor union in Honduras was the Sociedad Nacional de Mar-
ineros de Honduras (National Society of Honduran Seamen), incorporated in 1940.[42] Made up of seamen working on UFCO vessels, the union
had an unspecified number of members and very limited influence on
labor policies despite a contract between the union and the UFCO out-
lining conditions of employment, compensation, and other benefits.

Though the power of organized labor in the Honduran context was
limited, with previous efforts by organizations such as the IWW lacking
the cohesion and resources to galvanize workers, merchant seamen in
the United States engaged in much more spirited attempts to negotiate
better working conditions. This was most evident in the efforts of the
National Maritime Union (NMU). Founded in 1937 in New York City
by Joseph Curran, a seaman and boatswain originally employed by the
Panama Pacific Line, the union affiliated with the Congress of Industrial
Organizations (CIO) the same year and had amassed a membership of
more than seventy thousand workers by the end of the Second World
War. The NMU was an integrated union; as stated in its constitution,
one of its objects was to "unite in one organization regardless of creed,
color, nationality, or political affiliation all workmen eligible for membership directly or indirectly engaged in the shipping and maritime
transportation industry."[43] This mission also extended beyond the borders of the United States in the efforts of the organization "to assist the
seamen of other countries in the work of the organization and federation to the end of establishing a Brotherhood of the Sea."[44] The union's
constitution and the laws of the United States required that members be
legal entrants into the country and citizens of the United States.[45]

West Indian–born immigrants to the United States were no strangers
to the rank-and-file membership of the NMU, having been active in the
organization from its inception. The Jamaica-born avid communist Fer-

dinand Smith, a founding member and first national secretary-treasurer of the union, remained a prominent member until his expulsion in 1948. Following the second Red Scare, after the Second World War, the federal government compelled many labor unions to expel communist members. Smith rose through the steward ranks to hold national office, showing that on some level the union adhered to the nondiscriminatory policies stated in its original constitution. NMU records from the period indicate a strong stance on antidiscrimination within its ranks. In a report from the second biennial convention in New Orleans only two years after the union's founding, President Curran noted that since the formation of the union in 1937 more than a thousand blacks in the Atlantic region had lost their jobs. The numbers in the Gulf Coast region (of which New Orleans was a major center) were believed to be higher because of the reluctance of southern companies to hire blacks on integrated ships.[46] This reluctance partially explains why West Indians continued to work on ships based outside the United States or in northeastern ports. While New Orleans could operate as a base for family, the realities of racism in hiring practices meant that sustainable work was always abroad.

The NMU report also noted that shipping companies often laid off black workers at a higher rate, chose to go out of business rather than integrate, reclassified ships as freightliners to avoid hiring blacks, and acquiesced to white sailors (some of whom were union members) who refused black crew members.[47] In the face of these practices, the union conducted a national campaign to educate its workers about racial and ethnic discrimination, but it had limited success in New Orleans. As late as 1947 a special union report noted that blacks were discriminated against in every capacity on board ship and that a culture of intolerance toward blacks hindered elected union officials from performing their duties.[48]

As mentioned above, West Indians were also familiar with the city of New Orleans and the precarious race relations there. Immigration from the French West Indies was as old as the founding of the city. The roughly fifteen thousand whites, free people of color, and their enslaved Africans who arrived in New Orleans as refugees from Saint Domingue between 1791 and 1804 fleeing the Haitian Revolution, combined with the immigrants from the region who continued to trickle into the city following this period, added to the Caribbean flavor of the city. In the late nineteenth and early twentieth centuries, these French West Indians were joined by increased numbers of British West Indians. The intellectual and political members of the city's African American community, who were well versed in Caribbean political and economic issues, took notice. Many viewed the West Indies as a model for black advancement and saw the region as central to the economic progress of New Orleans as a whole. Black newspapers from the late nineteenth century reported on the commemoration of the emancipation of slaves in the British West Indies, among other things. In 1881 the former African American congressman General Robert B. Elliot, of South Carolina, gave the oratory at an Emancipation Day event.[49] Elliot himself was an immigrant to the United States of West Indian heritage whose parents had originally immigrated to Liverpool, England.

At an 1887 event in New Orleans, H. C. C. Astwood, the US consul to Santo Domingo, argued for US. expansion into the Caribbean through the burgeoning fruit, logwood, and railroad industries. Astwood believed that this economic expansion would benefit New Orleans and bring about racial equality in the city by providing blacks with opportunities for upward mobility and an increased standard of living. Astwood used the example of West Indians in northern US cities as evidence for his position that "color would no longer be the barrier to their civil and political rights, but condition (economic) would be the all-important factor." Astwood claimed that in northern cities West Indians found "no ostracism but were treated as men and gentlemen" largely for their economic success.[50] Though scholarship on West Indian immigration to the United States has long discredited such utopian notions of West Indian "exceptionalism" and racial inclusion in the United States, the West Indies were seen as the model for racial progress and uplift among elites in the African American community in New Orleans. This suggests that many in the city looked to the larger black Caribbean world for solutions to problems in the United States. Nonetheless, the majority of African Americans in the city, as evidenced by reports on working conditions in West Indian colonies such as Jamaica, rejected the West Indian approach to race relations and voiced concern about the "low wages and lack of opportunity in the sugar industry of the region."[51] An article relating to the plight of Jamaican workers in the *Weekly Planner* entitled "Slavery in Jamaica" noted that many workers (mostly blacks) emigrated to work on the Panama Canal project to escape the low wages and poor working conditions in Jamaica.[52]

While African American elites saw a model for racial and economic uplift in the Caribbean, the rest of the population linked the conditions of the black underclass in the region to the larger discourse on racism and colonialism, which curtailed the political and economic advancement of the majority of African descendants during the period. This was most evident among the working-class population, particularly as it pertained to the influence of Marcus Garvey and Pan-African discourse in New Orleans in the early twentieth century.

Garvey and the Universal Negro Improvement Association

Tony Martin, in his seminal work on the Universal Negro Improvement Association (UNIA), maintained that Louisiana was "far away the most Garveyite state" in the United States, with seventy-four UNIA branches.[53] Records from the organization throughout the 1920s substantiate this claim: the organization had between three thousand and five thousand members in New Orleans alone.[54] However, unlike the Eastern Seaboard, which had a significant population of West Indians from very early on and which was initially dismissed by detractors of the movement as West Indian in focus and not in tune with the realities of African Americans, the majority of the members of the Louisiana branches of the UNIA were native-born African Americans.

In New Orleans, West Indians were a minority within the UNIA. Most of the West Indian members were longshoremen and dockworkers, or those from headquarters who had been sent to work directly on Garvey's behalf. In fact, the UNIA leadership and rank-and-file members in the city were so overwhelmingly African American that in 1923 William Phillips, executive secretary of the New Orleans division, expressed dissatisfaction that Garvey was sending "another West Indian Negro to live on the people of New Orleans."[55] Thomas Anderson, the second assistant general at UNIA headquarters in New York City, chastised Phillips for his comments about West Indians, but Phillips's distinction between West Indians and native-born blacks suggests that the interests of the two groups were not always aligned.

In the South, the Pan-Africanist mission of the UNIA was in many instances the ideal rather than the reality. Local issues often superseded the organization's internationalist scope. Also, Phillips's reference to "another West Indian Negro" implies that UNIA headquarters had tried this strategy of hiring West Indians to head predominantly African American chapters before and failed. More importantly, Phillips's complaint possibly swayed the national office to acquiesce to local concerns. Though Anderson urged that distinctions between the "various groups of black people" needed to cease within the divisions, the UNIA leadership indicated that they had no intention of sending another West Indian to New Orleans anytime soon.[56] Much of this animosity toward West Indian leadership stemmed from the fact that the goals of the two groups in New Orleans were different. Often, roughly 50 percent of the members of the relatively small West Indian community in New Orleans were temporary residents. For African Americans, New Orleans (and the larger United States) was "home," and combatting racism and inequality in the city was their highest priority.

The economic and class differences among West Indians in New Orleans had decreased significantly by the 1930s. West Indians remained a small but visible part of the African American community in the city, but whereas in the past immigrants from the Caribbean and Central American enclaves had worked primarily in agriculture or on the Mississippi River docks, newer waves of immigrants chose to work on ships. As a result, the NMU's role in the city and its impact on West Indian assimilation into the larger society was even more significant.

West Indians, the National Maritime Union, and the Call for Americanization

New Orleans functioned as the headquarters of the NMU's Gulf Coast division. The city was the major hub of the Gulf Coast shipping industry and home to some of the largest commercial steamship lines in the country. The NMU had an immediate impact in New Orleans. Within a month of the union's founding, NMU delegates were permitted to board UFCO vessels to recruit members.[57] The company may have seen an opportunity to suppress the power of the ISU by supporting a rival organization overwhelmingly made up of former ISU members. Most of the rank-and-file members of the NMU had left the ISU because of its conservative approach to labor negotiations following a sit-down strike led by Joseph Curran on the Panama Pacific Line's SS *California*. The decision by the UFCO exacerbated the already existing animosities between the two unions. Other companies followed the lead of the UFCO. Less than a week after the recruitment initiatives of the NMU, sit-down strikes were called by the ISU on ships owned by the Lykes Brothers–Ripley Steamship Company, the Lykes Brothers Steamship Company, and the Tampa Interocean Company in retaliation for their allowing NMU delegates to recruit on their vessels.[58] The NMU delegates responded by striking to have the NMU recognized instead of the ISU on certain vessels.[59]

The numerous strikes and work stoppages in the initial months of the NMU's inroads on the New Orleans shipping industry culminated in a general election to determine which union would have the power to collectively bargain on behalf of all seamen in the city per the stipulations of the National Labor Relations Act of 1935. In January 1938, seamen on thirty-two ships based in New Orleans voted in favor of the NMU, and the organization became the major player in the industry.[60] In addition to establishing the NMU as a powerful union nationally, the strikes also revealed in part why so many seamen in New Orleans, particularly blacks, chose to join the union. The popularity of the NMU during this period also offers insight into why so many West Indian seamen in New Orleans applied for US citizenship during the period: it was a prerequisite to joining the union as a full member.

In July 1937 a sit-down strike by sixty-five NMU crew members on the UFCO passenger vessel the SS *Santa Marta* prevented the ship and its eighty-five passengers from sailing to Havana and Central America. The dispute was over the wages for forty-two members of the steward's department, including cooks and "negro waiters and room stewards," all

NMU members. Prior to the strike, the UFCO had resolved the griev-
ances of the deck and engine-room personnel (positions historically reserved for whites) over hours worked, but it had failed to address the
work hours of the stewards and waiters. The strikers wanted a nine-hour
workday at sea and an eight-hour workday while in port instead of the
standard ten-hour workday at all times. Fruit-company officials noted
that this was the first strike of its kind in New Orleans. This was perhaps
because the union, undoubtedly including several of its white members,
stood by its black members to the point that the national headquarters
of the NMU, in New York City, negotiated directly with the UFCO to re-
solve the situation.[61] Whereas in the past blacks had been excluded from
full membership in unions such as the ISU owing to discriminatory policies and customs—or relegated to the divisive and ostracized roles of
strikebreaker and day laborer—the actions of the NMU during the SS
Santa Marta strike indicated a genuine solidarity across racial lines.

Not surprisingly, the majority of the 271 petitions for naturalization filed by West Indians in the New Orleans East District Court
from roughly 1930 to 1943 involved West Indian and Central American
seamen employed as cooks and in the steward's department who had
entered the United States and lived in New Orleans since late in the
second decade and early in the third decade of the twentieth century.
Some had even married Americans but had failed to file a declaration
of intent to apply for citizenship until the late 1930s, a decision that
coincided with increased labor activity on the part of the NMU. In order
for foreign-born seamen to become full members in the union, they
first needed to file the paperwork to become American citizens. There
are several examples on US naturalization applications of sailors listed
on NMU rosters who had only recently become citizens of the United
States. Many were licensed and unlicensed seamen on UFCO vessels.
Table 3.1 illustrates the numbers of West Indians and Central Americans
who applied for US citizenship from 1930 to 1943.

Of the 271 naturalization applications surveyed, 109 were by West
Indians and 96 were by Spanish Americans. Of the Spanish Americans,
84 were Central Americans, while the others were British Hondurans of
Spanish American ancestry. Roughly 105 of the applicants (38 percent)

TABLE 3.1. Naturalization Applications, New Orleans, 1930–1943

Country of Origin	RACE (COLOR)		
	Black	White	Spanish American (White)
Anguilla	1	0	0
Barbados	9	1	1
Bermuda	1	0	0
British	0	2	0
British Guyana	2	0	0
British Honduras	25	20	11
Cayman Islands	1	15	0
Colombia	1	0	1
Costa Rica	2	2	6
Cuba	1	0	0
Dutch West Indies	1	0	0
Grenada	3	0	0
Guatemala	0	0	11
Honduras	10	14	36
Jamaica	35	8	0
Montserrat	1	0	0
Nicaragua	7	1	30
Panama	6	1	1
Saint Kitts	1	0	0
Saint Vincent	1	0	0
Trinidad	1	2	0
Total	109	66	96

Source: US Naturalization Applications, US National Archives at Fort Worth, TX.

were seamen on fruit-company vessels, with West Indians overrepresented.[62]

West Indians were also overrepresented as seamen in the 1930 merchant marine census for Jefferson and Orleans Parishes (Greater New

TABLE 3.2. US Merchant Marine Census, Jefferson Parish
       (New Orleans), 1930

| | RACE | |
Country of Origin	Black	White
British Guyana	0	1
British Honduras	9	0
British West Indies	9	0
Cayman Islands	2	4
Cuba	0	2
Dutch West Indies	4	0
Honduras	3	2
Jamaica	17	3
Nevis	0	1
Nicaragua	1	0
Panama	14	4
Trinidad	1	0
Virgin Islands (US)	6	1
Total	66	18

Sources: US Department of Commerce, *Fifteenth Census of the United States: 1930;* Census of Merchant Seamen, Jefferson Parish, New Orleans, National Archives and Records Administration, Washington, DC.

Orleans). The census was officially taken on April 1, 1930, but it was allowed to commence in October 1929 in some locales because of predictions of inclement weather. The census for New Orleans was conducted from March 4 to April 1, 1930. Unlike the standard US census, the merchant marine census was the first to include seamen on merchant vessels flying the US flag. In addition to information regarding the identity of individual seamen, the census also included the name of the vessel, the name of its owner, the port of embarkation, and the address of the seaman's next of kin. Surprisingly, none of the 105 sailors whose naturalization applications are included in table 3.1 appeared in the census.

TABLE 3.3. US Merchant Marine Census, Orleans Parish
      (New Orleans), 1930

	RACE	
Country of Origin	Black	White
Barbados	2	0
British Honduras	5	0
British West Indies	3	0
Cayman Islands	4	4
Cuba	0	4
Dutch West Indies	2	0
Honduras	2	3
Jamaica	7	2
Nicaragua	1	1
Panama	2	2
Virgin Islands (US)	6	0
Total	34	16

Sources: US Department of Commerce, Fifteenth Census of the United States: 1930; Census of Merchant Seamen, Orleans Parish, New Orleans, National Archives and Records Administration, Washington, DC.

Tables 3.2 and 3.3 indicate the country of origin and race of seamen on the various vessels at the Port of New Orleans during the census period.

In the censuses for Orleans and Jefferson Parishes, West Indians and Central Americans of African descent outnumbered their fellow countrymen who were classified as white. However, in both parishes the native-born blacks outnumbered their foreign-born counterparts. In Jefferson Parish, 97 blacks on board ship were native-born, compared with 66 West Indians and Central Americans. In Orleans Parish, 89 were native-born, compared with 34 West Indians and Central Americans. Such numbers support the works of Bolster and Fink, who emphasized the important role of African Americans employed on merchant vessels working in southern ports.

Very few of the sailors in the census resided in New Orleans. Addresses of next of kin encompassed much of the Eastern Seaboard. However, the data illuminate the varied nationalities of the crew on merchant vessels and the susceptibility of West Indians and Central Americans to the organizing efforts of labor unions such as the NMU. Several West Indians and Central Americans were signatories on two 1939 petitions to hold a joint meeting of licensed and unlicensed members of the NMU to discuss the intimidation and corruption of members by union officers at New Orleans. One petition comprised 111 signatures, without specific reference to ships of employment, while another petition comprised signatures of 52 seamen on the SS *Toloa,* a UFCO vessel.

One of the names on the SS *Toloa* petition was William Connor. Connor, born in Anguilla in 1896, arrived in Philadelphia in 1915 from San Juan, Puerto Rico, at the age of nineteen. By 1926 he was living in New Orleans. In May 1929, when Connor declared his intent to apply for US citizenship, he gave the name of his wife as Christina, a New Orleans native. While he listed Christina as his wife on his declaration of intent, Connor's US citizenship application in 1932 named his wife as one Viola Thomas, a native of New Roads, Louisiana, in Pointe Coupee Parish. The two were married in New Orleans in October 1929, suggesting that Connor and his first wife, Christina, divorced soon after he filed the initial declaration. Connor and Thomas had a son, Milton, who was born in New Orleans in 1930. Connor stated his occupation as both cook and seaman. One of the witnesses at his citizenship hearing was Baker Bryant, a career US coastguardsman. The other witness was a truck farmer named Eddie Pearl, from neighboring Jefferson Parish. Both witnesses were native-born African American men, indicating that Connor's associates were not limited to West Indians or sailors but included members of the broader African American community.[63]

Another petitioner, William Kelly, born in Buff Bay, Portland, Jamaica, in 1893, arrived at Norfolk, Virginia, from Nevitas, Cuba, in March 1921. Almost immediately after his arrival, Kelly settled in New Orleans, where he worked as a merchant seaman. Kelly did not file his declaration of intent to become a US citizen until 1935, and he was not naturalized until March of 1939. The witnesses who testified at his cit-

izenship hearing were Henry Edwards, a barber who may have spent
some time as a seaman or railroad worker, and Demus Wilson, an African American fruit-company porter. Though there is little information
available on the witnesses, their involvement in heavily unionized industries suggests that they may have influenced Kelly to acquire US citizenship. Since he lived in the country for fourteen years without even
filing a declaration of intent and waited another four years to apply for
naturalization, there was likely a catalyst that made Kelly suddenly want
to become a citizen. He was not married and had no children, so unlike
with other West Indians, family was not his motivation. The fact that
Kelly's signature appears on an NMU petition suggests that the desire
to be active in the union contributed to his decision to apply for citizenship, especially after the NMU committed resources to organizing across
racial lines in New Orleans.

The cases of Connor and Kelly are representative of the experiences
of other West Indians who signed the petitions. Their association with
the larger black community and their ties to railway workers, porters,
agricultural workers, and black professionals exposed them to every
facet of black political, economic, and cultural life in the city. Organized
labor was a key component in all of these interactions. Interestingly, the
issues of corruption and intimidation that union members wished to
address in a joint meeting sprang in part from accusations that one of
the New Orleans–based officers in the union, Arthur Thomas, was not
a US citizen and had forged his papers in order to seek membership and
ultimately assume a leadership role. Thomas, an African American and
professed New Orleans native, had a similar experience to other black
seamen based in the city. He worked on fruit-company vessels throughout Latin America and the Caribbean and on the Eastern Seaboard.
Thomas began his career in the steward's department, joined the NMU,
and eventually became a well-known figure within the local Gulf Coast
division. The charges against Thomas raise several questions about the
premium placed on citizenship within the unions, trumping national
and ethnic loyalties. How was it that at the height of Jim Crow in New
Orleans, when in all other areas of their lives they attempted to assimilate into the larger African American community, black West Indian sea-

men, many of whom had only recently become US citizens, sided with whites against another black seaman by questioning his citizenship? To what extent did union membership trump race among sailors and foster a sense of American nationalism within its membership?

In 1939, Arthur Thomas, Charles Degress, C. H. Applewhite, Frank Rinaldo, and William Duffy were brought before the NMU membership on fourteen counts and charged with conspiring to sabotage and break up the union.[64] Among the charges were the following:

1. Paying armed goons with funds of the Union to attack and intimidate membership of the Union into fear of their lives and personal safety if they at any time or in any way made statements derogatory to, or at all opposed to, their wishes.

2. Condoning assaults by armed men on members of the Union in good standing, both in the hall [meeting place] itself and out of it.

3. Not permitting the National Auditor, in whose appointment by the National Council nearly the whole membership had unanimously concurred, to properly audit the books of the Gulf Coast headquarters.

4. Using the funds of the Union to purchase automobiles for the private convenience of especially privileged members of the Union.

5. Attending National Council meetings where they [Thomas and Degress] voted concurrence with policies that they immediately returned home and attacked with the point in mind of solely discrediting the National Council and lowering Union morale.[65]

Subsequently, all fourteen charges were circulated among NMU branches nationwide, including the territory of Puerto Rico, and the accused members were voted out of the union, with the exception of Thomas, who resigned. As evidenced by crew lists from numerous vessels over a twenty-year period, Degress and Duffy were white, naturalized US citizens hailing originally from France and Ireland, respectively. Rinaldo and Applewhite were both native-born whites. Thomas's nationality, however, proved to be less clear, mainly because of an accusation by an unnamed union member about his legal status in the country. A survey of crew lists embarking and debarking at New Orleans during the period revealed only one seaman named Arthur Thomas. This Arthur Thomas was always listed as American and "Negro."[66]

Thomas worked almost exclusively on UFCO and Lykes Brothers vessels throughout the Caribbean and Central America. According to NMU accounts, he rose within the ranks of the Gulf Coast division and, along with Degress, was elected to represent New Orleans at the 1937 National Council meeting in New York. At the meeting, both New Orleanians played prominent roles, with Thomas serving as a member of the constitutional committee that drafted the union's governing document.[67] Upon his return from New York, Thomas was taken into custody by the New Orleans commissioner of immigration on the basis of testimony by an unnamed source that Thomas was in the country illegally.[68]

The accuser suggested that Thomas's employer, the UFCO, had sent him to Havana and that when he returned to New York (and later New Orleans) "he was a citizen of the United States of longstanding."[69] The implication was that the UFCO had forged Thomas's papers. The accuser appeared to be intimately familiar with Thomas's employment record. The serious allegations against Thomas, combined with his UFCO association and travel patterns, raised suspicion. Initially, the NMU president, Joseph Curran, chose not to investigate these claims. Thomas then became defensive and resigned from the union, citing his desire to not be party to a "dictatorship" of union officials and to "not be dominated by the Communist Party," which many (including the federal government) believed to be infiltrating the NMU and other organized labor unions.

Curran responded to Thomas's accusations in union media outlets, stating that every action taken by the union leadership had been ratified by the membership in an open and transparent process. He further noted that the NMU did not want to be dominated by the Communist Party or known as "an auxiliary of any political group, including the ship owners."[70] Curran did not deny that there were communists in the NMU but stated that the union itself was not an extension of the Communist

Party, a political move to both curtail further government scrutiny and increase membership among sailors (particularly in southern ports), who were more likely to be politically averse to communist causes. The sailors referenced an earlier plot in which several key union members had been found to be agents for the shipping companies, attempting to break up the union by instigating conflict within the rank-and-file membership. This reference was possibly a swipe at Thomas, who the accuser implied was an agent of the UFCO.

US immigration authorities, finding no evidence to substantiate the accuser's claims about Thomas's citizenship, released him. However, the fact that such accusations gained traction among the rank-and-file union members, combined with actual improprieties committed by Thomas, contributed to his demise. The Arthur Thomas affair and its fallout show the precarious position of foreigners within the labor movement and the role of citizenship in legitimizing its members. More importantly, how a person acquired citizenship was crucial. The questions regarding Thomas's citizenship focused on the allegation that the UFCO had sent him to Havana and that he had returned with citizenship papers, thus circumventing the federal process. Such actions by the UFCO throughout Latin America are well documented. These actions undoubtedly created resentment, since the majority of seamen went through the standard federal naturalization process, which involved a formal declaration of intent, a naturalization application, a federal court hearing that included calling witnesses and a background check, and the payment of applicable fees. Though seamen employed by the major fruit and shipping companies in New Orleans often acquired citizenship relatively swiftly after completing the application process, it was not guaranteed; there are several examples of denied applications and deportations.

The constant travel of sailors meant that their paperwork was frequently misplaced or lost. The most well known case nationally of lost paperwork was that of one of the founders of the NMU, Ferdinand Smith. Smith first arrived in the United States in 1919 from Jamaica as a crew member on the SS *Tuscan*, a fruit-company steamer. Discharged from the ship at New Orleans, in 1920 he filed a declaration of intent to apply for US citizenship in Mobile, Alabama. Smith then applied for citizenship papers in 1920 but was told he had to wait two years before the application would be approved. In the meantime, Smith ascended within the ranks of the Marine Workers Industrial Union and achieved prominence as a founding member of the NMU. When in 1946 his influence in the union proved problematic for the federal government, questions regarding his citizenship arose.[71] Curran spearheaded a national campaign within the union to prevent Smith's deportation from the United States. Smith's reapplication for US citizenship in 1946 was denied, and eventually, in 1951, he was deported to Jamaica, but not before being expelled from the union in 1948 in response to government pressure concerning his communist ties. What happened to Smith happened to countless other foreign-born seamen in the period of the second Red Scare. In the decades preceding World War II, a significant number of West Indians applied for US citizenship, with the largest increase followed the Thomas affair in the 1930s. This suggests that to the degree that race would allow, West Indians were as involved as European immigrants in the assimilation and acculturation processes that defined the interwar period in the United States.[72]

Saying Good-bye to the Union Jack: Americanization and the West Indian

Employment, union membership, and naturalization were important factors in determining the commitment of West Indians and Central Americans to their new nation. However, the willingness to serve in the US armed services and potentially die for the new nation was the ultimate commitment. Evidence from the First World War indicates that some West Indians in New Orleans were willing to sacrifice their lives for the United States years before organized labor expressed the virtues of citizenship and love of country. As table 3.4 shows, 91 West Indians residing in New Orleans during World War I registered for the military draft. Of this number, 48, or roughly 50 percent, had been born in Jamaica and gave their citizenship as British. The remaining registrants were from Central American nations (20) and other British West Indian colonies (23). Of the Jamaicans, 60 percent worked for the UFCO as sea-

TABLE 3.4. World War I Draft Registrants at New Orleans, 1918

	EMPLOYMENT			
Nationality	Draft Registrants	Fruit Companies	Other Employment	Unemployed
Barbados, BWI	5	4	0	1
British Honduras (Belize), BWI	10	8	2	0
Cayman Islands, BWI	3	3	0	0
Costa Rica	4	2	2	0
Grenada, BWI	5	5	0	0
Guatemala	1	1	0	0
Honduras	5	3	2	0
Jamaica, BWI	48	30	18	0
Nicaragua	4	3	1	0
Panama	6	5	1	0
Total	91	64	26	1

Source: World War I Draft Registration Cards, 1917–1918.

men on company vessels; the others were employed as laborers or porters for other New Orleans–based companies on the Mississippi River
waterfront.[73] Ten had declared their intent to apply for US citizenship,
and 3 were naturalized Americans.

The numbers for the Central Americans are very similar to those
for the Jamaicans in terms of employment with the fruit companies.
Of the 20 Central Americans, 14 were employed with the UFCO, while
the other 6 were laborers or professionals in other industries. Among
British subjects from other West Indian colonies, 20 of the 23 who declared for the draft were employed as seamen on UFCO or Standard
Fruit Company vessels, while the others were laborers in other New
Orleans industries. The draft numbers confirm that most West Indians in New Orleans during the period were employed as seamen on

fruit-company vessels. Furthermore, the decision to register for the US draft signaled that none of these men planned to serve the British government by registering for the West India regiment. Unlike in the settlements in Central America, the West Indian community in New Orleans considered themselves Americans, a conviction further demonstrated by their low level of engagement with the British Consulate in New Orleans. This contrasts with the situation in Honduras a few years prior, in which West Indians resisted military conscription and impressed service during the numerous internal conflicts in the country. In those encounters, West Indians were adamant in proclaiming their allegiance to the British Crown, whereas in the US example, West Indians were more than willing to embrace the United States.

The sociologist Ira Reid noted in his 1939 study of West Indian immigrants that West Indians often sought naturalization at a slower rate than did their European counterparts unless they had visibly assimilated into American life.[74] Social recognition as an individual did not occur in the United States to the same extent that it did in the Caribbean. Rather, it was often impeded by the issue of race. West Indians from the British territories who chose to be naturalized as Americans, according to Reid, were criticized by their countrymen for switching their political allegiance. There was also an added political disadvantage in becoming a US citizen, since they had to forgo the protection of the British Crown in cases of racism and discrimination. West Indians of African descent actually lost more political rights than would be gained from US citizenship.[75]

Lara Putnam, Michael Conniff, Philippe Bourgois, Baron Pineda, myself, and others who have worked extensively on West Indian migrant and immigrant populations in Central America have noted the high degree to which West Indians sought to maintain their British nationality.[76] These ties to British authorities could protect them against hostile Hispanic nationalism and also provided an advantage in gaining employment in American-dominated industries. Anne Spry Rush suggests that in the early twentieth century West Indians in the British colonies "re-fashioned themselves so as to fit British ideals," in the process creating a British imperial identity that was separate from, but closely related to, their local colonial identities.[77] To be "British" was held in high regard within the West Indian middle class and those aspiring to middle-class status. However, in New Orleans this was not the case, and West Indians were quick to forgo their British identity.

British consular records from New Orleans from 1856 to 1930 reveal only two West Indians claiming British nationality in New Orleans during the period. One was a Barbadian who worked as a missionary on the African continent. He applied for British citizenship for his son, who was born in New Orleans. The other was a merchant mariner from Grand Cayman also seeking citizenship for his young son.[78] In these two cases, the racial identity of the petitioners is unclear since race was not explicitly listed in consular registries. However, the fact that none of the previously mentioned West Indians in this study bothered to register with their consulate suggests that many chose to sever political ties with Great Britain. This break with British identity during the period, as well as embracing the labor movement, marrying Americans, and later seeking US citizenship, were some of the more notable ways in which West Indians in New Orleans, particularly those of African descent, created new identities in the city. However, the Spanish-speaking immigrants who arrived from the same Central American ports experienced a starkly different reception, largely owing to their racial and class status, a subject further explored in chapter 5.

CHAPTER FOUR

Inventing a New Life in the Midst of Uncertainty

* *

Navigating the Racial Divide in New Orleans

The existing immigration and labor records for West Indians in New Orleans between 1918 and 1939 reveal much about their public engagement with pressing political and economic issues in the city at the time. However, the documents are limited in what they reveal about the daily lives of the men and women who made New Orleans their home, largely because of the small size of the community and the fact that West Indians generally lived their lives under the radar. In their occupations as sailors on merchant vessels, laborers in the agricultural industries, and employees in service jobs (as porters, waiters, servers, cooks, and domestics), West Indians were an essential but indistinguishable group within the city. Their invisibility stemmed from their being black in a racially segregated society in which the white power structure paid little attention to the diversity within the black population unless it directly impacted them. Despite this invisibility, West Indian men and women had lives beyond their occupations. They participated in various aspects of New Orleans life and negotiated their identities as black and West Indian in unique but subtle ways. Through an analysis of residential patterns, military-draft records, census data, and civil and criminal court cases, it is possible to re-create aspects of West Indian life to gain a sense of their existence beyond the workplace. By reading between the lines, this chapter offers insight into the ways in which West Indians developed their own sense of community, challenging preexisting notions of race and its perceived limitations on economic advancement in the Jim Crow South.

As discussed in chapter 3, the bulk of the West Indian and West Indian–descent population living in New Orleans during the first half of the twentieth century arrived between the two world wars, with the years 1914–24 being the peak period. This pattern coincides with the experiences of European and Latino migrant populations in the United States. The 1924 federal legislation creating racial and nationality quotas that restricted the flow of nonwhite immigrants into the country caused the decline following the peak period. Steeped in the racial pseudoscience of eugenics, ideas of nationality and race were often conflated.[1] For example, to be French in nationality was also to be French in racial classification. Nation delineated history, culture, and origins as well as race. The immigration legislation, particularly the 1924 National Origins Act, was initially aimed at curtailing the immigration of eastern and southern Europeans. The fear among politicians and other elites was that these groups' increased presence would disrupt the political and cultural foundation of the nation established by the Anglo-Saxon and northern European "founders." Vice President–elect Calvin Coolidge expressed the sentiment of the times cogently in his 1921 essay "Whose Country Is This?," in which he asserted that American liberty was "dependent on quality in citizenship." According to Coolidge, it was the obligation of Americans of Anglo-Saxon and northern European descent "to maintain that citizenship at its best."[2] He said that there were "racial considerations too grave to be brushed aside for sentimental reasons." Biological laws, he argued, showed "that certain divergent people will not mix or blend."[3] The article's conclusions pointed to the need to limit the number of "undesirables" allowed into the United States and stated a preference for immigrants of Nordic and Anglo-Saxon extractions, which would ensure strong racial attributes for success. The federal government attempted to engineer this outcome with the 1924 legislation. Coolidge and others during the period disregarded the contributions of the roughly 10.5 million Americans of African descent to the development of the nation. This was most evident in later amendments to the National Origins Act that limited the number of people of Sub-Saharan African descent entering the country.

Though the federal government passed legislation that restricted the immigration of certain groups into the country, the enforcement of the law was left to immigration officials. For example, physicians employed on merchant vessels possessed a guide entitled "List of Races" to aid them in discerning the nationality and racial background of the crew. The guide listed forty-six racial categories and contained detailed instructions on how to determine an individual's racial background.[4] The instructions asserted that "race or people" was determined by the stock (blood) from which the "alien" sprang and the language he spoke. The original stock was the primary basis for classification; the native language assisted determination of the immigrant's ancestry.[5]

While race and nationality were synonymous for Europeans, there were clear distinctions when it came to immigrants of African descent. For instance, British West Indians were referred to by the nationality of their colonial government (British, Great Britain, or English) in the "nation" category on official US government documents. However, their race was always listed as "African (black) or Negro." The designations were similar for those from other Caribbean or Central American possessions. For instance, a black Cuban's nationality was listed as Cuban, but his or her race was always "African (black)." A "white" Cuban's race, however, was given as Spanish American and therefore legally white. These distinctions were not insignificant given that the National Origins Act specifically exempted immigrants from the Americas from immigration quotas.[6] However, those of African descent were specifically excluded in a subsequent amendment to the law and subject to increased scrutiny, rejection, and/or deportation.

While most West Indians and Central Americans of visible African descent were subjected to the new immigration laws, those employed as sailors were afforded some reprieve owing to the political and economic influence of the major shipping lines. For example, the only groups of seamen excluded from the United States were those from the "Continent of Asia and islands adjacent thereto," which only reaffirmed anti-Asian legislation dating back to the late nineteenth century.[7] That immigrants from the Americas were not excluded in part explains the tendency for West Indians to be employed as seamen on fruit-company vessels in New Orleans.

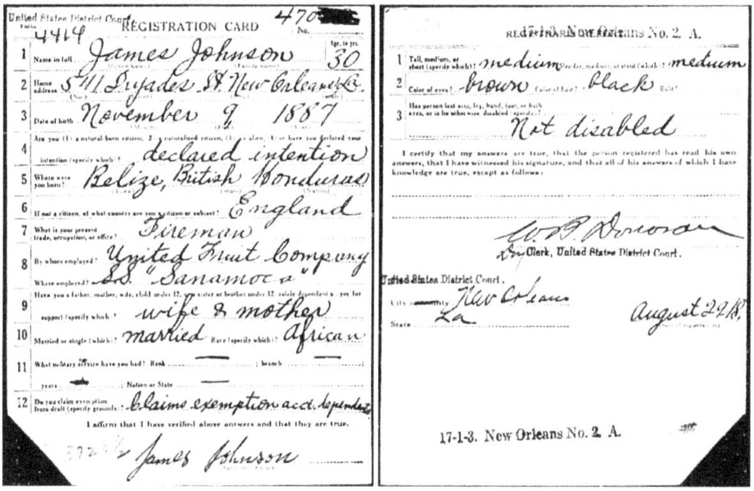

FIG. 4.1. World War I draft registration card, New Orleans. National Archives and Records Administration, Washington, DC.

There are no available data from the various fruit companies listing their employees. Many of the companies were small operations that existed for only short periods of time. The larger companies, such as the UFCO and Standard Fruit, have released exceedingly limited materials from their vast holdings. One must rely largely on US government documents for detailed information about the merchant-seaman population. The draft registrations referenced in chapter 3 offer insight. On the surface, the draft cards of these sailors contain merely the wonted data collected by US government officials during wartime. However, the amount of detail in the records helps us to reconstruct a West Indian community. Draft registration cards requested basic information similar to that contained in other government documents, such as full name, date of birth, address, alien status, place of birth, and country of citizenship (fig. 4.1). In addition, occupation, employer, marital status, and dependents were listed. Identifying characteristics such as race, height, color, and other relevant physical traits were included on most forms. How registrants responded to these questions reveals much about their lives, including family structure, residential patterns, political views and allegiances, and economic relationship to New Orleans and the larger Latin American and Caribbean world.[8]

Mae Ngai notes that in 1917, when the United States entered the First World War, all males aged 21 to 30 were required to register for the draft.[9] In September 1918 the draft age was extended to include men aged 18 to 44.[10] This later amendment to the draft incorporated the majority of West Indians in the city, as most ranged in age from 18 to 30. Not surprisingly, West Indian draft registrants came from throughout the Caribbean. However, immigrants from Jamaica and British Honduras were overly represented.

The preponderance of West Indians from particular locales was linked in part to the shipping routes established by the tropical fruit trade. Routes connecting New Orleans to the Caribbean and Central American republics were established by the fruit industry as early as the 1890s, when the Boston Fruit Company (later United Fruit) extended its routes from New York to Jamaica and Haiti to include New Orleans and Mobile. From New Orleans, further routes were established that linked the city to all of the Central American republics engaged in the cultivation of bananas.[11] Other companies expanded these routes to the point that virtually every Central American republic with Caribbean ports was connected to New Orleans. Mail routes and eventually passenger lines were established, and the trade in agricultural commodities quickly led to the movement of people and ideas for business and pleasure.[12]

Central City: A Little "Caribbean" Oasis Hidden in Plain Sight

Though West Indians from Jamaica and British Honduras represented the majority of draft registrants, the real story lies in the experiences of those from the smaller islands. Perhaps because of its limited numbers, this population was compelled to interact with both other West Indians and African Americans to a greater extent than they otherwise might have. Their ability to navigate multiple spaces, evident in the documents, reveals much about the larger community (and neighborhood) in New Orleans where most West Indians lived, Central City. Almost all the West Indians from the smaller islands who registered for the draft came from Grenada, Barbados, and the Cayman Islands, with the exception being one sailor from Saint Vincent. Of the ninety-one men, nine claimed dependents and four used this as cause for seeking exemption from military service. Of the dependents, a mother was almost always referenced, followed by a wife, a child, or younger siblings. For example, the assistant steward S. B. Bonpart, on the UFCO ship the SS *Cartago*, listed his grandmother along with an unnamed number of sisters and brothers under the age of twelve as dependents on his 1917 draft card, indicating that he was their sole means of financial support.[13]

Bonpart, like many of the other seamen, lived in the Central City neighborhood, a major commercial and entertainment district for African Americans in the first half of the twentieth century that counted famous jazz musicians such as Charles "Buddy" Bolden, Edward "Kid" Ory, and Henry "Professor Longhair" Byrd as residents at one time or another. As Louise McKinney notes, it was one of the few areas "beyond the *mêlée* of the French Quarter and the old-time (white) Creole sections" that experienced a cultural heyday whose influence reached beyond the city.[14] Many Irish, Italian, and Jewish immigrants settled in the neighborhood during the nineteenth century, and they were later joined by Caribbean and Latin American sailors and dockworkers, along with large influxes of African Americans, at the turn of the twentieth century. By the 1920s the neighborhood was overwhelmingly commercial, with a predominantly African American residential population and a significant Ashkenazi Jewish merchant and commercial class.

The map below shows the settlement patterns of West Indian and Central American immigrants in New Orleans, superimposed upon a base map originally drawn by the Home Owner Loan Corporation (HOLC), a company formed in 1933 as part of the New Deal to stave off foreclosures and promote development through financing and refinancing mortgage loans. The HOLC drew detailed maps of urban centers throughout the United States on which they showed neighborhoods' risk assessment for mortgages. The neighborhood maps were color coded and divided into four groups, labeled A, B, C, or D (corresponding to Best, Still Desirable, Definitely Declining, and Hazardous on the redrawn map pictured here):

A—"Hot spots": New, well-planned sections of the city not fully built up; areas where good mortgage lenders with available funds were willing to make their maximum loans, to be certified over a ten- to fifteen-year period up to 75–80 percent of the appraisal.

B—"Completely developed": Established neighborhoods holding their value, where good mortgages would hold loan commitments 10–15 percent under the appraisal limit.

C—"Transitioning": Areas characterized by age, obsolescence, change of style, expiring restrictions, infiltration of a "lower-grade" population.

D—"Transitioned": Areas with detrimental influences, undesirable population, low percentage of home ownership, unstable income, where lenders might refuse to extend mortgages and others might lend only on a conservative basis.[15]

West Indians and Central Americans mentioned in the available HOLC documents lived in areas labeled C or D. In addition to describing the physical and financial state of the areas, the documents also record the races and nationalities of the population in assessed areas. The populations in areas labeled C and D were increasingly black and majority black, respectively. These were neighborhoods with "cheaply constructed cottages occupied by Negroes" or where "a Negro slum project had been approved."[16] That the West Indians and Central Americans included in this study lived in these areas further racialized them as black (most already had been denoted as such in government documents) and lower class, in effect placing limitations on their upward mobility.[17]

Despite its federal designation as an undesirable area, Central City, like New Orleans, was a multicultural space in which immigrant and African American cultural influences merged, contributing much to the New Orleans cultural tradition.[18] Thomas Fiehrer asserted that many of the nineteenth-century West Indian "refugees" from Saint Domingue

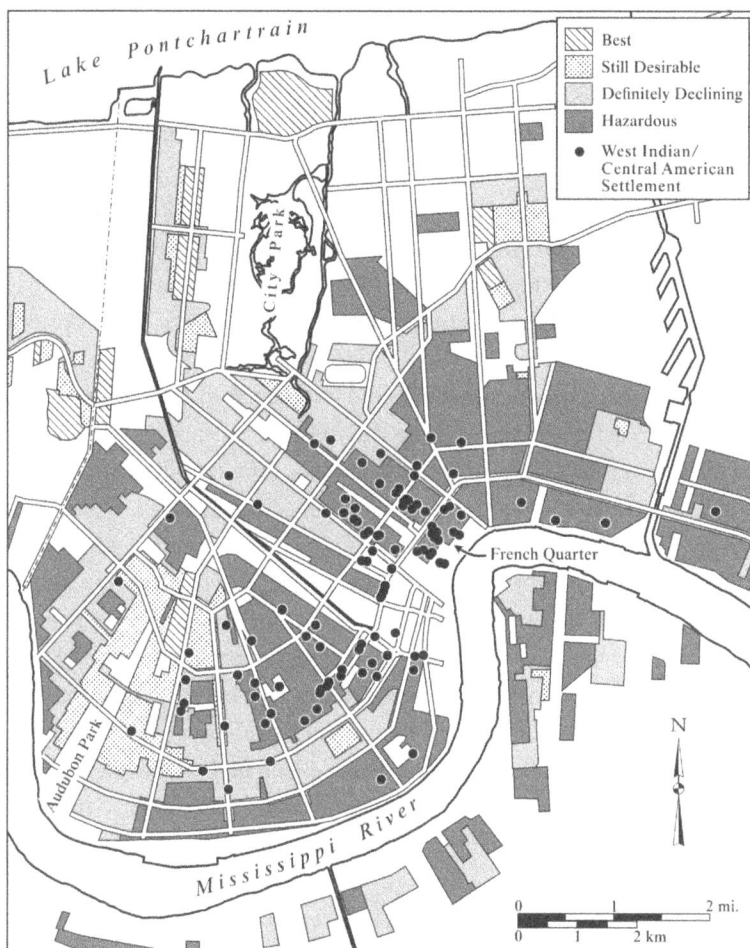

West Indian and Central American Settlement Patterns, Greater New Orleans, 1918–1940. Map drawn by Mary Lee Eggart.

who had converged on the city following the Haitian Revolution a century earlier (whites, blacks, and *gens de couleur*) had also added to New Orleans's culture. These "refugees" had maintained ties with their relatives who settled in Cuba, Jamaica, Mexico, and other Caribbean and Latin American nations.[19] These bonds, though weaker after the Civil War, never entirely ceased, and the West Indian and Central American immigrants and migrants simply continued a long tradition of Caribbean people seeking economic opportunity and in some cases escaping the diminished prospects in the Caribbean.[20]

It is unclear from the draft registration cards whether the previously mentioned Bonpart's family resided in New Orleans or remained in Grenada. His status as the primary means of support for his extended family and the fact that he was most often at sea suggest that Bonpart had little opportunity to take advantage of the extracurricular activities that Central City and other areas in the city offered. However, Emily Epstein Landau, in her seminal study on the Storyville district and prostitution in New Orleans, notes that while sailors docked in New Orleans did not play an active role in shaping daily life, they often patronized the bordellos and flophouses present throughout the city. The two professions frequently coexisted and offered opportunities for not only sexual activity but also cultural exchange.[21] This was often the case in port cities within Latin America and the Caribbean as well. For example, in early-twentieth-century Havana, dance schools known as *academias de baile*, run by black and mulatto women, taught elite men how to dance and also provided sexual favors. Because of their lower-class ownership and their location in the city, these schools made *son* (an Afro-Cuban musical form) the music of choice. These elite men began to identify *son* with their experiences at the *academias de baile*. Subsequently, many of the negative stereotypes of the music and those who performed it promoted by Cuban politicians and others in privileged circles diminished, allowing the music to gain national prominence.[22]

In her study of race and gender in the New Orleans Mardi Gras tradition, Kim Marie Vaz observes that in black New Orleans, men often worked on steamboats and in coal yards, sugar plants, sawmills, and blacksmith shops in addition to working as sailors. These men patronized prostitutes in the "Black Storyville" part of the city, the unofficial black section of the famous red-light district, which was in close proximity to where they lived.[23] Jazz music and black New Orleans culture were promoted in Storyville, and the houses of ill repute became the training ground for prominent musicians such as Jelly Roll Morton and Louis Armstrong. The former admitted to being heavily influenced by the music of Cuba, from which he acquired the "Spanish tinge" element of early jazz. The musicologist John Storm Roberts notes that the African American community was often the channel through which Latin American music entered popular US musical styles. Port cities such as New Orleans and New York were ground zero for such cross-cultural exchange. However, apart from the music of a few individual musicians and other anecdotal evidence, it is difficult to determine the exact relationship between Latin America and the music of New Orleans, particularly the Latin American influence on jazz. According to Roberts, because of the shared political and economic histories and common origins of the inhabitants in the two regions, similar styles existed in what he describes as the "polyglot musical language of the city."[24] Caribbean and Latin American cultural influences, and by extension its people, simply did not stand out in New Orleans.

West Indian Women at the Forefront of the Community

Judging from the scant references to women in the daily lives of the merchant seamen and those in related professions with the exception of references to prostitutes, one might assume that sailors only interacted with women as prostitutes. However, as Vaz indicates, women were often proprietors of boardinghouses and restaurants or employed as laundresses, seamstresses, and hairdressers.[25] Many worked as domestics for white families. The fact that sailors often gave their wives or mothers as reasons to avoid the draft in no way indicates that women were not at the forefront of West Indian and African American society in New Orleans. Several examples from the period reveal the diverse roles women played in New Orleans life. For example, Almina Salmon, a black woman from Westmoreland Parish in Jamaica, entered the United States at New Orleans in 1928 from Belize City, British Honduras. Identifying herself as a teacher, she applied for US citizenship in 1934. Salmon was single and never married. The available data suggest that she maintained a very low profile.[26] Witnesses at her citizenship hearing were one Mr. Fortunatus Ricard, principal at the Arthur P. Williams School, where she taught, and Ms. Noemie Marc, a teacher colleague. Both Ricard and Marc were African American New Orleans natives residing near Salmon in Central City.[27] The Arthur P. Williams School was named for the noted principal of the famous Fisk School for Boys in New Orleans, which employed many black Creole musicians as educators and later produced famous jazz musicians such as Buddy Bolden and Louis Armstrong. Williams was remembered as a strict disciplinarian who promoted a curriculum that incorporated music in daily instruction.[28] It is unclear whether Salmon was a musician, but she remained employed as a teacher at various African American schools in New Orleans at least through the 1950s.[29]

Anita McKay also represented the diverse experiences of West Indian women in New Orleans. McKay, also from Belize City, British Honduras, arrived in New Orleans in 1919. However, she gave her foreign address immediately prior to immigrating to the United States as Havana, Cuba.[30] Why McKay left Havana and sought opportunities in New Orleans is unclear, but one reason might be the increased opposition to West Indian immigration to Cuba during the period. Philip Howard describes a political and cultural environment in Cuba during the early twentieth century in which anti–British West Indian and anti-Haitian sentiment, expressed in nationalist rhetoric similar to that of Central American republics, manifested to the point that Cuban-led labor strikes targeted these populations throughout the 1920s and legislation was introduced at various points to ban West Indians from the country.[31] That McKay ended up in New Orleans and worked as a stewardess adds a new dimension to the role of women on merchant vessels.

Women were an anomaly on merchant vessels and underrepresented in labor-organizing efforts of organizations like the National Maritime Union. McKay was listed as a crew member on US passenger lists for vessels arriving at New Orleans on three separate occasions between 1923 and 1929. One vessel, the SS *Munplace,* was owned and operated by the Munplace Steamship Corporation, headquartered in New York City. However, the ship operated almost exclusively in Central America and the Gulf of Mexico.[32] McKay was working on the vessel when it arrived in New Orleans from the Mexican port of Progreso, on the Yucatán Peninsula. The other vessel that employed McKay, the SS *Comayagua,* was a

UFCO ship based at Puerto Cortes, Honduras. McKay worked on the *Comayagua* for nearly four years as it continued to make frequent voyages between Honduras, Belize City, the Caribbean, and New Orleans. After seven years of employment as a stewardess, McKay left the profession. It is unclear what prompted the change. However, when she applied for US citizenship in 1934, she identified herself as a housemaid at the rooming house where she resided in the French Quarter.

McKay's case is also noteworthy because unlike most West Indian women identified as black who immigrated to New Orleans, McKay was legally married when she arrived in the city. However, she claimed on her declaration of intent and her US citizenship application that her husband, William McKay, also from Belize, had abandoned her in 1919 after eighteen years of marriage. She also testified that she was unaware of his whereabouts. According to Anita's account, William had entered New Orleans a year before her arrival in the city. Within a year he was no longer in her life. It is plausible that her immigration to the city was precipitated by the desire to reunite with her husband and that after he left she was forced to make a life for herself. Anita McKay surfaced again in a 1956 New Orleans city directory, in which she was listed as the widow of William McKay, indicating that she never divorced him and at some point either found him or at least discovered what had happened to him.[33] As for William, available passenger records suggest that after he arrived in the United States, he moved to Alabama, where he briefly worked as a porter on a merchant vessel. In a passenger list from the SS *Lysepjord,* the Norwegian vessel arriving from Belize in 1924 on which William was employed, he gave his permanent residence as Birmingham, Alabama, hundreds of miles from New Orleans, where his wife was.[34] The SS *Lysepjord* had a history of hauling coal from Great Britain to Central America and the United States, and Birmingham, though inland, was a major hub for the coal industry in the South.[35]

Though Anita repeatedly stated on official documents that her husband had abandoned her, William identified himself as married on passenger lists. Whether he was referring to Anita or someone else as his wife is unclear. He named a male friend in Belize City, not Anita, as his nearest relative or friend to contact in case of an emergency. The accounts of William's and Anita's lives contain numerous twists and turns. From their origins in Belize to Havana, New Orleans, Birmingham, and the routes in between on merchant vessels, it is difficult to retrace their steps. However, the circuitous route by which they arrived in the United States and the centrality of New Orleans to their stories are representative of the lives of most West Indians in the city during the period. While Almina Salmon became a teacher at a well-known African American school that produced many notable figures in the African American community in New Orleans, Anita McKay adapted to inconstant circumstances and survived by her wits. Whether it was coming to terms with abandonment by her husband, seeking out a career on merchant ships, or settling for work as a maid in a rooming house in the city, McKay chose to make the city her home and adjusted to its economic realities. In this way, her story is similar to the stories of countless other blacks in New Orleans seeking a new life in uncertain political and economic times.

The account of another West Indian woman, Inez Flowers, offers a different perspective and in many ways demonstrates the transition from West Indian to African American for many of the immigrants. Flowers was born in Belize City, British Honduras, in 1914 and arrived in New Orleans from Puerto Cortés, Honduras, in 1919 with her parents and four siblings. Her father, Enoch, was a seaman for the Cuyamel Fruit Company; he had worked in New Orleans prior to the immigration of his family. Enoch registered for the World War I draft while working for Cuyamel even though he was still a permanent resident of Puerto Cortés at the time.[36] The fact that Enoch was willing to put his life on the line for the United States in the war despite not being a US citizen, as well as his failure to register with the British government, points toward a strong desire to establish himself in the United States. That the entire family arrived in New Orleans a year later from Puerto Cortés confirmed Enoch's commitment to the United States. Their move also endorsed the notion that the family participated in a secondary migration that began in British Honduras, continued to Spanish Honduras, and culminated with their permanent settlement in New Orleans. This constant movement very early in their childhood means that Inez and her younger siblings, unlike her oldest brother, who was ten years old at the time of their arrival in the city, would have had very few recollections of life in Belize City or Puerto Cortés. Their cultural identity would have been shaped largely by their experiences in New Orleans.

The Flowers family initially lived on Dumaine Street, in the French Quarter, surrounded by black migrants from all over the South as well as immigrants from Italy, Latin America, the Middle East, and Malta, among other places.[37] LaKisha Simmons argues that New Orleans during this period was home to many first- and second-generation white ethnic and nonwhite children.[38] Federal appraisers noted that New Orleans was a heterogeneous city in which it was impossible to create sizable or even small areas of exactly the same type. Exclusive streets and sections were prevalent, but the "character could change a block or two distant in any direction."[39] Despite strict segregation in many forms of political and social interaction, whites and blacks often lived in close proximity to each other in almost every neighborhood of the city, particularly in areas such as the French Quarter and Central City, where many of the West Indian and Central American immigrants initially settled. Inez and her siblings arrived in the city at such an early age and grew up in New Orleans with the contrasts and contradictions of its ethnic and racial diversity, yet given legally codified Jim Crow segregation,[40] they must have been well aware of the social limitations of their West Indian ethnicity. In fact, the family was mistaken for Louisiana natives in the 1930 US census. According to that census, Enoch was no longer living with the family. His wife, Cecilia, was listed as the head of household, and the family had relocated to Urquhart Street in the Seventh Ward, the historic section of the city where Creoles of color lived. By 1940 the family had relocated yet again, to nearby North Derbigny Street, also in the Seventh Ward.[41]

Unlike William McKay, Enoch Flowers did not abandon his family but remained in contact with them. He surfaced as an employee of the Clyde Mallory Steamship Company in New York City, where he registered for the draft in 1941. He gave his permanent residence as New Orleans and Cecilia Flowers as the "person who will always know his address" on the registration form.[42] Perhaps the nature of his profession forced Enoch to be away from the family. The instability of the banana industry in the 1930s, owing to the global economic depression and the prevalence of a banana disease that decimated banana crops throughout Central America, forced many industry workers to pursue other means of employment. This situation worsened when the major fruit companies transitioned their fleets to supply the US military during World War II, and many seamen sought employment on any ship that was hiring, regardless of its port of call.[43]

When Inez Flowers applied for US citizenship in 1939, at the age of twenty-five, she had not left the United States since her arrival in New Orleans twenty years earlier. She was single, a college graduate, and employed as a teacher with the Works Progress Administration School Project. Her name appeared on a list of 215 teachers available to fill vacancies at various "Negro schools" throughout the city in June 1939.[44] Perhaps it was this impending opportunity that prompted her to declare her intention to apply for US citizenship in March of that year and submit her formal application a few months later. Inez eventually married an African American migrant from nearby Woodville, Mississippi, and lived the remainder of her life in New Orleans.

Inez Flowers's story is not atypical of many first- and second-generation Americans. The experiences of her parents and siblings, though equally compelling for the immigration narrative, shed light on why the West Indian community in New Orleans remained relatively small and was nonexistent beyond the French Quarter and Central City. Inez's father was constantly away because of the nature of his profession. Her mother resided in the city and listed her occupation as housewife, indicating that either her husband continued to support the household from afar or her children provided for her. Over time, all of Inez's siblings left New Orleans. Her oldest brother, who initially worked in the shipyards and as a longshoreman, returned to Belize City. Her sister disappeared from the record entirely. Another brother migrated to Los Angeles, where their mother eventually joined him and lived out the remainder of her life. Inez's youngest brother relocated to Detroit, Michigan.[45] The departure of Inez's siblings coincided with the mass exodus of African Americans from the South to points north and west. As previously discussed, black Louisianans were often statistically overrepresented among migrant populations traveling to California during and after the Second World War. Because they integrated into black New Orleans life and encountered the same realities that faced native-born African Americans in the city, the Flowers family and others like them participated in the Great Migration, seeking better opportunities elsewhere in the United States. The fact that the oldest brother chose to move back to the country of their birth also suggests that the family did not completely sever ties with their native country after immigrating to the United States.

Those West Indians who immigrated to New Orleans as families or married soon after their arrival in the city often experienced an easier transition into New Orleans life. They were rooted in communities, their children adapted, and they became a part of the city's economic and cultural landscape despite the limitations placed on them by Jim Crow. Those who arrived single or left their families behind in the Caribbean often drifted in and out of various situations, never firmly settling in the city. For example, S. B. Bonpart, who attempted to use his Grenadian family as grounds for an exemption from the US military draft, disappeared from the historical record after January 4, 1918. He had no military record, indicating that he may have returned to Grenada or moved somewhere else outside the United States after registering for the draft. He was last recorded as working on the UFCO vessel the SS *Abangarez*, which arrived in New Orleans after passing through the ports of Cristóbal and Bocas del Toro, Panama, and Havana, Cuba. Bonpart received his pay upon arrival but was not discharged from the vessel, suggesting that he may have continued to work for the company in another country.[46] What is known is that Bonpart registered for the draft as required but roughly six months later was no longer in the United States.

Another Grenadian, Flood Alexander, also registered for the draft in 1917. He too lived in the Central City neighborhood, but unlike Bonpart, he listed no dependents. Alexander claimed an exemption from the draft on the grounds that he was a seaman, even though the occupation was not excluded from service. Alexander had been employed by the UFCO since 1913 and was still active as late as 1920, when he appeared on the US census taken on board the UFCO vessel the SS *Excelsior,* on which he was employed as a waiter.[47] It does not appear that Alexander ever actually served in the military, and like Bonpart, he eventually disappeared from the historical record.

Forging New Identities

Several curious details emerge from the draft registration cards of a minority of sailors who registered for the draft, most notably the failure of some to list their island of birth or nationality. Depending on their age when they arrived in the United States, it can be speculated that some did not actually know the specific Caribbean colony from which they originated. Was it possible that some of these "West Indian" seamen were actually native-born African Americans claiming a foreign identity in order to advance their position or evade the draft? Or did many West Indians in New Orleans choose to forgo their distinct ethnic identity and ties to their old countries and start fresh in the United States? While it is impossible to answer these questions conclusively, the following individual narratives offer insight into the ways in which West Indians dealt with some of these realities.

Henry Foster, a marine fireman for the UFCO born in 1896, listed his place of birth as the British West Indies and his nationality as English on his 1917 draft registration. Foster had been employed on United Fruit vessels based in New Orleans since at least 1914 and was included on crew lists of vessels arriving from Central America, Puerto Rico, Brazil, England, and France throughout the 1920s. The crew lists revealed that Foster was Jamaican by birth, and he appears to have maintained ties with the island, as several of the ships on which he was a crew member docked in Jamaica prior to arriving in New Orleans. It is also plausible that Foster did not mention Jamaica on his draft registration form because anti–West Indian sentiment in the Latin American ports where many of the seamen worked prior to New Orleans focused on Jamaican nationals due to their large numbers.

Foster remained employed by the UFCO even following an incident in Bordeaux, France, in 1920, in which he deserted ship. Perhaps Foster, like the fictitious characters in Claude McKay's *Banjo,* chose to explore the trappings of the French port city. However, like many of the sailors in the book, Foster was a hired hand, paid and discharged after each voyage. In each port city visited, there was never a guarantee of further employment if one left the ship on which he had contracted to work. This potentially made for unstable but exciting work. Being a seaman for hire offered more flexibility. Foster traveled to ports throughout the world, in contrast to seamen employed on a more permanent basis by a single company.

Unlike Foster, who was in New Orleans for a relatively brief period before choosing to live his life elsewhere, other sailors who registered for the draft made the city their home and eventually sought US citizenship. John Ellis, a Jamaican seaman from Annotto Bay working on the UFCO vessel the SS *Baman,* listed his mother and two children as dependents on his draft registration card in March 1918. Ellis claimed an exemption from the draft on the grounds that he was the only means of support for his family, all of whom lived in New Orleans's Central City. He later filed a declaration of intent to become a US citizen.

While the lives of families and ordinary seamen are revealed in draft records, a part of the population that often goes unnoticed comprised those who ran afoul of the law. West Indians during the period were very rarely involved in major criminal activity. The offenses most often attributed to this group were drunkenness and disorderly conduct. One example is the case of Joaquin Aszousa, a twenty-one-year-old Jamaican laborer arrested for "fighting and disturbing the peace" in the Tremé neighborhood. Aszousa was arrested at 2:00 a.m. one day in January 1923; he was discharged the next day once he had "slept it off."[48] A similar incident involved one Daniel Isaac, a twenty-six-year-old Jamaican painter, who was arrested on an alcohol-related charge of "disturbing the peace" and subsequently discharged without prosecution.[49] In the arrest records for the city of New Orleans for the years 1910–40, the twelve West Indians arrested worked either as day laborers or in occupations other than that of merchant seaman. The records include identifying information such as name, address, age, sex, nationality of arrestee and of his or her parents, occupation, and marital status. Date and place of arrest, complaint and complainant, and disposition are also given. The records are segregated, with arrests of "whites" appearing before those of "coloreds."[50] The most serious offenses recorded were federal immigration violations, which resulted in deportation, and draft evasion.[51]

Though most West Indians registered for selective service, draft evasion was not uncommon. In the available draft records for the First World War, several West Indian men who registered were identified as prisoners; all were arrested on charges of evading the draft. According to an article in the *New Orleans Times-Picayune* in January 1918, city officials directed the police to arrest men who failed to respond to their selective-service summons, including foreigners. Once taken into custody, they were forced to register and in some cases had to serve prison terms. David Sterling, an unemployed laborer from Saint James Parish, Jamaica, registered for the draft as an inmate in the third precinct of the Orleans Parish prison. He was listed in the *Times-Picayune* article as a draft dodger.[52] At the time of his arrest, Sterling was single, listed his mother as a dependent, and resided in Central City. Sterling's example is unique given his journey to the United States. In 1914 he arrived in Philadelphia as a stowaway on the SS *Catherine Curres* from Port Antonio, Jamaica. Initially held by immigration services, he was eventually allowed to remain in the country.

A few years later, Sterling showed up in the New Orleans draft-evasion records as an unemployed laborer. What Sterling did for a living and how he came to reside in the city are unknown. Following his arrest for draft evasion, Sterling's name did not appear again until the 1930 US census, which shows him to be married and residing in Providence, Rhode Island, with his five-year-old son, who was born there.[53] The boy's mother, also from the British West Indies, did not live in the house with Sterling and their son. How Sterling came to reside in Rhode Island and the whereabouts of his wife are unclear. Sterling identified himself as a building wrecker for a lumber dealer, but at the time of the census he was unemployed. For Sterling, New Orleans represented a brief period in his life, a way station to somewhere else. However, Sterling's arrival in the country as a stowaway, his failure to voluntarily register for the draft, and his constant trouble finding work no matter where he resided are all reasons why it was difficult to trace his steps or those of any West Indians in New Orleans. Not all West Indians who arrived in the city wanted to be found; many lived significant portions of their lives under the radar. The bits and pieces of their lives that surface in archival data are part of a larger, incomplete puzzle. However, the ways in which they navigated these spaces demonstrate how black immigrants dealt with the complexities of citizenship, residency, the legal system, and daily life as workers.

The examples from the prison records indicate that West Indians not associated with the maritime industry found the transition to life in New Orleans difficult. Yet, many found steady work and established a permanent residence in the city. West Indian sailors gravitated not only to Central City but also to the Seventh Ward, Mid-City, the Faubourg Marigny, the Faubourg Tremé, and the Central Business District. All these areas were near the docks and wharves or fruit-company offices. Census data and naturalization petitions from these neighborhoods in the 1920s and 1930s reveal that West Indians often lived in close proximity to individuals from the same colonies, thus establishing relationships beyond work.

Strikingly absent from the census data are West Indians who did not identify as black. Roughly 20 percent of immigrants from the British West Indies and Central America who identified themselves as seamen gave their race as white. Almost all were from British Honduras, the Cayman Islands, or the Bay Islands (Honduras). Despite identifying as white, these seamen lived in close proximity to black West Indian seamen. Take, for instance, Ashley Ebanks, a marine engineer originally from Grand Cayman who declared his intent to apply for US citizenship in January 1933. Ebanks lived in the Faubourg Marigny, near the Bywater neighborhood. On his declaration, he gave his race as West Indian, his nationality as British, and his color as white. Ebanks first arrived in the United States in 1916 at Key West, Florida, where he worked on merchant vessels. Eventually he found his way to New Orleans, where he continued in this line of work. Just two years after his declaration of intent, on his 1935 naturalization application, Ebanks was still employed on merchant vessels. However, he was now listed as French, but with British nationality. His West Indian identity vanished during his two years in New Orleans. Witnesses at Ebanks's citizenship hearing were fellow seamen George Rusch, white and originally from New York, and Charles Leo, a white, naturalized US citizen originally from Canada. Both Rusch and Leo lived close to Ebanks. This was not unusual given the history of interracial cooperation on merchant vessels and residential patterns in New Orleans during the period. However, Ebanks's embrace of a French identity suggests how some immigrants may have circumvented racial and ethnic barriers. To be white and of French descent in New Orleans carried more weight than a West Indian identity and its ambiguity regarding race.

Another seaman, James Arch, responded similarly to issues of race and nationality. Born in 1903 in French Harbour, Bay Islands, Honduras, Arch listed his nationality as Honduran but his race as English. Because the Bay Islands were settled largely by immigrants from the Cayman Islands in the early nineteenth century, Arch likely had distant English ancestry. However, rather than identifying racially as someone from Spanish America, as did most Honduran citizens, or as West Indian, as did many Bay Islanders, Arch chose to identify with England. His "English" identity would have immediately placed him in good position with immigration authorities, as northern Europeans, particularly those from Great Britain, were a preferred immigrant group. Like Ebanks, Arch lived in an area that was diverse ethnically, with a high concentration of West Indian seamen. However, the witnesses at his citizenship hearing were John Bender, a white New Orleanian, and Glen A. Smith, a fellow white seaman originally from Oklahoma.

These are but a few examples of West Indians forgoing their West Indian identity in favor of an English identity when applying for US citizenship. As we saw in relation to the National Maritime Union, this racialization process mattered most in negotiating the strict racial realities of New Orleans but had little impact on how seamen saw themselves and their colleagues in a larger context.

CHAPTER FIVE

Capitalists, Student Activists, and Everyday Citizens

Negotiating a Latin American Identity in a
"Diverse" Jim Crow City

In the early 1930s, an article entitled "Impresiones de Nueva Orleans" (Impressions of New Orleans) appeared in *Lucero Latino,* a monthly Spanish-language magazine published in New Orleans. In an effort to promote the city as a destination for middle- and upper-class tourists, the author described New Orleans as a Latin American city within the southern United States and invited tourists to experience the United States in a culturally analogous space.[1] The French and Spanish colonial legacy of the city, its architecture, its rich Catholic history, and its extensive trade with Caribbean and Latin American ports were given as evidence of the historical and cultural links between Latin America and New Orleans. Though the magazine was published in New Orleans, its main offices were located in Tegucigalpa, Honduras, with advertising and marketing based in New York City. The United Fruit and Standard Fruit Companies were the primary advertisers, indicating the publisher's strong ties to the companies and their subsidiaries. Central to the promotion of the companies were the numerous Central American passenger lines, with vessels traveling throughout the Caribbean, stopping at New Orleans and other Gulf Coast ports. While the article highlighted tourist attractions, the main goal was to attract Latin American business to New Orleans.

At the turn of the twentieth century, commercial publications in the city strategized about how to increase trade with Latin America; they decided to target citizens in the region who had money to buy products.[2] This plan not only led to an increase in trade but also created opportunities for Latin Americans to visit New Orleans and experience all that the city had to offer. When Latin American businessmen traveled to New Orleans to negotiate deals, the fruit companies, in need of translators and legal experts to interact with consumers, hired educated Latin Americans to work in the industry in upper-level positions. As a result of these business ties, several Latin American nations opened consulates in New Orleans to address the needs of its citizens living and working in the city, as well as to represent the economic and political interests of their nations. Thus a new type of Latin American and Caribbean immigrant entered the city. Unlike the West Indian seamen and Spanish-speaking immigrants of African descent, these new immigrants were lighter, whiter, and better connected both economically and politically, both in their home countries and in New Orleans, which enhanced their profile in the city. These social advantages facilitated their transition to whiteness upon their arrival and concurrently inhibited the semblance of a larger, racially inclusive Latin American community in the city.

In a master's thesis written in the late 1940s that was based largely on US census data and oral interviews, Norman Wellington Painter noted that from 1910 to 1940 the population of foreign-born, white Latin Americans in New Orleans averaged roughly 1,632 people. Most Latin Americans came from Mexico, Cuba, and the Central American republics of Honduras and Nicaragua. The year 1920 marked a peak, with 2,460 Latin Americans registered in the city.[3] This number declined significantly in 1930 (1,718) and again in 1940 (1,643) as a result of the Great Depression and ensuing regional and global conflicts. While their numbers were small, the occupations of many of the immigrants represented the realization of previous efforts by commercial interests to attract Latin American elites. Painter asserts that most subjects in his study were from middle-class families rather than laboring backgrounds. Of the sixty-seven participants in Painter's study, 15 percent of the respondents' fathers were members of the professions, roughly 6 percent of their fathers were in the service of their governments, and no less than 40 percent of their fathers were entrepreneurs engaged in commerce.[4] The majority of the respondents had initially left their countries for better educational opportunities, and others had left to advance their economic prospects. Many had come to New Orleans because it could be reached directly by ship. Others had family in the city. A smaller number, particularly women, had married Americans (most likely fruit-company employees) in their home countries and immigrated to New Orleans to be with their spouses.[5]

Corroborating the accounts in the *Lucero Latino,* Painter noted that many shipping companies in the city had Spanish departments that sought bilingual employees. He also noted that only 21 percent of immigrants were fluent in English, 42 percent spoke some English, and 37 percent spoke no English at all. Despite the large percentage of the immigrant population who spoke no English at all, there was not a sizable Latin American community in the city.[6] With the exception of a small pocket of Hondurans living in close proximity to each other, Latin Americans chose to live among other (particularly white) New Orleanians.[7] According to Painter, most Latin Americans chose to identify as white (as opposed to "colored") and were widely dispersed throughout the city. It is this lack of distinct community and the embracing of a larger "white" identity that is unique given the history of established white ethnic communities in the city. For example, because New Orleans was one of the few southern cities that received sizable numbers of immigrants during the late nineteenth and early twentieth centuries, there were well-defined Italian, Irish, and Jewish areas within the city. Alan Gauthreaux maintains in his study on Italian immigrants in New Orleans that Italians were subjected to lynch law and mob violence during the late nineteenth and early twentieth centuries, to the point that "violence against the Italian population must be placed within the context of the ongoing debate regarding whiteness of immigrants and how their racial classification changed over time."[8]

According to Gauthreaux, discrimination experienced by Italians in Louisiana was in part owing to well-established "racial" distinctions in Italy between the northern and southern areas of the country, those from the latter being perceived as less modern and racially inferior.[9] In

Louisiana, this stigma was exacerbated by the inability of Italian immigrants to embrace the post-Reconstruction notions of white supremacy. Italians worked alongside African Americans in the sugarcane fields, on the Mississippi River docks, and in early labor organizing. There were also reported instances of Italians and African Americans socializing outside work by virtue of living in the same neighborhoods and sending their children to the same schools.[10] Italians either did not understand the racial norms of the United States or chose to ignore them. In any event, their failure to assimilate into "whiteness" meant that they were treated more like African Americans than like other immigrants.

Lawrence Powell writes that in contrast to the Italian immigrant experience, Jewish immigrants assimilated into the larger white society in New Orleans at much higher rates than in other areas of the United States during the same period. The South in general had a smaller percentage of Jews, mostly residing in the major urban centers, of which there were very few in the nineteenth century. However, within these spaces, Jews maintained their distinct religious and cultural identity. This was a trend witnessed throughout the South as a "byproduct of pressures felt by Southern whites of all stripes to toe the line on matters of race and religion."[11] New Orleans Jews, according to Powell, achieved social and economic success and were visible in the upper echelons of society. Because of this, many "frowned on anything that called attention to their Jewish identity."[12] Few chose to abandon their religion or give up being Jewish, but for most, their religion and culture were a private matter, while publicly they became white. Unlike in the Northeast, this white identity was not predicated on disassociation from African Americans. There is not a tradition of Jews performing "blackness" through the racial and ethnic stereotypes of minstrelsy to assimilate.[13] Nor is there a tradition of overt hostility to working with African Americans. Instead, Jews in New Orleans in many ways exemplified assimilation through Americanization, "divest[ing] themselves of almost every cultural trait they brought from the Old World and firmly embrac[ing] the culture of the New."[14] This was the environment Latin American immigrants entered and navigated.

Because the majority of Latin American immigrants to New Orleans came from areas of Central America and the Caribbean that had a large US military and economic presence, they were well aware of the rigid racial classification system in the United States and the political, economic, and social barriers to those who identified as African American. Segregation was entrenched in the fruit-company structure in Honduras, Costa Rica, and the Panama Canal Zone in particular. The legal system reinforced Jim Crow racism in New Orleans, and the visible distinctions between white and "colored" were constant reminders that nonblack immigrants wanting to advance both socially and economically should assimilate into white society.

Interviews conducted by Painter revealed that some Latin Americans in New Orleans embraced the racial and ethnic stereotypes pertaining to African Americans, while others deplored the harshness and indignity of Jim Crow racism. Still others, as a result of their own racial ambiguity, were caught between the black and white worlds, which provided them a unique perspective on race relations in the city. Latin American responses to the racial situation in New Orleans were also closely tied to their own racial and class backgrounds in their home countries. Because many of the participants in Painter's study were Latin American elites, their views on African Americans reflected the antiblack sentiment that existed in Latin America. Painter reported that one person who claimed to have no prejudice against blacks upon first arriving in the United States "came to embody the same prejudices" after living in the city.[15] Another noted that in Panama, "Negroes can sit anywhere on the bus, the [street] car, and in the movies." However, the Panamanian situation was seemingly problematic given that this person concluded that "the separation in New Orleans (between black and white) was a good idea."[16]

Some embraced Jim Crow gradually. One interviewee noted initially being "horrified by the Negroes" because he had never seen one. However, he added, "I thought their situation was horrible, but now that I know the Negroes, well I have taken the same attitude held by Southerners. It is not fair, but there are too many of them. I don't like to sit with them because they smell different."[17] The black people this individual interacted with might have been day laborers, dockworkers, or workers performing other manual labor that might cause a person to "smell" after a long workday. It is possible that the individual interviewed aspired to a higher socioeconomic status and sought to create distance between himself and African Americans. The person's comment that there were "so many of them" implies consistent interaction and proximity, something that most well-to-do Latin Americans in New Orleans, like their white American counterparts, would not have had with African Americans outside a hierarchical economic relationship.

Work and education were the primary vehicles by which Latin Americans transitioned into whiteness. The sociologist Mary Bracken noted the high numbers of merchant seamen, stevedores, clerks, agents, and other types of workers passing through the port of New Orleans throughout the early twentieth century.[18] She also suggested that many Latin Americans in foreign branches of US companies were transferred to New Orleans home offices. This was especially the case with workers in the UFCO and the Standard Fruit Company. While many of these Latin American immigrants were already middle-class, secondary schools, colleges, and universities that catered to them offered opportunities for further advancement.

The preponderance of Catholic institutions in New Orleans provided an opportunity for Latin American immigrants to sustain religious traditions from their home countries. The Catholic Church in New Orleans welcomed these new immigrants, who helped reinvigorate an institution suffering from decades of religious indifference on the part of many in the city who were "culturally Catholic" but rarely attended services or contributed to religious life. Michael Doorley argues that immigrants in nineteenth-century New Orleans generally failed to take control of the Church the way they did in northern cities, since the mostly French and Creole clergy dominated the religious culture in the city.[19] Church leaders in New Orleans viewed the arrival of earlier Catholic immigrants, such as the Irish, as a chance to strengthen the Catholic Church against the expansion of Protestantism in the state, which had been a problem for the Church since the Louisiana Purchase and the rapid Americanization of New Orleans and its vicinity. However, instead of reinvigorating the Church, the Irish were absorbed into the Creole culture of New Orleans and became indifferent to the religion. While there is scant evidence indicating a surge in Catholic devotion upon the influx of Latin Americans in the city, Catholic schools welcomed and actively recruited the new arrivals.

In Spanish-language publications in New Orleans during the period, advertisements for Catholic institutions were prominently displayed. For example, the monthly magazine *Simpatia* promoted Holy Angels Academy as a school that welcomed Latin Americans.[20] Primarily an art school, the institution stressed its music program and granted scholarships for exceptional students. The school clearly sought to attract new students from this community, as it placed full-page advertisements in Spanish-language publications. While primary and secondary schools attracted elite students from Latin America, it was the universities that appealed to Latin American students. Beatrice Rodriguez Owsley asserts that young men and women from wealthy families came to New Orleans to be educated at Dominican College, Tulane, and Loyola.[21]

Despite a notable disdain for African Americans by some Latin Americans detailed in Painter's study, there were others who were exposed firsthand to the negative impact of US racism through the same institutions of higher learning that actively recruited them. They witnessed the complexities of the US system and articulated its hypocrisy. One interviewee noted that "Americans think that every dark-skinned person is colored" and treated them as such. This same interviewee gave as an example a white professor at an unnamed medical school who had failed a student from Latin America because he suspected that the student was black. The interviewee noted that the student was "quite dark and had definite traces of Indian (heritage)."[22] Whether the student was of legitimate indigenous ancestry or of African descent and "passing" as indigenous is unclear. However, the fact that the injustice to the student was observed by others and attributed to the student's racial background is evidence that even in elite spaces the racial background of Latin Americans was questioned.

One of Painter's interviewees said that there was "open war between Latins and Americans" in one of the area boarding schools. He cited an incident in which one of his countrymen (a Honduran) suffered prejudice because he was "rather dark." At the same institution, an incident occurred in which an American Jew and a Honduran got into a fight. The Americans cheered for the Jewish student to win, shouting "Kill the Nigger!" in reference to the Honduran.[23] In addition to conveying the level of antiblack vitriol and violence present in all elements of New Orleans society, the incident revealed that though American Jews suffered intense anti-Semitism and other forms of discrimination in larger white spaces, their "whiteness" was affirmed when they were pitted against groups deemed inferior, such as African Americans and Latin Americans. The fact that the Honduran student was racialized as a "Nigger" despite attending a well-known elite school that specifically excluded African Americans also indicates that having the financial means and legal status as "white" to attend these institutions did little to curtail the suspicions on the part of some Americans that Latin Americans in New Orleans were in fact "Negroes" passing as white. Furthermore, those described as American in these incidents were always considered to be white; African Americans and Latin Americans were the "other."

While some Latin Americans openly embraced Jim Crow and others struggled to cash in on their "white" status, the racially ambiguous Latin Americans, who were neither white nor black within the US racial system in New Orleans, had difficulty transitioning. The inability of education and economic status to supersede race continued to perplex many of the Latin Americans in Painter's interviews. One interviewee remarked that in his native Colombia "the Negro children go to school together with the white and there's no trouble over it." He spoke of a bank manager and an English professor in Colombia who were black and said that "Negroes were also represented in government positions."[24] Though these examples are anecdotal, they do speak to the complexities of race in Latin America and how it differed from race in the United States, particularly in the South. Racial and economic inequality were not foreign concepts in Latin America. However, upward mobility was possible for Latin Americans of African or indigenous backgrounds who exhibited certain qualities, such as the proper education, social and cultural backgrounds, and connections. In New Orleans this was not possible.

Latin American students in New Orleans continued to embrace their national identity and culture despite negative encounters with

US racism and xenophobia. Students were active in organizations that spoke to their particular needs as foreign students in the United States. However, they also sought to foster Pan-American unity among Latin American students. The concept of Pan-Americanism was rooted in the anticolonial movements of the late eighteenth and nineteenth centuries that led to the establishment of independent republics throughout the Americas. It focused on promoting strong political, economic, and commercial relationships between American nation-states. With the rise of the United States in the late nineteenth and early twentieth centuries, particularly after the Spanish-American War of 1898 and its increasingly interventionist policies toward Latin America, many Latin Americans sought an alternative means to strengthen regional identities that did not include the United States. In an article entitled "There Will Be No Pan-Americanism While Yankee Imperialism Exists," the author articulated the hypocrisy of American leaders such as President Calvin Coolidge calling for unity among the nations, when he (Coolidge) represented US capitalists, whose "hearts lay on Wall Street and ideals are centered on extending their political and economic power throughout the globe" to the detriment of Latin Americans.[25] According to this view, the predatory nature of US capitalism undermined any notion of Pan-American unity.

Major Latin American intellectuals of the period such as José Martí, José Mariátegui, and José Enrique Rodó crafted a new form of Latin American nationalism in response to US expansion that spoke to the unique historical and cultural realities of Latin America. They promoted homogeneity and inculcated an independent national spirit to combat US encroachment on Latin Americans' sovereignty.[26] Despite studying and residing in the United States, many Latin American students in places like New Orleans remained invested in these ideals and rallied around political causes in their home countries, where they hoped to effect change. For instance, there was a project to start a Latin American student house (La casa del estudiante latinoamericano), whose mission was to work in collaboration with the twenty-one countries in Latin America to promote student exchange, scholarships, and involvement in cultivating the political and cultural development of their respective

nations.[27] Latin American fraternities such as "FI IOTA ALFA" served
this purpose by promoting cultural relationships, spiritual consciousness, and the economic and political union of Latin Americans.[28]

The initial attempts of Latin American students in New Orleans to
organize collectively might be viewed as demonstrations of naïveté on
the part of idealistic and privileged college students in search of community away from home. However, events surrounding the political situation in Honduras in 1919 revealed a more nuanced understanding of
politics and engagement with their home country. Following the efforts
of the then Honduran president Francisco Bertrand to forgo presidential elections and name his Salvadoran brother-in-law, Nazario Soriano,
as his successor, the Union Patriótica Hondureña (Honduran Patriotic
Union) was formed in the United States to protest the action. Events
leading up to President Bertrand's actions were reported in the New
Orleans press, as Bertrand and Soriano summarily dismissed government officials unwilling to accept the new regime.[29] The institution of
martial law prior to the elections and the disruption of the banana industry created concern on the part of the fruit companies and the US
political establishment. Darío Euraque argues that the greatest growth
in US investments in Honduras in the years 1897–1919 occurred from
1908 to 1919,[30] a significant portion occurring during the administration
of Francisco Bertrand, who was seen by many Hondurans as a puppet of
the United States.

While the US government was concerned about its investments and
those of the fruit companies, few institutions lobbied on behalf of Honduran citizens in the United States. In a small way, the Union Patriótica
did so. The organization was made up of fifty-four Honduran nationals,
all students at universities and colleges throughout the United States,
who "could not simply remain spectators" while the constitution of their
country was being violated.[31] Twenty-five of these students were in New
Orleans, all but one matriculating at Tulane University. The others were
students at universities in Georgia, Pennsylvania, Indiana, New York,
Maryland, and California. Their ability to form a student organization
across multiple states demonstrates their efforts to remain connected
and politically engaged with their country and its citizens. According

to the students, the organization was founded to "(1) Protest against the interference of Nazario Soriano, whose personality does not align with the national life of Honduras; (2) Vow to maintain the Political Constitution [of Honduras]; (3) Call upon the sanity and patriotism of our countrymen in order to fight tirelessly for the triumph of law; (4) Promote the idea of 'Country first, political parties second, and nepotism never.'"[32] The actual effects of the students' efforts are unclear. However, the strong degree of patriotism exhibited and the desire to change the situation in their country explain why many of these Latin American students did not settle in the United States. Their intent was always to return home.

Apart from their efforts to organize politically, many students at Tulane and Loyola engaged in more traditional aspects of student life. A survey of university yearbooks from throughout the 1920s and 1930s revealed a small but active Latin American student body. Mostly male, these students were active members of the Sigma Iota Latino fraternity. Founded at Louisiana State University in 1904, the fraternity expanded to Tulane and Loyola in 1924 and 1927, respectively. More important than their revelations about the composition of Sigma Iota, the yearbooks revealed much about the makeup of the Latino student body. For instance, of the thirty-six Latin American students listed in Loyola University yearbooks from 1926 to 1931, all but one were male. Central America, Cuba, and Mexico were overwhelmingly represented. Most of the students majored in dentistry, pharmacy, and law. The only woman listed majored in "Arts and Sciences."[33] Both Tulane and Loyola were segregated institutions, reserved for whites only. Loyola did not allow African Americans to attend as full-time students until 1962, and Tulane followed suit in 1963.[34] The Latin American students enrolled in the institution during the period of study would have been white or nonwhite passing as white.

Working-Class Women and the Americanization of Latin New Orleans

Not all Latin Americans in New Orleans were university students. While men were overrepresented at the universities, Latin American women emerged in almost every other aspect of life in the city. Like their West Indian counterparts, Latin American women worked as housewives, nurses, seamstresses, teachers, and stenographers, among numerous other professions. The following examples offer a glimpse into the experiences of these women.

Enriqueta Bonney, originally from Puerto Cortés, Honduras, arrived in New Orleans in 1932 with her young son, Pablo. Her husband (Pablo's father), Pablo Mercado, had died in Honduras in 1929; the cause of his death is not known. In 1935 Enriqueta married Henry Bonney, a UFCO employee originally from Iowa and based in New Orleans. Henry was a merchant seaman who traveled between New Orleans and Honduras and was living in Honduras when Enriqueta applied for US citizenship in 1936. Henry worked as a utility man on ships traveling between Puerto Cortés, Honduras, and New Orleans exclusively.[35] The job was stable but not prestigious. The couple eventually settled in New Orleans, and Enriqueta remained in the city until her death in 1985. On her citizenship application she identified herself as a housewife, and there is no indication that she ever sought employment outside the home. Her marriage to Henry did not last, and she eventually married another white American. Her son, Pablo, who later Anglicized his name to Paul, was raised in New Orleans. As an adult, he worked as a merchant seaman as his stepfather did. However, unlike other seamen, Paul worked mainly in the Northeast, ultimately settling in Massachusetts. There is very little information available about Enriqueta's and Paul's shifting identities. However, it is clear from the records that both identified as white and lived in white spaces from the time of their arrival in the United States. Enriqueta's marriages to white Americans and Pablo's assimilation into American society—through the act of changing his name and settling in an area without a large population of Central Americans at the time—are consistent with the larger narrative of Americanization. Whiteness provided a degree of access and stability not afforded to the majority of Latin American and Caribbean immigrants.

Another Central American, Elida Corcoran, arrived in New Orleans under different circumstances but navigated the city in similar ways. Corcoran was born in Tegucigalpa, Honduras, in 1907, and entered the

United States at New Orleans in 1923, when she was fifteen. It is unclear whether she arrived alone or with family members. However, she lived in the city for fifteen years prior to applying for citizenship in 1938, a year after marrying John Corcoran, a researcher and native of New Orleans. On her citizenship application she identified herself as a nurse, indicating that she had been educated and trained in the United States.

Despite her previous training and employment as a nurse, in 1940 Elida listed her occupation as housewife and resided with her husband in the Mid-City neighborhood. The residents of the area were predominantly white, native-born Americans from Louisiana and other southern states; Elida was the only foreign-born, Latin American resident.[36] Given that Elida married a white American, had no known family in the city, and settled in an overwhelmingly Anglo space, it would have been difficult for her to maintain a strong bond with other Latin Americans. Perhaps this was by choice; perhaps Elida sought to distance herself from her Central American origins. Another possibility is that because she arrived in New Orleans at a relatively young age, she was caught between cultures and not completely grounded in either.

The sociologist Jessica Vazquez notes in her study of Mexican American immigrants over multiple generations in the United States that marriage can be a significant factor in assimilation among immigrants, particularly intermarriage with non-Latinos.[37] For Vazquez, marriage can serve as a measure of social distance between groups and explains tendencies of either thinned attachment or cultural maintenance.[38] Enriqueta's and Elida's marriages to white American men in Jim Crow–era New Orleans had long-term implications for retaining cultural traditions. The likelihood of Spanish being spoken in the home decreases if neither parent is a native speaker. And the imparting of cultural traditions diminishes if they are not reinforced by the parents and the larger community. In Vazquez's study, some women who sought marriage partners outside the Latino community did so because they were critical of what they described as a patriarchal culture within traditional Latin American families. Marriage to a white American male in the South during the 1930s would not necessarily have alleviated such constraints, but it might have lessened the impact of racism. The ability to "choose white" and be embraced as such by the larger community became more important than the commitment to maintaining strong ethnic and cultural ties. This may explain why Elida, who was a working nurse prior to her marriage, afterwards became a housewife despite having no children. After her marriage, her life resembled that of other white, married women in her community.

Esmeralda Renasco, a Nicaraguan seamstress, entered New Orleans in 1932 and declared her intent to apply for US citizenship four years later. She arrived in New Orleans a widow with a two-year-old child. Though from her citizenship application it would appear that Renasco was in the United States alone, the 1940 census for New Orleans lists her as living in a house with her mother, brother, grandmother, two children, and a Mexican lodger. By this point, Renasco was an artist working on the Public Emergency Library Project, a local offshoot of the New Deal's Federal Art Project. Her brother worked as an auto mechanic, and Manuel Naboa, the lodger, worked in a paper factory. While the family lived in a white area of the city, their working-class status, large family structure, Latin American birth (Nicaragua), and willingness to associate with other Latin Americans, as evidenced by accepting a Mexican lodger who spoke little English, demonstrated a strong commitment to the larger Spanish-speaking community.[39] In addition, Renasco was the only member of her family who had applied for US citizenship, which was granted in 1939. The others retained their Nicaraguan status. In this case, cultural preservation proved important even though the family lived in a predominantly white space. This implies that assimilation was a choice for some Latin American immigrants.

Not all Latin American immigrants quickly assimilated into white society. The examples of Amanda Balladares and Anita Velasquez further demonstrate the efforts of some Latin Americans in New Orleans either by choice or circumstances to maintain cultural connections with others from the region. Balladares and Velasquez, both Nicaraguans, immigrated to the United States from Bluefields, Nicaragua, in 1910 and 1911, respectively. Bluefields is a city situated on the Atlantic coast of Nicaragua historically made up of Anglo-dominated British, African, Spanish-speaking mestizo, and Amerindian communities. According to the anthropologist Edmund Morgan, US firms dominated commercial trade as well as most services and industries in Bluefields and the larger Atlantic coastal region during the first half of the twentieth century.[40] Bluefields therefore resembled many other coastal areas in Central America. The city's economic, political, and cultural histories made women like Balladares and Velazquez especially equipped to navigate a city like New Orleans.

Balladares and Velazquez were fourteen and eight when they arrived in New Orleans. Though they arrived separately, they declared their intent to apply for US citizenship together in 1929; they completed their applications and were granted citizenship in 1932. On their applications, both women listed the same witnesses, who were Latinas employed as beauticians. According to the 1920 census, Amanda Balladares resided in New Orleans with her mother, three brothers, and three nieces, all of whom had been born in Nicaragua and spoke Spanish as their primary language in the home. The Balladares family rented a home in the downtown area along with another Nicaraguan family. Their neighbors were immigrants from Armenia, Germany, and Ireland, as well as migrants from throughout the South and the Midwest. Amanda's brothers worked as a carpenter, an auto mechanic, and a tailor, respectively, while she was not employed.[41] Twenty years later, at the time of the 1940 census, Amanda was still single but living with other Nicaraguans in a rented home and working as a beautician.[42]

Anita Velasquez most likely met Amanda Balladares when the former was a lodger in a home that Balladares occupied with her nephew. According to the 1930 census, Velasquez and four other boarders from Nicaragua lived with Balladares in a rented home in Mid-City. Velasquez was unemployed at the time, but later she too would become a beautician, working in the same shop as Balladares.[43] That these two women lived and worked together, maintained strong ties with other Nicaraguans despite the young ages at which they immigrated to the United States, and appear to have had limited interactions outside the Latin American community suggests that it was possible to settle in New Orleans and remain in touch with one's origins. Like those mentioned above, these women and their families and associates were legally "white" and navigated spaces similar to those navigated by other Latin Americans. Their working-class background would have limited access to the upper levels of white society as equals. Most Latin American women who moved up the social ladder did so through marriage to American men, education, or their professions.

Class, though largely absent from discussions of the West Indian community in New Orleans, was often an issue for Latin Americans. While most Latin Americans who arrived during this period were privileged, coming as professionals or college students, those like the Balladares and Velasquez families came as traditional immigrants in search of a better opportunity and planned to build a new life in New Orleans. They worked regular jobs, lived in transient communities where they usually rented lodgings, and negotiated every aspect of daily life. Nothing was certain for them. Nevertheless, their racial classification as white provided these immigrants with access to opportunities not afforded to their West Indian and Afro-Latin counterparts. Among these were educational resources and employment training through publicly funded evening schools.

Public Evening Schools and the Americanization of Latin Americans

Evening schools began in New Orleans in 1905 as a means to educate the general population and improve the overall production of the local workforce. The schools were seen by some politicians and other city leaders as a vehicle to enable "the man or boy who would have otherwise had little to look forward to except a position as a laborer . . . to become a skilled workman."[44] The schools offered basic courses for Americans such as reading, writing, spelling, and arithmetic. They also offered English-language instruction for foreigners. Male students who made good progress had access to bookkeeping and advanced mathematics. Women and girls also attended evening schools. They studied the same basic curriculum as the men with the exception that advanced female students took typing and stenography classes. While men had to demonstrate proof of employment in order to be eligible for the schools, women did not. In addition to helping the students acquire a basic education, the schools also aimed to facilitate the Americanization process and help immigrants transition into Anglo-American society. Lectures on American citizenship were an integral part of the curriculum for foreigners.[45]

Judging by their growth rate, the evening schools were relatively successful in New Orleans. In 1909 there were 3,038 registered students. By 1912 the number of schools had increased from two to nine. However, the city continued to have difficulty providing places for students and finding instructors as enrollment swelled to 4,333 students in 1913.[46] In some areas, the number of adults attending evening classes outnumbered students in the public-school system.[47] The core curriculum remained the same, but classes in dressmaking, cooking, and "domestic science" (home economics) were added for women and girls.[48]

In 1915, three of the nine schools were relocated to the downtown area. As the neighborhoods around the schools became more African American demographically with the arrival of migrants from other parts of Louisiana and the rural South, the schools were transferred to "safe" white spaces.[49] This action exposed an unspoken reality of the time. Blacks were not allowed access to educational opportunities in the evening schools. For foreigners from Central America and the Caribbean, classification as "not black" was essential for access to these free and life-changing resources.

The demographics of the foreign student population reflected the demographics of the larger immigrant population in the city. The schools drew attendance from two very different classes of students and were organized under two different plans. The uptown schools were patronized chiefly by Latin Americans, while students at the downtown branches were mainly Syrians, Italians, and eastern Europeans. The uptown schools were in closer proximity to Mid-City and Central City, neighborhoods with higher concentrations of Latin Americans. Of these, the majority were Central Americans, with Hondurans, Nicaraguans, Costa Ricans, and Guatemalans statistically overrepresented, followed by Mexicans, Cubans, and Puerto Ricans.[50]

One reason city officials gave for the rapid growth in the evening schools was the economic prospects associated with the completion of the Panama Canal. Because of New Orleans's geographic location and its role as a major port for trade with Latin America and the Caribbean, many believed that the opening of the canal would create a demand for bookkeepers, clerks, and stenographers, particularly those with a knowledge of Spanish. As a result, most Latin Americans attending evening schools were there to acquire those skills, and enrollments in Spanish-language courses increased among Americans and other non–Latin Americans.[51] This in part explains why the majority of Latin American and white Caribbean applicants for US citizenship during the period were employed in these professions.

As the evening schools expanded, so did the curriculum. Bookkeeping, chemistry, business arithmetic, typing, and printing remained important areas of study. However, enrollments were highest for commercial English.[52] Despite this expanded curriculum, by the early 1920s evening-school enrollments were on the decline, and the schools closed permanently in the spring of 1922. The decline in enrollments coincided with an overall decline in the number of European immigrants to the city as a result of changes to US immigration law and limited economic opportunity. While Latin American and Caribbean immigrants continued to trickle in, the economic promise of the Panama Canal did not materialize for New Orleans. As Burton Kaufman asserts, commerce in the United States continued to flow from east to west, with New York City being the economic center of the nation. While New Orleans had an established port, it did not have the industry, population, banking infrastructure, or rail lines necessary to establish itself as the nation's central port of trade.[53] Equally important, while the city was able to ship US goods to Latin America and the Caribbean, the lack of established shipping lines and solid business contracts in the region limited the number of imports. Even though major fruit companies such as the UFCO built major operations in New Orleans, their headquarters and primary base of operations remained in Boston and New York, respectively. The hope had been that the Panama Canal would boost New Orleans's economy, but the amount of international commerce flowing through the city remained the same as it had prior to the canal's completion.[54] Outside the fruit industry, which offered a limited number of skilled jobs, there was little prospect of gainful employment in the city for immigrants. Thus, the majority of Latin American and Caribbean immigrants continued to seek opportunities in the Northeast.

Immigrants who chose to remain in New Orleans lived largely unassuming lives. They worked, studied, married, and lived among New Orleanians of all different racial, ethnic, and social backgrounds and were subjected to the economic and political realities that impacted all of the city's residents. However, whether through concerted efforts to assimilate on the part of Latin American immigrants or because the American racial-classification system created second-class citizens of immigrants of African descent, Latin Americans had to choose whether to embrace all of who they were or to embrace the status quo and assume a white identity.

Epilogue

As we have seen, the ways in which individuals and families transitioned into US constructions of race were at times the result of conscious decisions. In other instances, race was determined by the realities of everyday life in the Jim Crow South, in which whiteness translated into access and opportunity, and nonwhites were relegated to a subordinate position. The West Indians and Central Americans impacted by this system learned to navigate it with precision, to the point that many all but disappeared from the historical record. Only by combing the archives does one discover that the doctor or businessman with the vaguely Anglo-sounding name was actually Honduran or Nicaraguan and had changed his name to one that sounded "more American" when he became naturalized.

In cursory conversations with African American staff in the many libraries, archives, and hotels in New Orleans over my years of research for this book, passing references to an influential neighbor, teacher, pastor, or barber in their community sometimes revealed that they were originally from Jamaica, Belize, or Panama. The fact that their national origins did not play a more prominent role in their identity is critical to understanding the ways in which the city embraces and incorporates newcomers. The experiences of subsequent generations of Central American immigration to New Orleans from the 1970s on are a logical point of departure for future studies. West Indians and Central Americans during the first half of the twentieth century entered a United States in which nationalism was at a high. The two world wars and the

ensuing Cold War helped to solidify a sense of American identity centered on conforming to a proscribed set of core values that left little
room for compromise. With the shift to multiculturalism during the
later decades of the twentieth century, there was an understanding, at
least in principle, that one could be equally Latino or West Indian and
American.

Biological notions of race have long been discredited by scientists.
However, culture, though not fixed, can be central to one's identity. The
fact that immigrants from Central America several generations removed
from the British Caribbean still referred to themselves as West Indian on
arrival in New Orleans speaks to this. Though Jamaicans, British Hondurans, or Barbadians in the homeland may not have recognized (or embraced) the claims of cultural continuity with their compatriots in exile,
the fact that the latter continued to claim a political and cultural affinity
to the Caribbean demonstrates the power of culture and memory among
migrant populations. When thousands of Central Americans fleeing political and economic strife in the region arrived in New Orleans in the
late 1970s and early 1980s, many of those who came to their aid were
the descendants of earlier waves of Central American immigrants. Suddenly, a group that many in the city never knew existed emerged in
tangible and sustained ways.

A week-long series of articles in the *New Orleans Times-Picayune* in
1983 titled "The Latin Link" drew attention to the emergence of this
"new, but old" New Orleans community. The articles chronicled the increase in the number of Latin Americans arriving in the city in search of
refuge from the political and economic struggles impacting the region
at the time. Just as in the previous generation, there was considerable
diversity among the new arrivals. Nicaraguans, particularly the professional classes, fled the Sandinista Revolution and its socialist agenda.
Guatemalans sought refuge from the rampant killings taking place as
warring political factions sought control of a fragile government. The
Salvadoran civil war displaced thousands of farmers and other civilians.
The perpetual state of economic decline in Honduras motivated many
of its citizens to seek opportunities abroad.[1] The author, Joan Treadway,
noted that proximity by air (direct flights to New Orleans from Central

American capitals) and sea (via merchant and passenger lines) encouraged Latin Americans to try New Orleans. Treadway also emphasized
that New Orleans had received roughly two thousand Cubans as part of
the 1980 Mariel Boatlift. The city's successful response to this population, Treadway argued, had helped prepare it for the influx of Central
Americans that was to follow.

In 1983, reportedly 48,415 new "Hispanics" were living in the city
of New Orleans, with larger numbers in the surrounding area. Of this
number, an estimated 40,000 were undocumented, the majority hailing
from Central American nations. The unsubstantiated claims regarding
the legal status of these migrants notwithstanding, the drastic increase
in the number of Spanish-speaking Latin Americans in the city strained
resources and pushed the city to improve its political and social infrastructure to assist the new arrivals. Religious organizations were at the
forefront in creating institutions to assist Latin American immigrants.
Ecumenical Immigration Services was a joint effort of agencies of the
Lutheran, Baptist, and Catholic churches. The group provided legal
counsel to those having problems regarding their immigration status.
The Latin American Apostolate of the Archdiocese of New Orleans provided clothing, food, housing, job assistance, and other necessities. Over
time, many of these Central Americans adjusted to life in the city, and
most made it their home. However, it is clear from "The Latin Link" that
there was never a unified, pan–Latin American community on the scale
of those in southern cities such as Miami or Houston.

Several people Treadway interviewed for her series of articles noted
that unlike in Miami, in particular, the immigration of Latin Americans
to New Orleans was slow and gradual. Whereas Miami ultimately lost
its southern cultural identity as large waves of Cubans and other Latin
American and Caribbean populations took up residence in the city, New
Orleans remained a southern city. There were no barrios or designated
sections of the city in which Latin Americans were the majority. New
Orleans, noted one individual interviewed by Treadway, was a city in
which people integrated into the broader society. In fact, some argued
that there was often conflict between the various Latin American groups
based on historically deep-rooted regional rivalries, heightened nation-

alism, class distinctions, and legal status in the United States. For many, the Spanish language and a shared colonial past were the only ties that bound the groups.[2] If Treadway's articles are accurate, then Norman Wellington Painter's conclusions in his 1949 thesis were correct in that Latin Americans in New Orleans became a part of the city to the point that their identities were indistinguishable from those of others in the city. While such arguments reinforce the assimilationist narratives of US immigration myth, there is one caveat: New Orleans itself.

The ethnomusicologist Matt Sakakeeny asserts in an article on New Orleans music that while music "includes an amorphous collection of interrelated styles . . . they are bound together through an association with race, place, and functionality to such a degree that even a disaster of immeasurable consequences [in this case Hurricane Katrina] which disproportionately affected that race and dislocated them from that place, has not threatened its cohesiveness."[3] New Orleans's unique historical past, its connections to the larger Caribbean and Latin American world, combined with the central role that race played in shaping its political, economic, and cultural traditions, allowed for the development of a distinct, cohesive culture that recognized the importance of a group identity but allowed for individuality. Though Sakakeeny was assessing the musical traditions of New Orleans, I argue that this approach applies to people as well. West Indians and Central Americans in New Orleans were able to be black or white *and* Latino long before these categories appeared in US census data. They did this within the context of a society in which the racial and class lines were clearly delineated. As scholars embark on studies of West Indian and Latin American immigrants to the United States in locations outside the Northeast, Florida, and the Southwest with large population figures, the challenge of how to convey the history of the group without compromising the complexities of individuals and the choices they make in navigating foreign (and at times hostile) spaces remains. It is my hope that New Orleans offers one example of how this can be done.

Notes

Introduction

1. McKay, *Banjo*, 5.
2. Fussell, *Great War and Modern Memory*, 38–39.
3. Chaney, "Traveling Harlem's Europe," 68.
4. Abernethy, "Beauty of Other Horizons," 448.
5. Fiehrer, "From La Tortue to La Louisiane," 1.
6. Hall, *Africans in Colonial Louisiana*, 5–6.
7. Hall, 9.
8. Dessens, *From Saint Domingue to New Orleans*, 23.
9. Dessens, 24.
10. See Hall, *Africans in Colonial Louisiana*, 8, 14. The author notes that from 1717 to 1721 some seven thousand French colonists were sent to Louisiana. Roughly 2,000 of these died on the voyage from France or deserted. In 1726 the first official census revealed that there were 1,952 French citizens in the entire colony of Louisiana. By 1740 the white population had been reduced to 1,200, which included troops and settlers. Hall also indicates that when the population had rebounded somewhat by 1746, during King George's war between France and England, there were 3,200 whites and 4,730 blacks, the majority of whom were enslaved Africans. While the white population was consistently on the decline, the black population was increasing.
11. Powell, *Accidental City*, 104.
12. Dessens, *Creole City*, 143.
13. Lachance, "1809 Immigration of Saint-Domingue Refugees to New Orleans," 246.
14. Ferrer, *Freedom's Mirror*, 236, 253.
15. See Johnson, *Slavery's Metropolis*, 37. Johnson maintains that Saint Domingue migrants who were white or of African descent with documentation of freedom colluded with the US government and the state of Louisiana to classify roughly one-third of the Saint Domingue immigrants who were black as slaves despite the abolition of the foreign slave trade and the fact that these blacks had been free prior to their arrival in Louisiana.
16. Berry, *We Are Who We Say We Are*, 18–19.
17. Scott, *Degrees of Freedom*, 172.
18. Powell, "Why Louisiana Mattered," 394.
19. Dominguez, *White by Definition*, 102.
20. Barthelemy, "Light, Bright, Damn *Near* White," 257.
21. Dessens, *Creole City*, 24–25.

22. For an analysis of Creole-of-color identity in rural Louisiana, see Brasseaux, Fontenot, and Oubre, *Creoles of Color in the Bayou Country*; and Brasseaux, "Creoles of Color in Louisiana's Bayou Country, 1766–1877.Ð

23. Weise, *Corazón de Dixie*, 14.

24. Weise, 3.

25. Martel, "Storms Payback From God, Nagin Says," *Washington Post*, 17 January 2006.

26. Chaney, "Malleable Identities," 128.

27. See US Department of Commerce, *Fifteenth Census of the United States: 1930*, 70, 250; and US Department of Commerce, *Fourteenth Census of the United States: 1920*, 729.

28. Johnson, *Slavery's Metropolis*, 19. See also Scott, *Degrees of Freedom*, 172, and Cooper, Holt, and Scott, *Beyond Slavery*, 61–106; both works focus on families and other prominent individuals who shaped municipal societies in both Cuba and Louisiana. Through an examination of individuals, it was possible for Scott to make national and international connections to larger movements throughout the Atlantic world.

29. Greenbaum, *More Than Black*, 1–2.

30. Greenbaum, 12.

31. Arthur, *African Diaspora Identities*, 10.

32. Johnson, *Slavery's Metropolis*, 23.

33. Johnson, 21.

34. Lipsitz, "New Orleans in the World," 261.

35. Lipsitz, 263.

36. Bedasse, *Jah Kingdom*, 3.

37. Patterson and Kelley, "Unfinished Migrations," 24.

38. Palmer, "Defining and Studying the Modern African Diaspora," 28.

39. Hall, "Who Needs Identity?," 2.

40. There is a growing historiography related to the role of Caribbean immigrants and migrants in internationalist circles, particularly in Harlem, during the period of study. See Turner, *Caribbean Crusaders and the Harlem Renaissance*; Makalani, *In the Cause of Freedom*; and James, *Holding Aloft the Banner of Ethiopia*.

41. Patterson and Kelley, "Unfinished Migrations," 27.

42. Howard, *Black Labor, White Sugar*, 6–7.

43. I place *West Indian* in quotation marks here to indicate that while this population was historically and culturally connected to the British West Indies, politically their identity was more complex because according to British law, unless they had been born in Great Britain or one its colonial possessions, children of British citizens abroad had to formally petition for British citizenship. It was not a birthright, as many West Indians in Central America thought. In many cases, the British government ruled that the citizenship of their birth nation superseded any claim to British citizenship as long as they lived outside British territory. Therefore, to be British and West Indian only had meaning to British authorities when the person resided in a British territory. See British Chargé

d'Affaires Armstrong to British Legation in Guatemala, 27 November 1911, FO 632/ 20, no. 2607, British National Archives.

44. Meléndez Obando, "Slow Ascent of the Marginalized," 335.

45. See Gudmundson and Wolfe, *Blacks and Blackness in Central America*, 9. This collection is the first of its kind to explore several facets of the black experience in all of Central America. Some additional works on the subject include Herrera, *Natives, Europeans, and Africans in Sixteenth Century Santiago de Guatemala*; Lohse, "Africans in a Colony of Creoles"; and Lokken, "Marriage as Slave Emancipation in Seventeenth Century Guatemala."

46. Liberals throughout postindependence Latin America closely associated the social and economic success of a nation with its ethnic and racial composition. For a further analysis of the impact of liberal policies on Honduran racial attitudes, see Chambers, *Race, Nation and West Indian Immigration to Honduras*, 31–36.

47. The scholarship on West Indians in Central America gained significant attention in the 1980s with works centered on Panama and Costa Rica, countries having the largest population of West Indians as a result of the Panama Canal projects and the agricultural industries. On Panama, see Conniff, *Black Labor on a White Canal*. This study remains a seminal work, though Szok's *"La última gaviota"*; Richardson's *Panama Money in Barbados*; and Newton's *Silver Men* have expanded the debate. In Costa Rica, Bourgois, *Ethnicity at Work*; Chomsky, *West Indian Workers and the United Fruit Company in Costa Rica*; Harpelle, *West Indians of Costa Rica*; and Putnam, *Company They Kept*, focus on varying aspects of the political, economic, and cultural implications of the growing West Indian presence on the Caribbean coast. These works built on the foundation of works by Costa Rican scholars such as Duncan and Melendez Chaverri, *Negro en Costa Rica*; and later Martínez Montiel, *Presencia africana en Centroamérica*.

48. See Putnam, "Eventually Alien," 278–79.

49. The scholarship on West Indian immigration is vast and based largely on the political relationship between West Indian labor and US corporate interests. Because British West Indians arrived in Central America to work on North American construction projects and in the banana industry, their history in the region has often been tied to the expansion of US hegemony in the social, political, and economic spheres of Central American society. In Honduras, fruit companies such as the Standard Fruit and Steamship Company, the United Fruit Company and its subsidiaries, and the Cuyamel Fruit Company, among others, have been blamed for the destruction of the Central American political oligarchy and for the increased presence of foreign workers and their negative impact on national-identity construction. Local animosity toward this foreign influence materialized in numerous ways, most notably in the anti–West Indian sentiment prevalent throughout the twentieth century. For a complete review of the recent scholarship on West Indian immigration, see Chambers, *Race, Nation, and West Indian Immigration to Honduras*, 1–17.

50. See Euraque, *Conversaciones históricas con el mestizaje*; and Payne Iglesias, "Identidad y nación."

51. The history of the Bay Islands and their population of mostly British West Indian descent distinguishes the West Indian experience in Honduras from that in other Central American nations. Cayman Islanders and Jamaicans settled in large numbers beginning in the 1830s, and the territory was a British crown colony from 1851 until it was returned to Honduras in 1859. The islands were not fully integrated into the Honduran nation until 1913. Though many of the English-speaking inhabitants trace their ancestry back to these early settlers, most claimed British ancestry well into the 1930s even though they were legally Honduran citizens. In addition, the growth of the banana industry in the early twentieth century and the cultural reinvigoration brought on by the influx of new immigrants from the British West Indies contributed to the distinctiveness of the islands. For a further analysis, see Davidson, *Historical Geography of the Bay Islands;* and Chambers, *Race, Nation, and West Indian Immigration to Honduras,* 77–83.

52. Vinson, "Introduction."

53. See Murdoch, *Creolizing the Metropole,* 15–20.

54. Putnam, "Eventually Alien," 290.

CHAPTER ONE

New Orleans and Latin America: Disparate Destinies and Shared Imaginaries in the Late Nineteenth and Early Twentieth Centuries

1. See Chambers, *Race, Nation, and West Indian Immigration to Honduras.*

2. See Watkins-Owens, *Blood Relations;* Showers-Johnson, *Other Black Bostonians;* and Putnam, *Radical Moves.*

3. See James, *Holding Aloft the Banner of Ethiopia;* and Makalani, *In the Cause of Freedom.*

4. Reid, *Negro Immigrant,* 85.

5. Reid, 86–88.

6. Manning, "British West Indians in the United States," 27.

7. Manning, 27.

8. "The Golden Lure of Ambition Draws Many from the Islands," *Daily Picayune,* 2 August 1903, 19.

9. Bayor, *Encountering Ellis Island,* 27.

10. Bayor, 28.

11. De la Fuente, *Havana and the Atlantic in the Sixteenth Century,* 11.

12. See May, *Southern Dream of a Caribbean Empire;* Simmons, *Confederate Settlements in British Honduras;* and RosenGarten, *William Walker y el ocaso del filibusterismo.*

13. Silva Gruesz, "Gulf of Mexico System and the 'Latinness' of New Orleans."

14. Silva Gruesz, *Ambassadors of Culture,* 109.

15. Guterl, "I Went to the West Indies," 446.

16. Guterl, 448.

17. The history of slavery in the Latin American and Caribbean region is well doc-

umented. For works that focus on African slavery in the mining areas of early colonial Latin America, see Bennett, *Africans in Colonial Mexico;* Palmer, *Slaves of the White God;* and Rout, *African Experience in Spanish America.* R. Douglas Cope breaks down the formation of racial castes in *Limits of Racial Domination.*

18. RosenGarten, *William Walker y el ocaso del filibusterismo,* 35.

19. One of the most widely known and most well documented scholarly assessments of southerners' preoccupation with Central America and the Caribbean is May's *Southern Dream of a Caribbean Empire.* For more on the exploits of US filibusters such as William Walker or the exploits of later individuals such as General Lee Christmas, see Yuscarán, *Gringos in Honduras.*

20. F. E. Frye, US Consul, to Secretary of State William Hunter (9/30/1875), Despatches from Roatan, Omoa, and Truxillo, 1870–1880.

21. The 1866 immigration law, introduced under the government of President José María Medina on 26 February, offered lands and tax exemptions to foreigners who relocated to Honduras. Most of the immigrants came from the United States, England, Germany, France, and Italy. Later immigration laws of 1895 and 1906 were designed to attract principally white immigrants from Europe and the United States. See Amaya Banegas, *Los judíos en Honduras,* 33–37. A 1912 legislative decree indicates that the lenient immigration policies of the Honduran government extended far beyond the three immigration laws. The 1912 decree maintains that foreigners would be tax exempt for a period of ten years and could freely import any tools necessary for the establishment of their settlement, colonization, or industrial enterprises. See "Decreto Núm. 99," *La Gaceta,* 10 July 1912, 639.

22. Gonzalez, *Dollar, Dove, and Eagle,* 69.

23. "People Met in Hotel Lobbies," *Washington Post,* 11 October 1902, 6.

24. For the decree pertaining to the abolition of slavery in Central America, see Leiva Vivas, *Tráfico de esclavos negros a Honduras,* 155–57.

25. "The Land of the Banana: Glimpses at Village Life in Honduras," *New York Times,* 30 November 1884, 14.

26. "Land of the Banana."

27. Acker, *Making of a Banana Republic,* 19.

28. Hair, *Bourbonism and Agrarian Protest,* 141.

29. Palmer, *Central America and Its Problems,* 142.

30. For an analysis of the trials of former Confederate settlers in British Honduras, see Simmons, *Confederate Settlements in British Honduras.* Although Simmons fails to adequately address the racial attitudes of the Confederates and how they played out in relations with nonwhite British Hondurans, he does discuss the fact that Confederate settlers tried to re-create the South as much as possible by settling in isolated communities away from the black and mestizo populations.

31. Brasseaux, *Creoles of Color in the Bayou Country,* 81.

32. Brasseaux, 81.

33. An article from the *Sugar Planters' Journal*, published in New Orleans, details the success of Frank Hidalgo and Louis M. Barlow, both of Assumption Parish, Louisiana. Barlow, a former sugar engineer, revamped the local sugar mill, built a twelve-mile railroad, and erected two bridges in order to produce more sugar than had ever been produced in the town of San Luis Potosi. See "Louisianans in Mexico," 40.

34. "Valentine Contratas de 1892 y Solicitud de 1893," *El Observador*, 16 August 1911, 8.

35. MacClintock, "Refunding the Foreign Debt of Honduras," 216.

36. "Bases de propuesta del ferrocarril interoceánico por Washington S. Valentine y Henry L. Springer," *La Gaceta*, 12 March 1897, 102.

37. Legajo: Notas Varias, 1881–1912. I thank Darío Euraque for providing me with the notes and proper citations to these documents gathered by John Soluri.

38. Legajo: Ministerio de Relaciones Exteriores, Notas Varias, 1917. Request for colonization by J. R. Miller.

39. Penney, "Notes and Comments on Travels Through Mexico and Central America," 65.

40. Penney, 65.

41. Penney, 89–90.

42. Bodden, *Cayman Islands in Transition*, 17–18.

43. Bolland, *Colonialism and Resistance in Belize*, 202.

44. Bolland, 145.

45. "Some Plain Truths," *Cleveland (OH) Gazette*, 19 February 1898, 2. See also "Race Hatred in Honduras: Blacks Seek to Drive Out Whites," *Parsons (KS) Weekly Blade,* 19 March 1898, 3.

46. Under the advanced truck system, workers received a wage advance prior to each season of forestry employment and then purchased the remainder of what they needed on credit from company stores. Prices at these company stores were deliberately exorbitant, to the point that most workers could never repay their debt, which grew exponentially from season to season. For more on the system, see Moberg, *Myths of Ethnicity and Nation*, 4–5.

47. Dunk, *British Honduras Report of the Census of 1921*; Bowen, *Census of British Honduras, 1931*.

48. Bowen, *Census of British Honduras, 1931*.

49. Bodden, *Cayman Islands in Transition*, 17–18.

CHAPTER TWO

Criminalizing Blackness: Liberals, Modernization, and the West Indian "Problem" in Honduras

1. O'Reggio, *Between Alienation and Citizenship*, 143–45.

2. Pine, *Working Hard, Drinking Hard*, 4.

3. Graham, *Idea of Race in Latin America*, 2.

4. Aguirre and Buffington, *Reconstructing Criminality in Latin America*, xvi.

5. American Vice Consul William Beaulac to Secretary of State, 23 August 1923, enclosing "The Negro Problem," which had appeared in *El Precursor,* 18 August 1923, Records of the US Department of State Relating to the Internal Affairs of Honduras, 1910–1929.

6. Streeter, Weaver, and Coleman, *Empires and Autonomy,* 12–13.

7. "Officials Support a Movement to Eject Colored Laborers from Honduras," 10 July 1916, Records of the US Department of State Relating to the Internal Affairs of Honduras, 1910–1929.

8. "Officials Support a Movement to Eject Colored Laborers from Honduras."

9. "Officials Support a Movement to Eject Colored Laborers from Honduras."

10. "Officials Support a Movement to Eject Colored Laborers from Honduras."

11. Alanen, *Morgan Park,* 8.

12. Alanen, 1.

13. Alanen, 8.

14. Warren, *Bethlehem Steel,* 81–82.

15. Warren, 82–83.

16. Harpelle, "White Zones," 319–20.

17. Building on the precedents of the 1929 immigration law, which required blacks to deposit upwards of five thousand US dollars into a Honduran bank before being allowed to immigrate, which in effect curtailed immigration, chapter 3, article 14, of the 1934 immigration law strictly forbade the entrance of blacks, East Indians, gypsies, and Chinese into Honduran territory under any circumstances. Article 4 of the law even forbade these groups from entering the country as tourists. The government also began to intensify the registration of immigrants with the proper authorities, a practice that was enforced inconsistently for much of the period. See "Ley de Inmigración de 1934," in Republic of Honduras, *Recopilación de leyes migratorias;* and Selected Documents Pertaining to Entrance Visas, 1934–1947.

18. Appelbaum, *Race and Nation in Modern Latin America,* 4.

19. Appelbaum, 4.

20. Peloso and Tenenbaum, *Liberals, Politics, and Power,* 1.

21. Aguirre and Buffington, *Reconstructing Criminality in Latin America,* xvi.

22. Payne Iglesias, "Identidad y nación," 86.

23. Sir Harold Baxter Kittermaster to Colonial Office, London 14 April 1932, CO 318/406/1, British National Archives.

24. Luis Rivera, Gobernación in Trujillo, to Ministro de Gobernación, Tegucigalpa, 1 July 1895, Honduras Telegrafos Nacionales, Latin American Library, Tulane University.

25. Luis Rivera, Gobernación in Trujillo, to Ministro de Gobernación, Tegucigalpa, 19 June 1895, Honduras Telegrafos Nacionales, Latin American Library, Tulane University.

26. Carbajal, Trujillo, to Ministro de Gobernación, Tegucigalpa, 28 August 1895, Honduras Telegrafos Nacionales, Latin American Library, Tulane University.

27. Republica de Honduras, *Recopilación de leyes migratorias,* 33–35.

28. González, Gobernación de Atlántida, to Gobernación Política en Tegucigalpa, 10 August 1928, Legajo: Telegramas de Departamento de Atlántida de 1928; Francisco Mejía, Secretario de Estado, "Informe del Gobernador Político del Departamento de Atlántida, La Ceiba, October 28, 1916," in Republic of Honduras, *Memoria de gobernación y justicia, 1915–1916,* 137.

29. Euraque, "Banana Enclave, Nationalism, and Mestizaje in Honduras," 152.

30. Lambert, "Myth, Manipulation, and Violence," 29.

31. Lambert, 26.

32. Euraque, "Banana Enclave, Nationalism, and Mestizaje in Honduras," 161.

33. Froylán Turcios, "Inmigrantes Innecesarios II," *El Nuevo Tiempo,* 15 July 1916, 6490.

34. Froylán Turcios, "Inmigrantes Innecesarios III," *El Nuevo Tiempo,* 18 July 1916, 6498.

35. Francisco Mejía, Legajo: Informe de Gobernador Política del Departamento de Cortés, 27 October 1916, Archivo Nacional de Honduras. Ironically, the political debates on West Indian immigration failed to acknowledge that the region was also home to the Garifuna. an Afro-Carib people who have resided in Honduras since their deportation from Saint Vincent by the British in 1797, after their defeat in a series of Carib Wars to evade the colonization of the island by Great Britain. Traditionally, the Garifuna have dominated popular and scholarly discussions of blackness in Honduras.

36. The exact number of West Indians in Honduras from 1910 to 1940 is difficult to determine, as some entered the country legally and registered with government agencies, while others entered illegally or through the channels of fruit companies, most of which reported few statistics to the Honduran government. Elisavinda Echeverri-Gent, using British government documentation, maintains that there were upwards of ten thousand West Indians on the North Coast during the period of study. See Echeverri-Gent, "Forgotten Workers," 283. Available Honduran census data for 1926 and 1930 give the number of West Indians in all North Coast departments as 3,673 and 4,215 persons, respectively. However, these numbers are based only on official data collected by Honduras. See "General Census of the Population of Honduras, 1926," Records of the US Department of State Relating to the Internal Affairs of Honduras, 1910–1929; and Republic of Honduras, *Resumen del censo general de población levantado el 29 de junio de 1930.*

37. Mendoza, "La desmitologización del mestizaje en Honduras," 259.

38. H. Grant Watson, British consular agent (Guatemala), to Colonial Office, London, 8 April 1932, FO 371 A2561/2561/A, British National Archives.

39. Sir Harold Baxter Kittermaster to British Colonial Office, London, 14 April 1932, CO 318/406/1, British National Archives.

40. H. Grant Watson to Sir John Simon, Foreign Office, Report on Situation in Honduras and Guatemala, 8 April 1932, CO 318/406/1, British National Archives.

41. H. Grant Watson to Sir John Simon.

42. Mr. Wilton, British Consul at Tegucigalpa, Honduras, to British Foreign Office, London, 20 April 1931, FO 371 A2610/2354/8, British National Archives.

43. For an in-depth discussion on the intellectual response to West Indian immigra-

tion in Honduras and its implications for fomenting a national response, see Chambers, *Race, Nation, and West Indian Immigration to Honduras*, chap. 3, which outlines the debate on West Indian immigration as it played out in the Honduran press, in the national government, and in the response of the fruit companies to changing perceptions of the West Indian community as an impediment to the Honduran nation-building process.

44. "Ley de Policía," *La Gaceta*, 10 February 1906, 73.

45. "Ley de Policía."

46. British Vice Consul Jack Armstrong to Foreign Office, 24 October 1911, Correspondence: Sent Out Letters to H.M. Legation, Guatemala, Consuls and Foreign Office Honduras Government Departments, July–December 1911, no. 2210, British National Archives.

47. British Vice Consul Jack Armstrong to Registrar General, Somerset House, London, 8 January 1912, Correspondence: Sent Out Letters to H.M. Legation, Guatemala, Consuls and Foreign Office Honduras Government, January–May 1912, no. 2307,British National Archives.

48. Mr. Wilton, Tegucigalpa, to British Foreign Office, 27 August 1931, enclosing "Situation in Honduras," FO 371 A 2707/2354/8, British National Archives.

49. "Ley sobre Misiones Consulares Extranjeras," *La Gaceta*, 27 March 1906, 2679.

50. For more on the La Masica incident and its impact on diplomatic relations between Honduras and Great Britain, see Chambers, *Race, Nation, and West Indian Immigration to Honduras*, 103–7.

51. British Vice Consul Jack Armstrong to Mariano Vazquez, Honduran minister of foreign affairs, 20 May 1912, Correspondence: Sent Out Letters to H.M. Legation, Guatemala, Consuls and Foreign Office Honduras Government, January–May 1912, no. 2500, British National Archives.

52. Armstrong to Vazquez, 20 May 1912, Correspondence: Sent Out Letters to H.M. Legation, Guatemala, Consuls and Foreign Office Honduras Government, January–May 1912, no. 2501, British National Archives.

53. Armstrong to Vazquez, no. 2501.

54. Armstrong to Vazquez, no. 2501..

55. Argueta, *Tres caudillos, tres destinos*, 62–63.

56. Willard L. Beaulac, American Vice Consul at Puerto Castilla, to US Department of State, 21 July 1924, US Department of State Records Relating to the Internal Affairs of Honduras, 1910–1929.

57. Beaulac to US Department of State, 21 July 1924.

58. Beaulac to US Department of State, 21 July 1924.

59. Beaulac to US Department of State, 21 July 1924.

60. Beaulac to US Department of State, 21 July 1924.

61. Dosal, *Doing Business with the Dictators*, 119.

62. Opie, *Black Labor Migration in Caribbean Guatemala*, 85–86.

63. Beaulac to US Department of State, 21 July 1924.

64. Villars, *Lealtad y rebeldía*, 54.

65. Willard L. Beaulac, American Vice Consul at Puerto Castilla, to US Department of State, 19 July 1924, US Department of State Records Relating to the Internal Affairs of Honduras, 1910–1929.

66. Beaulac to US Department of State, 19 July 1924.

67. Beaulac to US Department of State, 19 July 1924.

68. Beaulac to US Department of State, 19 July 1924.

69. Beaulac to US Department of State, 19 July 1924.

70. Foreign Office to Sir Esme Howard, British Ambassador to the United States, 21 July 1924, British National Archives.

71. Foreign Office to Sir Esme Howard.

72. Mr. Birch to Foreign Office, 3 February 1938, enclosing "Honduras: Labour," from *Annual Report: Central American Republics*, 1937, FO 371 A1500/1500/8, British National Archives.

73. Legajo: Informe de Estadísticas de Policía, 1933–1943.

74. Mr. Birch to Mr. Eden, Foreign Office, 3 February 1938, London, Annual Report: Central American Republics, 1937, FO 371 A1500/1500/8, British National Archives.

75. Chambers, *Race, Nation, and West Indian Immigration to Honduras*, 74–96.

76. The historiography on trade unionism and its role in the political process that led to decolonization in the British Caribbean in the second half of the twentieth century is exhaustive. For a comprehensive but concise analysis of the period, see Bolland, *Politics of Labour in the British Caribbean;* chapters 5 and 6 focus on the institutionalization of labor politics during the Second World War and the eventual establishment of self-rule within these Caribbean colonies.

77. British Chargés d'Affaires Armstrong to British Legation in Guatemala, 27 November 1911, FO 632/20, no. 2607, British National Archives.

78. "Treatment of British Subjects in the Bay Islands of Honduras," 20 February 1939, FO 371 A2411/2411/8, British National Archives.

79. "Treatment of British Subjects in the Bay Islands of Honduras."

CHAPTER THREE

West Indians and the Call to Citizenship in Early-Twentieth-Century New Orleans

1. *List of Races of People*, 1936, US Immigration and Naturalization Administration, National Archives and Records Administration, Washington, DC.

2. Kelley, *Right to Ride*, 15.

3. Reed, "Lumberjacks and Longshoremen," 54–55.

4. Vanderveer, "On the Fruit Wharf of New Orleans," *New Orleans Times-Picayune*, 11 July 1920, 17.

5. Arnesen, *Waterfront Workers of New Orleans*, 6.

6. Arnesen, 6.

7. Studies on African American migration to the Midwest and the West such as Grossman, *Land of Hope*, and Moore, *To Place Our Deeds*, emphasize the important role of migrants from Louisiana in the establishment of black communities in these regions. Grossman in particular notes the importance for migrants of New Orleans and its railroad line to Chicago by way of Memphis.

8. Opie, *Black Labor Migration in Caribbean Guatemala*, 19, 21–25.

9. Bolster, *Black Jacks*, 2–4.

10. Bolster, 5–6.

11. Fink, *Sweatshops at Sea*, 51–52.

12. "Colored Sailors," *Weekly Louisianan*, 16 April 1881, 1.

13. "Mexico; New Orleans; Caribbean," *People's Advocate*, 10 December 1881, 1.

14. Wilfred Levy, naturalization application, Records of the District Courts of the United States, 1685–2004.

15. List or Manifest of Aliens Employed on the Vessel as Crew Members, New Orleans, 1910–1945, *Coppename*, arriving at New Orleans 17 July 1929, sheet no. 21; New Orleans Passenger Lists, 1813–1945; Crew Lists of Vessels Arriving at New Orleans, Louisiana, 1910–1945.

16. Burnis Davis, naturalization application, Records of the District Courts of the United States, 1685–2004.

17. List or Manifest of Aliens Employed on the Vessel as Crew Members, New Orleans, 1910–1945, SS *Omoa* (Honduran), arriving at New Orleans 23 April 1923 from Puerto Cortés (Honduras), sheet no. 1; New Orleans Passenger Lists, 1813–1945; Crew Lists of Vessels Arriving at New Orleans, Louisiana, 1910–1945.

18. Records of the Selective Service System, 1926–1975, Louisiana, Record Group 147; World War II Draft Cards (4th Registration) for the State of Louisiana, National Archives and Records Administration, Washington, DC.

19. Amy Agnes Nash, naturalization application, Records of the District Courts of the United States, 1685–2004.

20. Horne, *Red Seas*, 7.

21. Horne, 17.

22. Horne, 14.

23. Horne, 14.

24. P. D. Parks, Assistant Vice-President of the United Fruit Company, to Vicente Williams, Consul General of Honduras, 1 August 1934, Legajo: Consulado General de Honduras en Nueva Orleans, January–December 1934.

25. Solicitud de Pasaporte, Visa de Pasaporte, Dorothy May Davis, 7 August 1934, Legajo: Consulado General de Honduras en Nueva Orleans, January–December 1934.

26. SS *Atenas*, sailing from Puerto Castilla, Honduras, 13 August 1936, Crew Lists of Vessels Arriving at Boston, Massachusetts, 1917–1943.

27. José Tomas Idiáguez, naturalization application, Records of the District Courts of the United States, 1685–2004.

28. Francisco Herrera, naturalization application, Records of the District Courts of the United States, 1685–2004.

29. SS *Ceiba* (Honduran), arriving at New Orleans 9 November 1918, Crew Lists of Vessels Arriving at New Orleans, Louisiana, 1910–1945.

30. SS *Nicarao* (Honduran), arriving at New Orleans 5 September 1925, Crew Lists of Vessels Arriving at New Orleans, Louisiana, 1910–1945.

31. MS *Elizabeth Lykes*, arriving at New York City 21 August 1945, Crew Lists of Vessels Arriving at New Orleans, Louisiana, 1910–1945.

32. American steamer *Gretna Victory*, arriving 6 August 1953, California Passenger and Crew Lists, 1882–1959.

33. *Report of the United States Merchant Marine Commission*, 208.

34. Reed, "Lumberjacks and Longshoremen," 54.

35. "Adjustment Board Without Chairman Postpones Session," *New Orleans Times-Picayune*, 26 October 1919, 10.

36. *Report of the United States Merchant Marine Commission*, 347.

37. Villars, *Lealtad y rebeldía*, 54.

38. Julio C. Castro, General Secretary of the Central American Labor Confederation, to Lee Tulin, General Secretary and Treasurer at IWW headquarters in New York, 3 April 1927, Industrial Workers of the World Collection, Series III—General Organization, III A General File.

39. Tulin to Castro, 4 June 1927, Industrial Workers of the World Collection, Series III—General Organization, III A General File.

40. "The Great White Graft," *Marine Worker*, 1 March 1922, 2.

41. "A Todas Las Uniones de Transporte Maritimo del Hemisferio Oeste," *Marine Worker*, 1 June 1925, 1.

42. John D. Erwin, US Ambassador, to Secretary of State, 30 December 1943, replying to questionnaire regarding labor matters in Honduras, US Confidential Diplomatic Records, 1930–1945.

43. Objectives, Article I, Section 3(a), *Constitution of the National Maritime Union of America, Affiliated with the CIO* (N.p.: National Maritime Union, 1937), 7.

44. Objectives, Article I, Section 3 (j), *Constitution of the National Maritime Union of America*, 8.

45. "Joint Membership Meeting of the National Maritime Union held at Jerusalem Temple, New Orleans, Louisiana, June 23, 1939," 6, National Maritime Union: Minutes of Meetings and Convention Sessions Held in New Orleans, folder 6, Louisiana Collection, New Orleans Public Library.

46. Joseph Curran, Report of President Joseph Curran to the Second Biennial Convention of the National Maritime Union of America, Jerusalem Temple, NOLA, July 1939, Box 90, National Maritime Union Papers, Rutgers University.

47. Curran.

48. Chester Young, NMU vice president, Report on Investigation of the Port of New Orleans, 20 June 1947, Box 97, National Maritime Union Papers, Rutgers University.

49. Local, *Weekly Louisianan,* 30 July 1881, 3.

50. "Consul Astwood at Home. A Complimentary Dinner Given Him. Louisiana Honors Her Adopted Son," *Weekly Pelican,* 21 May 1887, 2.

51. "Sugar Problem," *New Orleans Weekly Planner,* 4 December 1886, 3.

52. "Slavery in Jamaica," *New Orleans Weekly Planner,* 15 January 1887, 2.

53. Martin, *Race First,* 15.

54. "Report by Harry D. Gulley, January 1923," in Hill, *Marcus Garvey and Universal Negro Improvement Association Papers,* 5:178; "Speech by Marcus Garvey, Liberty Hall (NYC), July 4, 1922," in Hill, *Marcus Garvey and Universal Negro Improvement Association Papers,* 4:693–94.

55. "Thomas W. Anderson, U.N.I.A. Second Assistant Secretary General to William Phillips, Executive Secretary, New Orleans Division. October 10, 1922," in Hill, *Marcus Garvey and Universal Negro Improvement Association Papers,* 5:45.

56. "Thomas W. Anderson, U.N.I.A."

57. "NMU Delegates Can Board Fruit Ships," *New Orleans Times-Picayune,* 14 May 1937, 2.

58. "Sit-Down Strikes on Ships of Three Lines are Called," *New Orleans Times-Picayune,* 18 May 1937, 27.

59. "Sit-Down Strike is Called on Ship Here: S.S. Cayo Mambi Held in Port When Seamen Quit Work," *New Orleans Times-Picayune,* 12 May 1937, 2.

60. "Seamen on 32 Ships Vote for CIO Union," *New Orleans Times-Picayune,* 26 January 1938, 10.

61. "Sit-Down Strike Ties Up Vessel About to Depart," *New Orleans Times-Picayune,* 11 July 1937, 22.

62. US Naturalization Petitions, New Orleans East District Federal Court, microfilm 7RA 232 23, rolls 23–31, 1930–43, National Archives at Fort Worth, TX.

63. William Connor, declaration of intent and naturalization application, Records of the District Courts of the United States, 1685–2004.

64. "Joint Membership Meeting of the National Maritime Union held at Jerusalem Temple, New Orleans, Louisiana, June 23, 1939," 13.

65. "Joint Membership Meeting of the National Maritime Union held at Jerusalem Temple, New Orleans, Louisiana, June 23, 1939," 13,

66. List or Manifest of Aliens Employed on the Vessel as Crew Members, New Orleans, 1910–1945, SS *Cartago,* Cristóbal, Panama, United Fruit Company, 1922; SS *Atenas,* Havana, Cuba, September 1921, September 1922; SS *Abangarez,* Cristóbal, Panama, November 1920; SS *Parismina,* Havana, Cuba, 1920.

67. Minutes, 1st Constitutional Convention, National Maritime Union of America, July 19, 1937–July 30, 1937, Box 89, National Maritime Union Papers, Rutgers University.

68. "Joint Membership Meeting of the National Maritime Union held at Jerusalem Temple, New Orleans, Louisiana, June 23, 1939," 11.

69. "Joint Membership Meeting of the National Maritime Union held at Jerusalem Temple, New Orleans, Louisiana, June 23, 1939," 11.

70. Joseph Curran, "Gulf Officials Should Be Glad Crooks Are Driven Out, Not Protect Them," June 1939, National Maritime Union Papers, Rutgers University.

71. "The Facts About Ferdinand Smith: Read the Facts and Know the Truth," *N.M.U. Pilot*, 27 February 1948.

72. Mirel, *Patriotic Pluralism*, 25.

73. World War I Draft Registration Cards, 1917–1918, New Orleans.

74. Reid, *Negro Immigrant*, 160.

75. Reid, 160.

76. See Putnam, *Radical Moves*, 204–7. There were clear limits to British identity and citizenship for "nonwhite" subjects of the British Empire coming from the various colonial possessions. Scholars such as Putnam note the debate around this issue related to children of West Indians born abroad claiming the citizenship of their parents, as well as concerns around interisland movement within the region and the authenticity of citizenship. British Foreign Office and consular agents drove much of this political debate. However, the situation in New Orleans was different, since on US documents citizenship and nationality were always listed as British for West Indians from the British Empire regardless of race or the position of the British government. Before becoming US citizens, West Indians had to renounce their British citizenship.

77. Rush, *Bonds of Empire*, 2.

78. Register of Births, New Orleans. British Consulate, British Foreign Office, FO 585/16. British National Archives.

CHAPTER FOUR

Inventing a New Life in the Midst of Uncertainty: Navigating the Racial Divide in New Orleans

1. Bayor, *Encountering Ellis Island*, 14–15.

2. Coolidge, "Whose Country Is This?," 14.

3. Coolidge, 14.

4. M. D. Rojas, "Affidavit of Surgeon," 20 August 1936, SS *Atenas*, List or Manifest of Aliens Employed on the Vessel as Crew Members, New Orleans, 1910–1945. Each alien, whether arriving as an immigrant or as a temporary visitor to the United States, had to undergo a medical inspection to determine whether he was physically and mentally fit to enter the United States. Sailors on merchant vessels were often examined by company physicians either at their port of embarkation or upon arrival at a US port. The list of races in this instance was given to a Honduran doctor employed by the Truxillo Railroad

Company at the port of Puerto Castilla, Honduras. The doctor had to sign a sworn affidavit regarding his qualifications, and the document was notarized by the Guatemalan consul because there was no American consular agent at the port.

5. Rojas.

6. Immigration Act of 1924 (Johnson-Reed Act), 68th Cong., 1st sess., 1924, chaps. 185, 190, p. 155.

7. Immigration Act of 1924, 167.

8. World War I Draft Registration Cards, 1917–1918, New Orleans.

9. Ngai, *Lucky Ones,* 189.

10. Ngai, 189.

11. Boston Fruit Company Papers.

12. "Departure of Mails," *New Orleans Times-Picayune,* 4 January 1890, 3.

13. S. B. Bonapart, registration card, World War I Draft Registration Cards, 1917–1918, New Orleans.

14. McKinney, *New Orleans,* 111, 118.

15. "Summary of Economic, Real Estate, and Mortgage Survey and Security Area Descriptions of New Orleans Louisiana," 28 April 1939, Division of Research and Statistics, Federal Home Loan Bank Board, Home Owner Loan Corporation, Washington, DC. "Hot spots" and "Completely developed" represent the language of the HOLC, whereas "transitioning" and "transitioned" are my own labels, based on HOLC descriptions of the areas.

16. "Area Description, New Orleans Areas D-5 and D-7," 28 April 1939, 1A–2A, Division of Research and Statistics, Federal Home Loan Bank Board, Home Owner Loan Corporation.

17. Woods, "Federal Home Loan Bank Board," 1048–49.

18. The famed early jazz musician Jelly Roll Morton is credited with learning to play Spanish (Cuban) rhythms on the streets of New Orleans and merging it with blues, ragtime, European classical music, and other popular music. Morton added these Spanish rhythms as part of the musical vocabulary that would become jazz. See Sommerville and Morgan, "King of the Underworld," 90–91.

19. Fiehrer, "From Quadrille to Stomp," 30–31.

20. See Chambers, *Race, Nation, and West Indian Immigration to Honduras;* chapters 4 and 5 detail the economic and social conditions within the British Caribbean that fostered intense emigration to Central America and later the United States.

21. Landau, *Spectacular Wickedness,* 22.

22. Moore, *Nationalizing Blackness,* 98–99.

23. Vaz, "Baby Dolls," xviii.

24. Roberts, *Latin Tinge,* 34–35.

25. Vaz, "Baby Dolls," xviii.

26. Almina Salmon, application for US citizenship, US Naturalization Petitions, New Orleans East District Federal Court, 1933–35, National Archives at Fort Worth, TX.

27. Entries for Fortunatus P. Ricard in the 1926 New Orleans City Directory, 1177, and for Noemie Marc and Almina Salmon in the 1928 New Orleans City Directory, 1044 and 1228.

28. Kennedy, *Chord Changes on the Chalkboard*, 1–3.

29. Entry for Almina Salmon, New Orleans City Directory, 1956, 688.

30. Anita Gonzales McKay, application for US citizenship, US Naturalization Petitions, New Orleans East District Federal Court, 1933–35, National Archives at Fort Worth, TX.

31. Howard, *Black Labor, White Sugar*, 209.

32. US Department of Commerce, *Fifty-Fourth Annual List of Merchant Vessels*, 54.

33. Entry for Anita McKay, New Orleans City Directory, 1956, 701.

34. List or Manifest of Alien Passengers for the United States, *S.S. Lysepjord*, 5 December 1924.

35. "Vessel Rates from North American Ports and Cardiff and Quotations for Welsh Coals," *Coal Trade Journal* 47 (September 1915): 1080.

36. Enoch Elijah Flowers, registration card, World War I Draft Registration Cards, 1917–1918.

37. US Department of Commerce, *Fourteenth Census of the United States: 1920*.

38. Simmons, *Crescent City Girls*, 20.

39. "Summary of Economic, Real Estate, and Mortgage Survey and Security Area Descriptions of New Orleans, Louisiana," 1A.

40. "Summary of Economic, Real Estate, and Mortgage Survey and Security Area Descriptions of New Orleans Louisiana," 1A.

41. US Department of Commerce, *Fifteenth Census of the United States: 1930*; US Department of Commerce, *Sixteenth Census of the United States: 1940*.

42. Enoch Elijah Flowers, registration card.

43. On the impact of plant diseases on Central American agriculture during the period, see Marquardt, "Green Havoc," 49, 57.

44. "Eligible Teacher Names for Negro Schools Issued," *New Orleans Times-Picayune*, 24 June 1939, 25.

45. Obituary for Cecilia Flowers, *New Orleans Times-Picayune*, 22 March 1983, 15.

46. "S. B. Bonpart," SS *Abangarez*, 4 January 1918, List or Manifest of Aliens Employed on the Vessel as Crew Members, New Orleans, 1910–1945.

47. Flood Alexander, registration card, World War I Draft Registration Cards, 1917–1918.

48. Arrest record of Joseph Aszousa, 1925, New Orleans Police Department Arrest Records, 1881–1966.

49. Arrest record of Daniel Isaac, 3rd Precinct, 5 January 1923, New Orleans Police Department Arrest Records, 1881–1966.

50. The complete arrest records are for the years 1881–1966. I chose to focus on the period of the study. Most of the microfilm related to the arrest records is not usable

because of its deteriorated state. However, the arrest records were available in abbreviated form. I initially searched the arrest records for the names of the 271 West Indians and Central Americans of all races and nationalities who applied for US citizenship or declared intent to apply in the years 1910–40 and found none. I also searched the records for the 2nd and 3rd Precincts, which included Central City, Mid-City, the French Quarter, Faubourg Marigny, and Tremé, areas where West Indians and Central Americans were known to reside. Only twelve names emerged from that search.

51. See arrest record of Philip Ingram, 5th Precinct, 9 April 1926, New Orleans Police Department Arrest Records, 1881–1966.

52. "Police Directed to Make Arrests for Local Board: Forty-Three Men Registered in Division No. 11 Fail to Answer Calls," *New Orleans Times-Picayune*, 9 January 1918.

53. US Department of Commerce, *Fifteenth Census of the United States: 1930*.

CHAPTER FIVE

Capitalists, Student Activists, and Everyday Citizens: Negotiating a Latin American Identity in a "Diverse" Jim Crow City

1. Nott, "Impresiones de Nueva Orleans."

2. "Exports from New Orleans," *Revista Comercial Americana,* May 1906, 7.

3. Painter, "Assimilation of Latin Americans in New Orleans, Louisiana," 40.

4. Painter, 14.

5. Painter, 24.

6. Painter, 18, 54.

7. Owsley, *Hispanic American Entrepreneur,* 3.

8. Gauthreaux, "Inhospitable Land," 42.

9. Gauthreaux, 52–53.

10. Gauthreaux, 52–53.

11. Powell, "When Hate Came to Town," 393.

12. Powell, 393.

13. The growing literature on the evolution of whiteness in the United States, particularly as it pertains to European immigrants during the late nineteenth and early twentieth centuries, notes a tendency among immigrants considered "inferior" within the US racial and ethnic paradigm to seek inclusion in white society on the backs of groups deemed inferior in the country, such as African Americans, Native Americans, and Mexican Americans (Southwest), by performing racial norms accepted by the dominant society and/or through labor organization. See Jacobson, *Whiteness of a Different Color;* Roediger, *Working toward Whiteness;* and Roediger, *Wages of Whiteness.*

14. Mirel, *Patriotic Pluralism,* 25.

15. Folder 9, "Prejudice," Norman Wellington Painter Research Material, 1948–49, Manuscript Collection, Latin American Library, Tulane University. This collection com-

prises interview notes and transcripts related to the field research Painter conducted on Latin Americans in New Orleans after the First World War.

16. Folder 9, "Prejudice."

17. Folder 10, "Impressions," Norman Wellington Painter Research Material, 1948–49.

18. Bracken, "Restructuring the Boundaries," 41–42.

19. Doorley, "Irish Catholics and French Creoles," 38–39.

20. "Academia Holy Angels," *Simpatia: Revista Mensual Ilustrada*, August 1935, 2, 15.

21. Owsley, *Hispanic American Entrepreneur*, 3.

22. Folder 9, "Prejudice."

23. Folder 9, "Prejudice."

24. Folder 10, "Impressions."

25. Mejía, "No habrá panamericanismo mientras exista el imperialismo yanki," *Luz y Patria: Revista Independiente*, 30 May 1926, 1.

26. See Krauze, *Redeemers*. Krauze demonstrates how in late-nineteenth- and early-twentieth-century Latin America intellectuals and politicians constructed national narratives as a means of uniting the citizens in their respective nations in order to combat the encroachment of US political, cultural, and economic influence.

27. "La casa del estudiante latinoamericano," *Simpatia: Revista Mensual Ilustrada*, August 1935, 5.

28. "FI IOTA ALFA," *Simpatia: Revista Mensual Ilustrada*, August 1935, 19. Interviewees in Painter's study also noted that they were never invited to join fraternities and sororities at the universities and boarding schools they attended. Some of the men were able to maintain an active social life through participation in athletics (baseball in particular) or through house parties or other social events organized by fellow Latin American students. See Folder 9, "Prejudice."

29. "Intense Politics and Martial Law Worry Hondurans," *New Orleans Times-Picayune*, 6 May 1919, 6.

30. Euraque, *Reinterpreting the Banana Republic*, 48.

31. "Union Patriótica Hondureña," *Revista Mexicana*, 29 June 1919, 1.

32. "Union Patriótica Hondureña," 1, my translation.

33. *The Wolf: Yearbook of Loyola University.*

34. See Bruce Albert, "Former New Orleans assessor helped integrate Loyola University in 1962, but not its basketball team," *New Orleans Times-Picayune*, 28 August 2013; and Jasmin, "Desegregation of a University." Though Loyola entered into a partnership with Xavier University, the historically African American Catholic university in the city, to allow students from the latter institution to enroll in certain classes at Loyola beginning in the late 1940s, it was not until 1962 that the university allowed African Americans to matriculate.

35. Henry S. Bonney, application for seaman's protection certificate, Records of the Bureau of Marine Inspection and Navigation, Box 114, New Orleans.

36. Record for Elida Corcoran, in US Department of Commerce, *Sixteenth Census of the United States: 1940.*

37. Vazquez, *Mexican Americans across Generations,* 91.

38. Vazquez, 91.

39. Record for Amanda Balladares, in US Department of Commerce, *Sixteenth Census of the United States: 1940.*

40. Morgan, *Disparate Diasporas,* 63, 115.

41. Record for Anita Velazquez, in US Department of Commerce, *Fourteenth Census of the United States: 1920.*

42. Record for Amanda Balladares, in US Department of Commerce, *Sixteenth Census of the United States: 1940.*

43. Records for Amanda Balladares and Anita Velazquez, in US Department of Commerce, *Sixteenth Census of the United States: 1940.*

44. E. M. Daniel, "In the Public Evening Schools," *New Orleans Times-Picayune,* 2 March 1913, 3.

45. "Night Schools to Open this Week," *New Orleans Times-Picayune,* 29 October 1905, 1.

46. Daniel, 67.

47. "Evening Schools Transferred," *New Orleans Times-Picayune,* 2 November 1915, 10.

48. "Evening Schools Open," *New Orleans Times-Picayune,* 1 October 1912, 6.

49. "Evening Schools Transferred," 10.

50. Annual Report of the New Orleans Public Schools, 1920–1921, Orleans Parish School Board Papers.

51. Daniel, 67.

52. Meeting Minutes, 10 May 1918, Orleans Parish School Board Papers.

53. Kaufman, "New Orleans and the Panama Canal," 344.

54. Kaufman, 344.

Epilogue

1. Joan Treadway, "The Latin Link: Latins flock to New Orleans for haven, prosperity," *New Orleans Times-Picayune,* 13 November 1983, 18.

2. Joan Treadway, "Hispanics found on every rung of success ladder," *New Orleans Times-Picayune,* 15 November 1983; Treadway, "Soccer orients newcomers into N.O. Latin community," *New Orleans Times-Picayune,* 14 November 1983, 8.

3. Sakakeeny, "New Orleans Music as a Circulatory System," 291.

Bibliography

GOVERNMENT DOCUMENTS
United States

California Passenger and Crew Lists, 1882–1959. National Archives and Records Administration, Washington, DC.

Census of Merchant Seamen, Jefferson Parish, New Orleans. National Archives and Records Administration, Washington, DC.

Crew Lists of Vessels Arriving at Boston, Massachusetts, 1917–1943. National Archives and Records Administration, Washington, DC.

Crew Lists of Vessels Arriving at New Orleans, Louisiana, 1910–1945. National Archives and Records Administration, Washington, DC.

Crew Lists of Vessels Arriving at New York City, 1897–1957. National Archives and Records Administration, Washington, DC.

Despatches from Roatan, Omoa, and Truxillo, 1870–1880. Record Group 59. National Archives and Records Administration, College Park, MD.

Federal Home Owner Loan Corporation Papers. National Archives and Records Administration, College Park, MD.

List or Manifest of Alien Passengers for the United States, *S.S. Lysepjord,* 5 December 1924. National Archives and Records Administration, Washington, DC.

List or Manifest of Aliens Employed on the Vessel as Crew Members, New Orleans, 1910–1945. National Archives and Records Administration, Washington, DC.

New Orleans Passenger Lists, 1813–1945. National Archives and Records Administration, Washington, DC.

Records of the Bureau of Marine Inspection and Navigation. Record Group 41. National Archives and Records Administration, Washington, DC.

Records of the District Courts of the United States, 1685–2004. Group 21. National Archives at Fort Worth, Fort Worth, TX.

Records of the Selective Service System, 1926–1975. National Archives and Records Administration, Washington, DC.

Records of the US Department of State Relating to the Internal Affairs of Honduras, 1910–1929. National Archives and Records Administration, College Park, MD.

Report of the United States Merchant Marine Commission. Washington, DC: Government Printing Office, 1905.

US Confidential Diplomatic Records, 1930–1945. National Archives and Records Administration, College Park, MD.

US Department of Commerce. *Fourteenth Census of the United States: 1920. Population, Volume III, Population, Composition and Characteristics of the Population by States.* Washington, DC: Government Printing Office, 1923.

———. *Fifteenth Census of the United States: 1930. Population, Volume II, General Report, Statistics by Subjects.* Washington, DC: Government Printing Office, 1933.

———. *Fifty-Fourth Annual List of Merchant Vessels of the United States with Official Numbers and Signal Letters and List of Vessels Belonging to the United States Government with Distinguishing Signals for the year ended June 30 1922.* Washington, DC: Government Printing Office, 1922.

———. *Sixteenth Census of the United States: 1940. Population, Volume II, Characteristics of the Population.* Washington, DC: Government Printing Office, 1943.

World War I Draft Registration Cards, 1917–1918, New Orleans. National Archives and Records Administration, Washington, DC.

Honduras

Legajo: Consulado General de Honduras en Nueva Orleans, January–December 1934. Archivo Nacional de Honduras, Tegucigalpa.

Legajo: Informe de Estadísticas de Policía, 1933–1943. Archivo Nacional de Honduras, Tegucigalpa.

Legajo: Ministerio de Relaciones Exteriores, Notas Varias, 1917. Archivo Nacional de Honduras, Tegucigalpa.

Legajo: Notas Varias, 1881–1912. Archivo Nacional de Honduras, Tegucigalpa.

Legajo: Telegramas de Departamento de Atlántida de 1928. Archivo Nacional de Honduras, Tegucigalpa.

Republic of Honduras. *Memoria de gobernación y justicia, 1915–1916.* Tegucigalpa: Tipografía Nacional, 1917.

———. *El negocio Valentine: El ferrocarril nacional de Honduras y el muelle y faro de Puerto Cortés, colección de articulos publicados por el diario El Observador.* Tegucigalpa: Tipografía Nacional, 1911.

———. *Recopilación de leyes migratorias y afines procedimientos prácticos.* Teguci-galpa: Departamento de Inmigración, 1967.

———. *Resumen del censo general de población levantado el 29 de junio de 1930.* Tegucigalpa: Tipografía Nacional, 1932.

Selected Documents Pertaining to Entrance Visas, 1934–1947. Alcaldía Munic-ipal de Olanchito, Departamento de Yoro, Honduras.

British Honduras

Bowen, Frederick Charles. *Census of British Honduras, 1931.* Belize City: Gov-ernment Printing Office, 1933.

Dunk, Herbert. *British Honduras Report of the Census of 1921 taken on the 24th of April 1921.* Belize City: Government Printing Office, 1922.

United Kingdom

British Consulate, Honduras: General Correspondence, 1861–1965. FO 632. British National Archives.

British Consulate, United States of America: General Correspondence and Various Registers, New Orleans, 1850–1938. FO 585. British National Archives.

Political Departments, General Correspondence, 1906–1966. FO 371. British National Archives.

UNIVERSITY ARCHIVES

Boston Fruit Company Papers. Volume III: Register of Ships, 1898–1901. Harvard Business School Library, Cambridge, MA.

Honduras Telegrafos Nacionales. Latin American Library, Tulane University.

Industrial Workers of the World Collection, Series III—General Organization. Walter P. Reuther Library, Wayne State University, Detroit.

National Maritime Union Papers. Alexander Library, Rutgers University, New Brunswick, NJ.

Orleans Parish School Board Papers. Louisiana Collection, University of New Orleans.

The Wolf: Yearbook of Loyola University, 1924–26, 1927–29, 1931–33. Loyola University, New Orleans.

NEW ORLEANS PUBLIC LIBRARY

National Maritime Union Papers. Louisiana Collection.
New Orleans City Directory, 1928–1956. Louisiana Collection.
New Orleans Police Department Arrest Records, 1881–1966. Louisiana Collection.

TRAVEL ACCOUNTS

Palmer, Frederick. *Central America and Its Problems: An Account of a Journey from the Rio Grande to Panama, with Introductions, Chapters on Mexico, and Her Relations to Her Neighbors.* London: T. Werner Laurie, 1916.
Penney, William T. "Notes and Comments on Travels Through Mexico and Central America, being the personal happenings to and experiences of yours sincerely." Guatemala City, 1913. Louisiana Collection, Tulane University Library, New Orleans.

BOOKS

Acker, Allison. *The Making of a Banana Republic.* Boston: South End Press, 1988.
Aguirre, Carlos, and Robert Buffington, eds. *Reconstructing Criminality in Latin America.* Wilmington, DE: Scholarly Resources, 2000.
Alanen, Arnold R. *Morgan Park: Duluth, U.S. Steel, and the Forging of a Company Town.* Minneapolis: University of Minnesota Press, 2008.
Amaya Banegas, Jorge. *Los judíos en Honduras.* Tegucigalpa, Honduras: Editorial Guaymuras, 2000.
Appelbaum, Nancy P., Anne S. Macpherson, and Karin Alejandra Rosemblatt, eds. *Race and Nation in Modern Latin America.* Chapel Hill: University of North Carolina Press, 2003.
Argueta, Mario. *Tres caudillos, tres destinos, 1919–1932.* Tegucigalpa, Honduras: Subirana, 2007.
Arnesen, Eric. *Waterfront Workers of New Orleans: Race, Class, and Politics, 1863–1923.* New York: Oxford University Press, 1991.
Arthur, John A. *African Diaspora Identities: Negotiating Culture in Transnational Migration.* Lanham, MD: Lexington Books, 2010.

Bayor, Ronald H. *Encountering Ellis Island: How European Immigrants Entered America*. Baltimore: Johns Hopkins University Press, 2014.

Bedasse, Monique A. *Jah Kingdom: Rastafarians, Tanzania, and Pan-Africanism in the Age of Decolonization*. Chapel Hill: University of North Carolina Press, 2017.

Bennett, Herman L. *Africans in Colonial Mexico: Absolutism, Christianity, and Afro-Creole Consciousness, 1570–1640*. Bloomington: Indiana University Press, 2003.

Bennett, James B. *Religion and the Rise of Jim Crow in New Orleans*. Princeton, NJ: Princeton University Press, 2005.

Berry, Mary Frances. *We Are Who We Say We Are: A Black Family's Search for Home across the Atlantic World*. New York: Oxford University Press, 2015.

Bodden, J. A. Roy. *The Cayman Islands in Transition: The Politics, History, and Sociology of a Changing Society*. Kingston, Jamaica: Ian Randle, 2007.

Boelhower, William, ed. *New Orleans in the Atlantic World: Between Land and Sea*. New York: Routledge, 2010.

Bolland, O. Nigel. *Colonialism and Resistance in Belize: Essays in Historical Sociology*. Kingston, Jamaica: University of the West Indies Press, 2003.

———. *The Formation of a Colonial Society: Belize, from Conquest to Crown Colony*. Baltimore: Johns Hopkins University Press, 1977.

———. *The Politics of Labour in the British Caribbean: The Social Origins of Authoritarianism and Democracy in the Labour Movement*. Princeton, NJ: Markus Wiener, 2001.

Bolster, W. Jeffrey. *Black Jacks: African American Seamen in the Age of Sail*. Cambridge, MA: Harvard university Press, 1997.

Bourgois, Philippe I. *Ethnicity at Work: Divided Labor on a Central American Banana Plantation*. Baltimore: Johns Hopkins University Press, 1989.

Boyle, Kevin. *Arc of Justice: A Saga of Race, Civil Rights, and Murder in the Jazz Age*. New York: Henry Holt, 2004.

Brasseaux, Carl A., Keith P. Fontenot, and Claude F. Oubre. *Creoles of Color in the Bayou Country*. Jackson: University Press of Mississippi, 1994.

Chambers, Glenn A. *Race, Nation, and West Indian Immigration to Honduras, 1890–1940*. Baton Rouge: Louisiana State University Press, 2010.

Chomsky, Aviva. *West Indian Workers and the United Fruit Company in Costa Rica, 1870–1940*. Baton Rouge: Louisiana State University Press, 1996.

Conniff, Michael. *Black Labor on a White Canal: Panama, 1904–1981*. Pittsburgh: University of Pittsburgh Press, 1985.

Cooper, Frederick, Thomas C. Holt, and Rebecca J. Scott. *Beyond Slavery: Explorations of Race, Labor, and Citizenship in Postemancipation Societies.* Chapel Hill: University of North Carolina Press, 2000.

Cope, R. Douglas. *Limits of Racial Domination: Plebeian Society in Colonial Mexico City, 1660–1720.* Madison: University of Wisconsin Press, 1994.

Davidson, William V. *The Historical Geography of the Bay Islands, Honduras: Anglo-Hispanic Conflict in the Western Caribbean.* Birmingham, AL: Southern University Press, 1979.

D'Cruze, Shani. *Everyday Violence in Britain, 1850–1950: Gender and Class.* London: Longman, 2000.

de la Fuente, Alejandro. *Havana and the Atlantic in the Sixteenth Century.* Chapel Hill: University of North Carolina Press, 2008.

Dessens, Nathalie. *Creole City: A Chronicle of Early American New Orleans.* Gainesville: University Press of Florida, 2015.

———. *From Saint Domingue to New Orleans: Migrations and Influences.* Gainesville: University Press of Florida, 2010.

Dominguez, Virginia. *White By Definition: Social Classification in Creole Louisiana.* New Brunswick, NJ: Rutgers University Press, 1986.

Dormon, James H., ed. *Creoles of Color of the Gulf South.* Knoxville: University of Tennessee Press, 1996.

Dosal, Paul. *Doing Business with the Dictators: A Political History of United Fruit in Guatemala, 1899–1944.* Wilmington, DE: Scholarly Resources, 1993.

Duncan, Quince, and Carlos Melendez Chaverri. *Negro en Costa Rica.* San José: Editorial Costa Rica, 1974.

Euraque, Darío A. *Conversaciones históricas con el mestizaje y su identidad nacional en Honduras.* San Pedro Sula, Honduras: Centro Editorial, 2004.

———. *Reinterpreting the Banana Republic: Region and State in Honduras, 1870–1972.* Chapel Hill: University of North Carolina Press, 1996.

Faires, Nora, and Dirk Hoerder. *Migrants and Migration in Modern North America: Cross-Border Lives, Labor Markets, and Politics.* Durham, NC: Duke University Press, 2011.

Falola, Toyin, and Matt D. Childs, eds. *The Yoruba Diaspora in the Atlantic World.* Bloomington: Indiana University Press, 2005.

Ferrer, Ada. *Freedom's Mirror: Cuba and Haiti in the Age of Revolution.* New York: Cambridge University Press, 2014.

Fink, Leon. *Sweatshops at Sea: Merchant Seamen in the World's First Globalized Industry, from 1812 to the Present.* Chapel Hill: University of North Carolina Press, 2011.

Foner, Nancy. *Islands in the City: West Indian Migration to New York*. Berkeley: University of California Press, 2001.

Freund, David. *Colored Property: State Policy and White Racial Politics in Suburban America*. Chicago: University of Chicago Press, 2007.

Fussell, Paul. *The Great War and Modern Memory*. New York: Oxford University Press, 2013.

Gmelch, George. *Double Passage: The Lives of Caribbean Migrants Abroad and Back Home*. Ann Arbor: University of Michigan Press, 1992.

Gonzalez, Nancie L. *Dollar, Dove, and Eagle: One Hundred Years of Palestinian Migration to Honduras*. Ann Arbor: University of Michigan Press, 1992.

Graham, Richard, ed. *The Idea of Race in Latin America, 1870–1940*. Austin: University of Texas Press, 1990.

Greenbaum, Susan D. *More Than Black: Afro-Cubans in Tampa*. Gainesville: University Press of Florida, 2002.

Grossman, James R. *Land of Hope: Chicago, Black Southerners, and the Great Migration*. Chicago: University of Chicago Press, 1991.

Gudmundson, Lowell, and Justin Wolfe, eds. *Blacks and Blackness in Central America: Between Race and Place*. Durham, NC: Duke University Press, 2010.

Hahamovitch, Cindy. *No Man's Land: Jamaican Guestworkers in America and the Global History of Deportable Labor*. Princeton, NJ: Princeton University Press, 2013.

Hair, William Ivy. *Bourbonism and Agrarian Protest: Louisiana Politics, 1877–1900*. Baton Rouge: Louisiana State University Press, 1969.

Hall, Gwendolyn Midlo. *Africans in Colonial Louisiana: The Development of Afro-Creole Culture in the Eighteenth Century*. Baton Rouge: Louisiana State University Press, 1992.

Hall, Stuart, and Paul Du Gay, eds. *Questions of Cultural Identity*. London: Sage, 1996.

Harpelle, Ronald N. *The West Indians of Costa Rica: Race, Class, and the Integration of an Ethnic Minority*. Montreal: McGill-Queen's University Press, 2001.

Hathaway, Heather. *Caribbean Waves: Relocating Claude McKay and Paule Marshall*. Bloomington: Indiana University Press, 1999.

Henry, Frances. *The Caribbean Diaspora in Toronto: Learning to Live with Racism*. Toronto: University of Toronto Press, 1994.

Herrera, Robinson. *Natives, Europeans, and Africans in Sixteenth Century Santiago de Guatemala*. Austin: University of Texas Press, 2003.

Hill, Robert A., ed. *The Marcus Garvey and Universal Negro Improvement Association Papers*. Vol. 4. Berkeley: University of California Press, 1985.

———. *The Marcus Garvey Universal Negro Improvement Association Papers*. Vol. 5. Berkeley: University of California Press, 1987.

Hintzen, Percy. *West Indian in the West: Self-Representations in an Immigrant Community*. New York: New York University Press, 2001.

Hirsch, Arnold. *Making the Second Ghetto: Race and Housing in Chicago, 1940–1960*. New York: Cambridge University Press, 1983.

Hollandsworth, James G., Jr. *An Absolute Massacre: The New Orleans Race Riot of July 30, 1866*. Baton Rouge: Louisiana State University Press, 2001.

Horne, Gerald. *Red Seas: Ferdinand Smith and Radical Black Sailors in the United States and Jamaica*. New York: New York University Press, 2005.

Howard, Philip A. *Black Labor, White Sugar: Caribbean Braceros and Their Struggle for Power in the Cuban Sugar Industry*. Baton Rouge: Louisiana State University Press, 2015.

Jacobson, Matthew Frye. *Whiteness of a Different Color: European Immigrants and the Alchemy of Race*. Cambridge, MA: Harvard University Press, 1998.

James, Winston. *Holding Aloft the Banner of Ethiopia: Caribbean Radicalism in Early Twentieth Century America*. New York: Verso, 1998.

Johnson, Rashauna. *Slavery's Metropolis: Unfree Labor in New Orleans during the Age of Revolutions*. New York: Cambridge University Press, 2016.

Kelley, Blair L. M. *Right to Ride: Streetcar Boycotts and African American Citizenship in the Era of Plessy v. Ferguson*. Chapel Hill: University of North Carolina Press, 2010.

Kennedy, A. J. *Chord Changes on the Chalkboard: How Public School Teachers Shaped Jazz and the Music of New Orleans*. Lanham, MD: Scarecrow, 2005.

Kiely, Ray. *Empire in the Age of Globalisation: U.S. Hegemony and Neoliberal Order*. Ann Arbor, MI: Pluto, 2005.

Krauze, Enrique. *Redeemers: Ideas and Power in Latin America*. New York: HarperCollins, 2011.

Landau, Emily Epstein. *Spectacular Wickedness: Race and Memory in Storyville, New Orleans*. Baton Rouge: Louisiana University Press, 2013.

Leiva Vivas, Rafael. *Tráfico de esclavos negros a Honduras*. Tegucigalpa, Honduras: Editorial Guaymuras, 1982.

Macpherson, Anne S. *From Colony to Nation: Women Activists and the Gendering of Politics in Belize, 1912–1982*. Lincoln: University of Nebraska Press, 2007.

Makalani, Minkah. *In the Cause of Freedom: Radical Black Internationalism from Harlem to London, 1917–1939.* Chapel Hill: University of North Carolina Press, 2011.

Martin, Tony. *Race First: The Ideological and Organizational Struggles of Marcus Garvey and the Universal Negro Improvement Association.* Dover, MA: Majority Press, 1976.

Martínez Montiel, Luz. *Presencia africana en Centroamérica.* Mexico City: Consejo Nacional para la Cultura y Los Artes, 1993.

May, Robert E. *The Southern Dream of a Caribbean Empire, 1854–1861.* Gainesville: University Press of Florida, 2002.

McKay, Claude. *Banjo: A Story Without a Plot.* New York: Harcourt Brace Jovanovich, 1929.

McKinney, Louise. *New Orleans: A Cultural History.* New York: Oxford University Press, 2006.

Meyers, Stephen Grant. *As Long As They Don't Move Next Door: Segregation and Racial Conflict in American Neighborhoods.* New York: Rowman & Littlefield, 2000.

Mirel, Jeffrey. *Patriotic Pluralism: Americanization Education and European Immigrants.* Cambridge, MA: Harvard University Press, 2010.

Moberg, Mark. *Myths of Ethnicity and Nation: Immigration, Work, and Identity in the Belize Banana Industry.* Knoxville: University of Tennessee Press, 1997.

Moore, Robin D. *Nationalizing Blackness: Afrocubanismo and Artistic Expression in Havana, 1920–1940.* Pittsburgh: University of Pittsburgh Press, 1997.

Moore, Shirley Ann Wilson. *To Place Our Deeds: The African American Community in Richmond, California, 1910–1963.* Berkeley: University of California Press, 2000.

Morgan, Edmund T. *Disparate Diasporas: Identity and Politics in an African Nicaraguan Community.* Austin: University of Texas Press, 1998.

Murdoch, H. Adlai. *Creolizing the Metropole: Migrant Caribbean Identities in Literature and Film.* Bloomington: Indiana University Press, 2012.

Newton, Velma. *The Silver Men: West Indian Labor Migration to Panama.* Kingston, Jamaica: Ian Randle, 2004.

Ngai, Mae. *The Lucky Ones: One Family and the Extraordinary Invention of Chinese America.* New York: Houghton Mifflin Harcourt, 2010.

Opie, Frederick Douglass. *Black Labor Migration in Caribbean Guatemala, 1882–1923.* Gainesville: University Press of Florida, 2009.

O'Reggio, Trevor. *Between Alienation and Citizenship: The Evolution of Black*

West Indian Society in Panama, 1914–1964. Lanham, MD: University Press of America, 2006.

Owsley, Beatrice Rodriguez. *The Hispanic American Entrepreneur: An Oral History of the American Dream.* Woodbridge, CT: Twayne, 1992.

Palmer, Colin. *Slaves of the White God: Blacks in Mexico, 1570–1650.* Cambridge, MA: Harvard University Press, 1976.

Palmer, Ransford W. *Pilgrims from the Sun: West Indian Migration to America.* London: Prentice Hall International, 1995.

Peloso, Vincent C., and Barbara Tenenbaum. *Liberals, Politics, and Power: State Formation in Nineteenth-Century Latin America.* Athens: University of Georgia Press, 1996.

Pine, Adrienne. *Working Hard, Drinking Hard: On Violence and Survival in Honduras.* Berkeley: University of California Press, 2008.

Powell, Lawrence N. *The Accidental City: Improvising New Orleans.* Cambridge, MA: Harvard University Press, 2012.

Putnam, Lara. *The Company They Kept: Migrants and the Politics of Gender in Caribbean Costa Rica, 1870–1960.* Chapel Hill: University of North Carolina Press, 2002.

———. *Radical Moves: Caribbean Migrants and the Politics of Race in the Jazz Age.* Chapel Hill: University of North Carolina Press, 2013.

Reed, John Shelton. *Dixie Bohemia: A French Quarter Circle in the 1920s.* Baton Rouge: Louisiana State University Press, 2012.

Reid, Ira De A. *The Negro Immigrant: His Background, Characteristics and Social Adjustment, 1899–1937.* New York: Arno Press, 1969.

Richardson, Bonham C. *Panama Money in Barbados, 1900–1920.* Knoxville: University of Tennessee Press, 2004.

Roberts, John Storm. *The Latin Tinge: The Impact of Latin American Music on the United States.* New York: Oxford University Press, 1999.

Roediger, David. *The Wages of Whiteness: Race and the Making of the American Working Class.* New York: Verso, 2007.

———. *Working toward Whiteness: How America's Immigrants Became White.* New York: Basic Books, 2005.

RosenGarten, Frederic, Jr. *William Walker y el ocaso del filibusterismo.* Tegucigalpa, Honduras: Editorial Guaymuras, 2002.

Rout, Leslie B. *African Experience in Spanish America, 1502–Present.* New York: Cambridge University Press, 1976.

Rush, Anne Spry. *Bonds of Empire: West Indians and Britishness from Victoria to Decolonization.* New York: Oxford University Press, 2011.

Scott, Rebecca J. *Degrees of Freedom: Louisiana and Cuba after Slavery.* Cambridge, MA: Belknap Press of Harvard University Press, 2005.

Showers-Johnson, Violet. *The Other Black Bostonians: West Indians in Boston, 1900–1950.* Bloomington: Indiana University Press, 2006.

Silva Gruesz, Kirsten. *Ambassadors of Culture: The Transamerican Origins of Latino Writing.* Princeton, NJ: Princeton University Press, 2002.

Simmons, Donald C. *Confederate Settlements in British Honduras.* Jefferson, NC: McFarland, 2001.

Simmons, LaKisha. *Crescent City Girls: The Lives of Young Black Women in Segregated New Orleans.* Chapel Hill: University of North Carolina Press, 2015.

Storch, Randi. *Red Chicago: American Communism at Its Grassroots, 1928–1935.* Urbana: University of Illinois Press, 2007.

Streeter, Stephen M., John C. Weaver, and William D. Coleman, eds. *Empires and Autonomy: Moments in the History of Globalization.* Vancouver: University of British Columbia Press, 2009.

Szok, Peter A. *"La última gaviota": Liberalism and Nostalgia in Early Twentieth-Century Panama.* Westport, CT: Greenwood, 2001.

Thomas-Hope, Elizabeth. *Freedom and Constraint in Caribbean Migration and Diaspora.* Kingston, Jamaica: Ian Randle, 2009.

Turner, Joyce Moore. *Caribbean Crusaders and the Harlem Renaissance.* Urbana: University of Illinois Press, 2005.

Vaz, Kim Marie. *The "Baby Dolls": Breaking the Race and Gender Barriers of the New Orleans Mardi Gras Tradition.* Baton Rouge: Louisiana State University Press, 2013.

Vazquez, Jessica M. *Mexican Americans across Generations: Immigrant Families, Racial Realities.* New York: New York University Press, 2011.

Villars, Rina. *Lealtad y rebeldía: La vida de Juan Pablo Wainwright.* Tegucigalpa, Honduras: Editorial Guaymuras, 2010.

Warren, Kenneth. *Bethlehem Steel: Builder and Arsenal of America.* Pittsburgh: University of Pittsburgh Press, 2008.

Waters, Mary C. *Black Identities: West Indian Immigrant Dreams and American Realities.* Cambridge, MA: Harvard University Press, 2009.

Watkins-Owens, Irma. *Blood Relations: Caribbean Immigrants and the Harlem Community, 1900–1930.* Bloomington: Indiana University Press, 1996.

Weise, Julie M. *Corazón de Dixie: Mexicanos in the U.S. South since 1910.* Chapel Hill: University of North Carolina Press, 2015.

Weiss, Holger. *Framing a Radical African Atlantic: African American Agency, West*

African Intellectuals and the International Trade Union Committee of Negro Workers. Boston: Brill, 2014.

Wigan, Greg, and Jean T. Waldron. *Following the Northern Star: Caribbean Identities and Education in North American Schools.* New York: Nova, 2013.

Yuscarán, Guillermo. *Gringos in Honduras: The Good, the Bad, and the Ugly.* Tegucigalpa, Honduras: Nuevo Sol, 1995.

BOOK CHAPTERS

Barthelemy, Anthony G. "Light, Bright, Damn *Near* White: Race, the Politics of Genealogy, and the Strange Case of Susie Guillory." In *Creole: The History and Legacy of Louisiana's Free People of Color,* edited by Sybil Kein, 252–75. Baton Rouge: Louisiana State University Press, 2000.

Brasseaux, Carl A. "Creoles of Color in Louisiana's Bayou Country, 1766–1877." In *Creoles of Color of the Gulf South,* edited by James H. Dormon, 67–86. Knoxville: University of Tennessee Press, 1996.

Brown, Lawrence. "Black and British: Garveyism and British West Indian Migrant Communities across the Americas." In *Exploring the British World: Identity, Cultural Production, Institutions,* edited by Kate Darian-Smith, Patricia Grimshaw, Kiera Lindsey, and Stuart Mcintyre, 1–20. Melbourne: RMIT, 2004.

Butterfield, Sherri-Ann P. "'We're Just Black': The Racial and Ethnic Identities of Second-Generation West Indians in New York." In *Becoming New Yorkers: Ethnographies of the New Second Generation,* edited by Philip Kasinitz, 288–312. New York: Russell Sage Foundation, 2004.

Euraque, Darío. "The Banana Enclave, Nationalism, and Mestizaje in Honduras." In *Identity and Struggle at the Margins of the Nation State: The Laboring Peoples of Central America and the Hispanic Caribbean,* edited by Aviva Chomsky and Aldo Lauria-Santiago, 151–68. Durham, NC: Duke University Press, 1998.

Fiehrer, Thomas. "From La Tortue to La Louisiane: An Unfathomed Legacy." In *The Road to Louisiana: The Saint Domingue Refugees, 1792–1809,* edited by Carl Brasseaux and Glenn R. Conrad, 1–30. Lafayette: Center for Louisiana Studies, University of Southwest Louisiana Press, 1992.

Gmelch, George. "West Indian Migrants and Their Rediscovery of Barbados." In *Coming Home? Refugees, Migrants, and Those Who Stayed Behind,* edited by Lynellyn D. Long and Ellen Oxfeld, 206–23. Philadelphia: University of Pennsylvania Press, 2004.

Hall, Stuart. "Who Needs Identity?" In *Questions of Cultural Identity,* edited by Stuart Hall and Paul Du Gay, 1–17. London: Sage, 1996.

Harpelle, Ronald. "White Zones: American Enclave Communities of Central America." In *Blacks and Blackness in Central America: Between Race and Place,* edited by Lowell Gudmundson and Justin Wolfe, 307–33. Durham, NC: Duke University Press, 2010.

Lachance, Paul. "The 1809 Immigration of Saint-Domingue Refugees to New Orleans: Reception, Integration, and Impact." In *The Road to Louisiana: The Saint Domingue Refugees, 1792–1809,* edited by Carl Brasseaux and Glenn R. Conrad, 245–84. Lafayette: Center for Louisiana Studies, University of Southwest Louisiana Press, 1992.

Lambert, Peter. "Myth, Manipulation, and Violence: Relationships between National Identity and Political Violence." In *Political Violence and the Construction of National Identity in Latin America,* edited by Will Fowler and Peter Lambert, 19–36. New York: Palgrave Macmillan, 2006.

Lohse, Russell. "Africans in a Colony of Creoles: The Yoruba in Colonial Costa Rica." In *The Yoruba Diaspora in the Atlantic World,* edited by Toyin Falola and Matt D. Childs, 130–56. Bloomington: Indiana University Press, 2005.

Meléndez Obando, Mauricio. "The Slow Ascent of the Marginalized: Afro-Descendants in Costa Rica and Nicaragua." In *Blacks and Blackness in Central America: Between Race and Place,* edited by Lowell Gudmundson and Justin Wolfe, 334–52. Durham, NC: Duke University Press, 2010.

Putnam, Lara Putnam. "Eventually Alien: The Multigenerational Saga of British West Indians in Central America, 1870–1940." In *Blacks and Blackness in Central America: Between Race and Place,* edited by Lowell Gudmundson and Justin Wolfe, 278–306. Durham, NC: Duke University Press, 2010.

Tormala, Teceta Thomas, and Kay Deaux. "Black Immigrants to the United States: Confronting and Constructing Ethnicity and Race." In *Cultural Psychology of Immigrants,* edited by Ramaswami Mahalingam, 131–50. New York: Routledge, 2006.

ARTICLES

Abernethy, Graeme. "'The Beauty of Other Horizons': Sartorial Self-Fashioning in Claude McKay's *Banjo: A Story without a Plot.*" *Journal of American Studies* 48 (2014): 445–60.

Aymer, Paula. "Caribbean Women: Labor Migrants and Traders." *Ahfad Journal: Women and Change* 22, no. 1 (2005): 97–115.

Bauer, Elaine, and Paul Thompson. "'She's Always the Person with a Very Global Vision': The Gender Dynamics of Migration, Narrative Interpretation and the Case of Jamaican Transnational Families." *Gender & History* 16, no. 2 (2004): 334–75.

Benson, Janel E. "Exploring the Racial Identities of Black Immigrants in the United States." *Sociological Forum* 21, no. 2 (2006): 219–47.

Bonnett, Aubrey W. "The West Indian Diaspora to the USA: Remittances and Development of the Homeland." *Wadabagei: A Journal of the Caribbean and Its Diasporas* 12, no. 1 (2009): 6–32.

Bryce-Laporte, Roy Simon. "Introduction: New York City and the New Caribbean Immigration: A Contextual Statement." *International Migration Review* 13, no. 2 (1979): 214–34.

Butcher, Kristin F. "Black Immigrants in the United States: A Comparison with Native Blacks and Other Immigrants." *Industrial & Labor Relations Review* 47, no. 2 (1994): 265–84.

Butterfield, Sherri-Ann P. "Challenging American Conceptions of Race and Ethnicity: Second Generation West Indian Immigrants." *International Journal of Sociology and Social Policy* 24, nos. 7/8 (2004): 75–102.

Calliste, Agnes. "Race, Gender and Canadian Immigration Policy: Blacks from the Caribbean, 1900–1932." *Journal of Canadian Studies* 28, no. 4 (1993): 131–48.

Chaney, James. "Malleable Identities: Placing the Garínagu in New Orleans." *Journal of Latin American Geography* 11, no. 2 (2012): 121–44.

Chaney, Michael A. "Traveling Harlem's Europe: Vagabondage from Slave Narratives to Gwendolyn Bennett's 'Wedding Day' and Claude McKay's *Banjo*." *Journal of Narrative Theory* 32 (Winter 2002): 52–76.

Chioneso, Nkechinyelum A. "(Re)Expressions of African/Caribbean Cultural Roots in Canada." *Journal of Black Studies* 39, no. 1 (2007): 69–84.

Coolidge, Calvin. "Whose Country Is This? The Question of Vital Interest to Every Man and Woman in America, Is Answered Here by the Vice President—after March 4th—of the United States." *Good Housekeeping*, February 1921, 12–16.

Doorley, Michael. "Irish Catholics and French Creoles: Ethnic Struggles within the Catholic Church in New Orleans, 1835–1920." *Catholic Historical Review* 87, no. 1 (January 2001): 34–54.

Echeverri-Gent, Elisavinda. "Forgotten Workers: British West Indians and the Early Days of the Banana Industry in Costa Rica and Honduras." *Journal of Latin American Studies* 24 (1992): 275–308.

Fiehrer, Thomas. "From Quadrille to Stomp: The Creole Origins of Jazz." *Popular Music* 10, no. 1 (1991): 21–38.

Foner, Nancy. "Gender and Migration: West Indians in Comparative Perspective." *International Migration* 47, no. 1 (2009): 3–29.

———. "Race and Color: Jamaican Migrants in London and New York City." *International Migration Review* 19, no. 4 (1985): 708–27.

———. "West Indian Identity in the Diaspora: Comparative and Historical Perspectives." *Latin American Perspectives* 25, no. 3 (1998): 173–88.

Gauthreaux, Alan G. "An Inhospitable Land: Anti-Italian Sentiment and Violence in Louisiana, 1891–1924." *Louisiana History: The Journal of the Louisiana Historical Association* 51, no. 1 (Winter 2010): 41–68.

Gordon, Monica H. "In Search of the Means to a Better Life: Caribbean Migration to the United States." *Contributions in Black Studies* 5, no. 4 (1981): 28–42.

Griffith, David. "Peasants in Reserve: Temporary West Indian Labor in the U.S. Farm Labor Market." *International Migration Review* 20, no. 4 (1986): 875–98.

Gullick, Charles J. M. R. "Afro-American Identity: The Jamaican Nexus." *Journal of Geography* 82, no. 5 (1983): 205–11.

Guterl, Matthew Pratt. "'I Went to the West Indies': Race, Place, and the Antebellum South." *American Literary History* 18, no. 3 (2006): 446–67.

Hall, Schekeva P., and Robert T. Carter. "The Relationship between Racial Identity, Ethnic Identity, and Perceptions of Racial Discrimination in an Afro-Caribbean Descent Sample." *Journal of Black Psychology* 32, no. 2 (2006): 155–175.

Jackson, Jennifer V., and Mary E. Cothran. "Black versus Black: The Relationships among African, African American, and African Caribbean Persons." *Journal of Black Studies* 33, no. 5 (2003): 576–604.

James, Carl E. "African-Caribbean Canadians Working 'Harder' to Attain Their Immigrant Dreams: Context, Strategies, and Consequences." *Wadabagei: A Journal of the Caribbean and Its Diasporas* 12, no. 1 (2009): 92–108.

Jasmin, Alicia Duplessis. "The Desegregation of a University." *Tulane Magazine,* September 2013, 14–19.

Kaufman, Burton. "New Orleans and the Panama Canal, 1900–1914." *Louisiana History* 14, no. 4 (Autumn 1973): 333–46.

Lightfoot, Natasha. "A Transnational Sense of 'Home': Twentieth-Century West Indian Immigration and Institution Building in the Bronx." *Afro-Americans in New York Life and History* 33, no. 2 (2009): 25–46.

Lipsitz, George. "New Orleans in the World and the World in New Orleans." *Black Music Research Journal* 31, no. 2 (Fall 2011): 261–90.

Lokken, Paul. "Marriage as Slave Emancipation in Seventeenth Century Guatemala." *Americas* 58, no. 2 (2001): 175–200.

MacClintock, Samuel. "Refunding the Foreign Debt of Honduras." *Journal of Political Economy* 19, no. 3 (March 1911): 216–28.

Manning, Seaton W. "British West Indians in the United States." *West Indian Review* 1, no. 5 (January 1935): 27–28.

Marquardt, Steve. "Green Havoc: Panama Disease, Environmental Change, and Labor Process in the Central American Banana Industry." *American Historical Review* 106, no. 1 (February 2001): 49–80.

Mendoza, Breny. "La desmitologización del mestizaje en Honduras: Evaluando nuevos aportes." *Mesoamérica* 42 (2001): 256–79.

Mohl, Raymond A. "Black Immigrants: Bahamians in Early Twentieth-Century Miami." *Florida Historical Quarterly* 65, no. 3 (1987): 271–97.

Nott, G. William. "Impresiones de Nueva Orleans: Una ciudad latina dentro de los Estados Unidos." *Lucero Latino: Revista Mensual* 1, no. 6 (December 1933): 12–15.

Palmer, Colin A. "Defining and Studying the Modern African Diaspora." *Journal of Negro History* 85 (Winter–Spring 2000): 27–32.

Parker, Jason. "'Capital of the Caribbean': The African American–West Indian 'Harlem Nexus' and the Transnational Drive for Black Freedom, 1940–1948." *Journal of African American History* 89, no. 2 (2004): 98–117.

Patterson, Tiffany Ruby, and Robin D. G. Kelley. "Unfinished Migrations: Reflections on the African Diaspora and the Making of the Modern World." *African Studies Review* 43, no. 1 (April 2000): 11–45.

Payne Iglesias, Elizet. "Identidad y nación: El caso de la costa norte e islas de La Bahía en Honduras, 1876–1930." *Mesoamérica* 42 (2001): 75–103.

Powell, Lawrence N. "When Hate Came to Town: New Orleans' Jews and George Lincoln Rockwell." *American Jewish History* 85, no. 4 (December 1997): 393–419.

———. "Why Louisiana Mattered." *Louisiana History: The Journal of the Louisiana Historical Association* 53, no. 4 (Fall 2012): 389–401.

Putnam, Lara. "Provincializing Harlem: The 'Negro Metropolis' as Northern Frontier of a Connected Caribbean." *Modernism/Modernity* 20, no. 3 (2013): 469–84.

———. "The Ties Allowed to Bind: Kinship Legalities and Migration Restriction in the Interwar Americas." *International Labor and Working Class History* 83 (2013): 191–209.

Reed, Merl E. "Lumberjacks and Longshoremen: The I.W.W. in Louisiana." *Labor History* 13 (1972): 41–59.

Rogers, Reuel R. "Race-Based Coalitions among Minority Groups: Afro-Caribbean Immigrants and African-Americans in New York City." *Urban Affairs Review* 39, no. 3 (2004): 283–317.

Sakakeeny, Matt. "New Orleans Music as a Circulatory System." *Black Music Research Journal* 31, no. 2 (Fall 2011): 291–325.

Showers-Johnson, Violet. "'What, Then, Is the African American?' African and Afro-Caribbean Identities in Black America." *Journal of American Ethnic History* 28, no. 1 (2008): 77–103.

Silva Gruesz, Kirsten. "The Gulf of Mexico System and the 'Latinness' of New Orleans." *American Literary History* 18, no. 4 (Fall 2006): 468–95.

Sommerville, Kristine, and Speer Morgan. "The King of the Underworld: The Invention of Jelly Roll Morton." *Missouri Review* 35, no. 2 (Summer 2012): 87–112.

Springer, Jennifer Thorington. "Fractured Diaspora: Mending the Strained Relationships between African Americans and African Caribbeans." *Wadabagei: A Journal of the Caribbean and Its Diasporas* 13, no. 2 (2011): 2–34.

Taylor, Christopher Stuart. "Education is the Key to Prosperity: The Barbadian Education System and 20th-Century Black Barbadian Migrants in Canada." *Journal of Black Studies* 45, no. 5 (2014): 453–73.

Toney, Joyce. "The Perpetuation of a Culture of Migration: West Indian American Ties with Home, 1900–1979." *Afro-Americans in New York Life and History* 13, no. 1 (1989): 39–55.

Vinson, Ben, III. "Introduction: African (Black) Diaspora History, Latin American History." In "The African Diaspora in the Colonial Andes," edited by Ben Vinson III. Special issue, *Americas* 63, no. 1 (July 2006): 1–18.

Walter, John C., and James H. Rigali. "The Anglophone Caribbean Immigrant and Partisan Politics in New York City, 1900–1972." *Afro-Americans in New York Life and History* 30, no. 1 (2006): 19–75.

Woods, Louis Lee, II. "The Federal Home Loan Bank Board, Redlining, and

the National Proliferation of Racial Lending Discrimination, 1921–1950."
Journal of Urban History 38, no. 6 (2012): 1036–59.

THESES AND DISSERTATIONS

Bracken, Mary Karen. "Restructuring the Boundaries: Hispanics in New Or-
leans, 1960–1990." PhD diss., University of New Mexico, 1992.
Painter, Norman Wellington. "The Assimilation of Latin Americans in New
Orleans, Louisiana." Master's thesis, Tulane University, 1949.

NEWSPAPERS AND PERIODICALS

New Orleans

Daily Picayune
New Orleans Weekly Planner
Sugar Planters' Journal
Times-Picayune
Weekly Louisianan
Weekly Pelican

Central America

Coal Trade Journal
La Gaceta
Luz y Patria: Revista Independiente
El Nuevo Tiempo
El Observador
People's Advocate
Revista Comercial Americana
Simpatia: Revista Mensual Ilustrada

United States

Cleveland (OH) Gazette
Marine Worker (New York)

New York Times
N.M.U. Pilot (New York)
Parsons (KS) Weekly Blade
Revista Mexicana (San Antonio, TX)
Washington Post

Index

Bonilla, Policarpo, 57
Bonney, Enriqueta, 138
Bonney, Henry, 138
Bonpart, S. B., 111, 114, 121
Bourgois, Philippe, 18, 104
Bracken, Mary, 132
Brasseaux, Carl, 6, 32
British diplomacy and consular delega-
    tions: debate on children born abroad
    and, 164n76; West Indians in Hondu-
    ras and, 55–56, 64–65, 70
British Honduran "exception," 36–40
British Honduras (Belize): abolition
    of slavery in, 32; nurses in, 80;
    racial diversity and construction
    in, 36–40; US white settlement in,
    30, 32
British nationality and identity: Bay
    Islands and, 55, 70; in Honduras,
    55–56, 64–65, 70; in New Orleans,
    105, 126
Bryant, Baker, 97
Buffington, Robert, 43, 48
Burke, Glendy, 31
Byrd, Henry "Professor Longhair," 111

Carías Andino, Tiburcio, 57–59, 61
Cartago, SS, 111
Catherine Curres, SS, 124
Catholic Church, 132–33
Caymanian "exception," 36–40
Ceiba, SS, 82
census data: British Honduras, 38–39;
    US, 9–10, 10, 125, 151n10
Central American Federation, 28–29
Central American immigrants,
    Spanish-speaking. See Latin
    American immigrants and identity,
    Spanish-speaking
Central American Labor Federation

(Confederación Obrera Centroamer-
    icana), 86
Central American republics: black experi-
    ence in, 17–18; black migration from
    US to, 32–35; citizenship in, 16–17;
    racial exclusion strategies, 23; white
    migration from US to, 29–32. See also
    Honduras; Latin American immi-
    grants and identity, Spanish-speaking
Chaney, James, 8–9
Chaney, Michael, 2
Chomsky, Aviva, 18
citizenship: British, 104–5, 152; imaged
    sense of British nationality in
    Honduras, 68–70; rates of, 104;
    West Indian children born abroad,
    42, 68–70, 164n76; "West Indians"
    in Central American republics and,
    16–17; "Whose Country Is This?"
    (Coolidge), 107
citizenship and naturalization, US: case
    studies, 75–78, 81–83; English iden-
    tity and, 126; naturalization petitions
    in New Orleans, 93–94, 94; NMU
    and, 97–98, 101–2
Clyde Mallory Steamship Company, 119
Coleman, William, 44
Comayagua, SS, 116–17
communism, 100–101, 102
Confederación Obrera Centroamericana
    (Central American Labor Federa-
    tion), 86
Congress of Industrial Organizations
    (CIO), 87
Conniff, Michael, 18, 104
Connor, Christina, 97
Connor, William, 97
conscription, military, 66–68
conscription of labor, 55–56
Coolidge, Calvin, 107, 135